PENGUIN COOKERY LIBRARY

# ENGLISH SEAFOOD COOKERY

Rick Stein was born in 1947 on a farm near Chipping Norton in Oxfordshire, and was educated at Uppingham School. Having worked as a chef at the Great Western Royal Hotel at Paddington, he spent several years travelling and held a variety of occupations, from being a television studio assistant in Sydney to a deckhand on a German cargo ship. He returned to read English at New College, Oxford, but went on to find a practical outlet for his enthusiasm for the splendours of seafood when he and his wife Jill opened the Sea Food Restaurant in Padstow, Cornwall, in 1975. Since then the business has grown from one small harbour-side bistro into a number of establishments with a genuinely international reputation and clientele.

Over the last twenty-five years Rick Stein has become the household name in the UK for fish cookery, having written a number of popular cookbooks which have won numerous awards. *English Seafood Cookery* won the 1989 Glenfiddich Award for the Food Book of the Year. *Rick Stein's Taste of the Sea* won the 1995 André Simon Memorial Fund Book Award and the Good Food Award in 1996. He has made a number of television series and films which have also proved to be highly successful. *Rick Stein's Taste of the Sea* won the 1996 Glenfiddich Award for Best Television Programme of the Year.

The Steins live at Trevone Bay near Padstow with their three sons and their Jack Russell, Chalky, who has become something of a star in his owner's television appearances. Rick's passion continues to be for fresh, simply cooked fish and, as well practising his craft, he now hopes to spend more time supporting the causes of fishermen in the South West.

RICK STEIN

# ENGLISH SEAFOOD COOKERY

PENGUIN BOOKS

## PENGUIN BOOKS

Published by the Penguin Group
Penguin Books Ltd, 80 Strand, London WC2R 0RL, England
Penguin Putnam Inc., 375 Hudson Street, New York, New York 10014, USA
Penguin Books Australia Ltd, Ringwood, Victoria, Australia
Penguin Books Canada Ltd, 10 Alcorn Avenue, Toronto, Ontario, Canada M4V 3B2
Penguin Books India (P) Ltd, 11 Community Centre, Panchsheel Park, New Delhi – 110 017, India
Penguin Books (NZ) Ltd, Cnr Rosedale and Airborne Roads, Albany, Auckland, New Zealand
Penguin Books (South Africa) (Pty) Ltd, 24 Sturdee Avenue, Rosebank 2196 South Africa

Penguin Books Ltd, Registered Offices: 80 Strand, London WC2R 0RL, England

www.penguin.com

First published 1988
5

Printed in England by Clays Ltd, St Ives plc
Filmset in Linotron Goudy

# CONTENTS

# One

# INTRODUCTION

So many cookery books appear every year that one must explain the reason for writing yet another. This book is about the seafood I cook at my restaurant in Padstow. It doesn't aim to be comprehensive in its coverage of the cookery of fish and shellfish in Great Britain, and although it is called *English Seafood Cookery*, you won't find many traditional recipes in it. This is largely because there aren't many. Some English dishes like fish and chips, stargazey pie or potted shrimps are well-known and good; but one soon begins to run out of material. To fill a book with recipes with an English flavour, one has to look elsewhere than to traditional English cookery, and that is where the recipes from my restaurant come in.

The Seafood Restaurant, which I run, is in the small fishing port of Padstow on the North Cornish coast. My wife Jill and I started it twelve years ago in this part of England long dismissed as a gastronomic desert; but after a dozen years if you were to tell me that the English are not interested in seafood, I would say that was rubbish. The public's appreciation of good food has progressed incredibly fast in that period.

Just to give you an idea, twelve years ago we were selling sea bass as the unnamed fish in fish and chips; now we cannot buy enough of it to satisfy the demand, and it certainly doesn't go into fish and chips any more. A popular main course that we sold then called Seafood Thermidor used to be described as follows: 'Lobster, crab and prawns with sole and other white fish in a white wine sauce with cheese, mustard and mushrooms'. The 'other white fish' was monkfish, which now features as a main course in its own right and sells very well.

There are virtually no fish we cannot interest our customers in now, even conger eel and shark; but how many recipes in our traditional cuisine can be found for the unusual varieties? This book covers almost every type of fish, crustacean and mollusc available around our shores and presents them in a way I hope you will find inspiring. That's why it's *English Seafood Cookery* – the cooking by English chefs of fish from English coastal waters in an English fishing port for English people. I may borrow from France, Italy, and even China, India and Japan, but everything is finely filtered by the place where I work and the people I cook for. We may not have much culinary heritage to refer to in the cooking of seafood, but it's time we showed the French and Italians we can do it too!

## · THE SALE OF FISH TODAY ·

Now that I have begun on an optimistic note about the growing interest in fish, let me temper this with a couple of observations I made recently.

The supermarket in Wadebridge, six miles from the coast here in Cornwall, sells two types of fish: frozen plaice fillets and frozen cod fillets. Last time I was in Brittany, I went to a supermarket eight miles from the coast, between Dinard and Dinan. In addition to every type of wet fish commonly available, including John Dory and slip soles, arranged in glistening mounds with that natural flair for presentation of food for sale so obvious everywhere in France, they had live scallops, two sizes of fresh langoustine, squid, shrimps, palordes and praires, baskets of oysters and mussels, and a vivarium filled with lobsters, crawfish, crabs and spider crab.

If you think it unfair to contrast an area of France known for its seafood and an area of England which isn't (but should be and will be!), don't imagine that the situation is much better in London. Last March, I went into a large supermarket in the King's Road to see what fish they had. This shop was selling fresh root turmeric, tamarind, fresh basil, tarragon, lamb's lettuce, radicchio, frisé – a first-class selection of fresh produce, even in March. Yet this shop had just four types of fresh fish for sale – no shellfish, not even a mussel.

We must make more demands on our suppliers. That supermarket could sell much more. The fish shop here in Padstow, run by the Cornish Fishermen's Cooperative, sells magnificent fish, and not just cod and plaice, but John Dory, red mullet, monkfish, dogfish, conger eel. I think the speed with which they turn it all over astonishes them, but the public are confident because they know it comes straight off the boats.

This is not just the case in a fishing port. I talk to customers in our restaurant from all over Great Britain and find that anyone with a serious interest in cooking always knows somewhere now that sells good fresh fish. You have to be in the know, and generally it's still frozen plaice fillets everywhere else. But I sense a change; and it's about time too.

## · ABOUT THE RECIPES IN THIS BOOK ·

Much as I'm aware of the difficulties of cooking anything complicated and time-consuming these days, because of the extraordinarily frenetic life we all lead (me included), let me advise you to calm down!

In my opinion, good cookery owes far less to skill than many of my customers realize, and far more to good ingredients and good planning; and you cannot plan well unless you sit down and think. Most of the recipes in this book will not work well if you are hurriedly cobbling them together after work or in between bathing the children and dashing out to get the babysitter. You wouldn't expect a plumber to install your central heating like that, and it is not the right way to produce something delightful to eat.

Many people tell me they dislike cooking, and I believe it is because they don't give themselves enough time to enjoy it. There are plenty of recipes in this book which you can produce and cook very quickly but very few that don't need pre-planning. You will see that any recipe which needs some serious planning contains an 'Order of work' which will help you to organize a difficult dish.

More often than not, you will need to do more than begin at six o'clock. There's fish to be chosen, filleted perhaps, vegetables to be prepared, stock to be made; and before that – much before that – if you've got a garden there are herbs to be grown along with special vegetables and salads (see Chapter 5).

I know it's possible to buy imported red snapper, tuna, rascasse, Mediterranean prawns, soft-shelled crabs, swordfish and much more, all freshly flown in, but I decided a long time ago that the fish and shellfish sold in my restaurant should be limited to what I could get locally. This book includes only recipes for fish I've used in the restaurant. I hope you will forgive me if you find that I've missed lots of unusual varieties out; it's not that I haven't considered them, just that I want to concern myself only with what's fresh and good and to concentrate on fish that I know well.

I haven't normally bothered to specify what other fish a particular dish can be made with, but in most cases the named fish can be substituted by many others. For example, for the grilled red mullet with a tomato and tarragon dressing on p. 173 you could substitute red bream, black bream, shark, John Dory, monkfish, grey mullet, even mackerel or sardines – any fish, in fact, that you can imagine cooking over a charcoal grill.

With a few exceptions, the recipes in the book are written for four adult people. Quantities are given in both imperial and metric measurements, but in order to avoid fractions in transposing imperial (in which I still work) into metric, I have rounded up all the metric measurements; consequently you should use imperial or metric but not a mixture of the two.

# Two

# AN A-TO-Z OF FISH
# AND HOW TO BUY THEM

## · TELLING FRESH FISH FROM STALE ·

It is very easy to tell fresh fish from stale. If it looks bright, shiny and firm, and if it smells of the sea, it will taste as good as it looks. If fish has that smell that we generally know as 'fishy', it won't be fresh. The gills should be a nice pink, not brownish, the skin should be shining, and the scales (if any) should be tight. Some fish, such as megrim sole, have a rather washed-out appearance, and hake, being a dull dark silver in colour, can look a bit wan when still perfectly fresh; but on the whole, a tired-looking fish, even if not smelling, will have been on ice for too long. The eyes of a fresh fish are clear and bright, but as it stales they become cloudy and sunken. When you press the skin you should not be able to see the indent of your finger; the flesh underneath should spring back.

It is always best to buy fish whole, or, if you want fillets or steaks, have them cut from the whole fish while you wait. It is far easier to judge the freshness of a fish when it is whole, and if you are adept at filleting it is well worth buying whole fish, as it keeps much better.

## · HOW MUCH FISH AND SHELLFISH TO BUY ·

Wastage through skin, bone and shell varies from about thirty-five per cent for a monkfish tail to about seventy per cent for a lobster. Generally most flat or round fish have as much skin and bone as usable fillet; or, to put it another way, you should halve the weight of a whole fish to find out how much you will be able to eat.

At the restaurant, we work on portion sizes of 3–4 oz. (90–120 g) for a first course and 7–8 oz. (200–240 g) for a main course; so for each person allow 8 oz. (240 g) on the bone for a first course and 1 lb. (480 g) for a main course. If serving a whole large fish, you can get away with less, but I like to be generous. The exceptions to this rule are monkfish (because it's sold as a tail only), John Dory, gurnard and similar large-headed fish, and all shellfish: for details of how much to buy of all these, see the list on pp. 17–47.

## · WHAT FISH CAN YOU BUY? ·

The choice of fish in all but the very best of fish shops in Great Britain is poorer than on the Continent, but things are improving. You shouldn't have too much difficulty in getting hold of red mullet, black bream, John Dory and squid nowadays. If you can't find what you want, you will further the cause of better fresh fish supplies by ordering it. Any fishmonger will tell you that it's lack of demand that leads to a poor selection, not lack of supply.

Don't be too dogmatic about what you mean to buy at a fishmonger. If another fish looks fresher and shinier than the one you came in for, buy that. There are few recipes which can't be made with a different fish, so long as it is similar to the one named. In the Padstow fish shop the other day, I was standing behind a couple who asked if there was any monkfish. There wasn't. On the slab were some extremely fresh and cheap John Dory, which were pointed out to them. 'No,' they said. 'We really wanted monkfish.' They left with nothing. A man reading our menu another day said to me, 'Do they *ever* have John Dory up at the fish shop?' I said they did and added that they had some excellent small monk tails at the moment. But it was John Dory he wanted. Fish is wild food; you have to take what you can get, not necessarily what you want, and if you can't get what you want you just might find you get what you need!

Below is a list of fish, crustaceans, shellfish and others which are likely to be caught around the British Isles, with some ideas about how to cook them and some personal views about their culinary value.

I shan't bother you with a chart of when is the best time to buy each fish, since I've never seen such a list which was correct. As a general rule, fish are in poor condition after spawning but fine to eat at any other time of year when you can get them. If there are special times in the year when you can't get a particular fish or when it is cheap and in good condition, I've mentioned it. I add what sizes to buy if that's important and a maximum market size (which is not the biggest specimen ever caught, but rather the largest one you are likely to see on sale).

I have also listed any regional differences in names. Most of the information on this last point comes from *North Atlantic Seafood* by Alan Davidson (published by Penguin), the definitive work on the naming of fish.

## Angel fish
(*monkfish; angel shark; sea angel; sea devil; puppy fish*)

Weight up to 20 lb. (9 kg).

Somewhat confusingly, angel fish, like angler fish, is also called monkfish; but the angel fish is a bottom-feeding shark, a sort of cross between a dogfish and a ray. The most common name, angel, refers to its extended pectoral fins, which look like wings. I have bought angel fish a few times in Padstow and find it nice poached in a *court bouillon* and served with capers and *beurre noir*, as for skate (see pp. 223–4).

## Angler fish: see Monkfish

## Bass, sea bass

Weight up to 10 lb. (4.5 kg). Fish of about 1 lb. 4 oz. (600 g) or less must not be sold in Devon or Cornwall (to conserve stocks).

Sea bass is a beautiful-looking fish. With its firm, rounded but sleek shape and bright silver colouring, like worked stainless steel, it stands out in a fish shop; it looks as though it must be expensive, and it is. Bass are not fished on any large commercial scale, so the supply tends to be erratic, depending on the enthusiasm of anglers in pursuing their sport. We find that May to October are good months to buy bass, but they occasionally turn up in trawls in the winter. They are normally sold ungutted. Before you attempt to gut or fillet a bass, you should first snip off all the fins, since most of them are sharply spiked. Watch out too for the spikes on the gill covers. Remove the intestines as soon as possible; bass are voracious eaters of other quite large fish, so they have rather volatile innards which can burst and taint the flesh around the gut cavity.

It is often suggested that bass should be prepared and cooked in the same way as salmon, but apart from a passing similarity in the sleek, silver shape, they have little in common. Bass has a soft dense texture with a delicate flavour, whereas salmon has a much more open texture, falling into thick flakes, and a much richer flavour, being an oily fish. Bass is not especially well suited to being poached and eaten cold, unlike salmon.

Bass is particularly successful when simply cooked but well nurtured with unsalted butter. I think it is for this reason that bass with *beurre blanc* is something of a *nouvelle cuisine* classic (pp. 96–7). A whole bass, roasted and well basted with butter, is simple and effective, with, perhaps, my sorrel sauce (pp. 234–5). Try using bass in the recipe for steamed grey mullet and garlic, ginger and spring onions (pp. 166–7).

*Bib:* see *Pout*

*Bream: red sea bream and black sea bream*

Weight up to 6 lb. (2.7 kg); normal weight 8 oz.–2 lb. (240–960 g).

Like such fish as the red mullet and John Dory, bream seems to me to be more commonly associated with the Mediterranean. But in the south of England bream is available during the summer months, though not, unfortunately, the best of all the bream family, the gilt-headed bream, or daurade, as it is probably better-known. Both types of bream are similar in shape, being what one might call flat round fish. They should be filleted like round fish, but in fact they are quite thin. They are all good to eat; my recipe for fillet of bream with a retsina sauce (p. 161) is intended to suggest the Mediterranean connection, a small culinary conceit!

We quite often buy small black bream from the fish markets at Plymouth and Newlyn. They are an ideal size to be cooked on our charcoal grill and served as a first course with a simple tomato, chive and vinaigrette dressing, or as part of our *grillade* (pp. 242–3). The only other people who seem to buy them at these markets are the Chinese, who certainly know what is good.

*Brill, kite*

Weight up to 8 lb. (3.6 kg).

Brill used to be a really good buy for restaurateurs, because it was much cheaper than turbot but almost as good. Now, unfortunately, with the growing awareness of different varieties of fish, it is much closer in price. But it is still about 25 per cent cheaper and of excellent quality, producing good firm bone-free fillets.

If you have difficulty telling the difference between brill and turbot, just rub the top, dark skin. Brill doesn't have little bony bumps like tiny limpets on its back; turbot does. Brill is more oval in shape than turbot, and it has scales.

*Catfish:* see *Wolf fish*

*Clams: bean clam or wedge shell, carpet shell or palourde, golden carpet shell, hard clam or quahog, otter shells, razor shell, soft-shelled clam or long neck or steamer or sand mussel, tellin, trough shell, venus shell, warty venus or praire, wedge shell*

Average size 2 inches (5 cm). Allow ten of this size per person.

All the clams of one sort or another listed above are prepared in the same way. They are briefly opened by being heated in a covered pan with a splash of white wine, and are then served in the half shell with a filling of, say, garlic butter (p. 102) or my spinach stuffing for cockles (p. 180). They are also all excellent eaten raw, with maybe some shallot vinegar (p. 106), or very lightly steamed.

We use local soft-shelled clams in our *fruits de mer* and buy in hard-shelled clams which are the North American quahog from the Duchy of Cornwall Oyster Farm at Port Navas Constantine (telephone 0326 40210). They send off clams, oysters and mussels by train.

*Coalfish:* see *Coley*

*Cockles*

Allow about 20 average-sized (1½-inch, 3-cm) cockles per person for a first course.

It would be nice to be able to buy cockles still alive in the shell, but I've never seen them. They are easy to dig anywhere around our coasts. They should be opened in the same way as clams (see above) and similarly stuffed or eaten raw. If you've only eaten cockles pickled in acetic acid, you're in for a treat.

*Cod*

Weight up to 30 lb. (13.5 kg).

I suspect it is the price of cod and the fact that it produces big flaky fillets, with no small bones to catch in the throat, rather than any enthusiasm about its flavour, that make it so popular.

Cod needs to be perfectly fresh to be worth buying – the same goes for most fish, of course, but the duller it is, the more this is true. However, as long as you follow the guidelines for choosing fresh fish, particularly in ensuring that the gills are a nice light pink, you may not be buying the most exciting fish on the slab, but is it always necessary for the main ingredient in a dish to be full of flavour? I don't think so. What about fillet steak, for example? It's not particularly full of flavour, but it makes a pleasant contrast to a good strong sauce – perhaps a Rioja sauce with ceps and chopped spring onions. My recipe for mussel and cod chowder (pp. 129–30) is a case in point, where the salt pork with lots of flavour and the mussels and their salty juice allow the cod to shine through as an unsalty, indeed slightly sweet contrast.

To me, though, cod is a fish of supreme worth because when salted down and then soaked in cold water, it becomes a totally different and far more interesting fish. I include a recipe for making your own salt cod (or *morue*, as the French call it) because it is far nicer when made from a piece of cod which is known to be perfectly fresh and which is not salted for too long.

We are lucky in Padstow to be able to buy cod from local boats which don't go out for more than two or three days at a time, so that it is always in excellent condition. If you are sure that you can buy the freshest cod I would recommend my recipe for cod *en papillote* (pp. 202–3). If you are faced with the Icelandic deep-sea trawled variety, I would suggest using it for the cod and mussel chowder (pp. 129–30).

## Coley, coalfish, saithe

Weight up to 20 lb. (9 kg).

A lesser member of the cod family which seems to be bought more for cats than humans. The fillets are a bit grey and therefore don't look too exciting. Nevertheless, if you get some really fresh coley, you can use it in fish cakes or pies, or you might try it as a substitute for pollack in our battered, marinated pollack with raita and kachumber (pp. 218–20).

## Conger eel

Weight up to 20 lb. (9 kg).

Conger eels are a sort of by-product of lobster fishing in that they are normally caught in lobster pots. They are extremely cheap and full of body. By 'body' I mean that quality found in such cuts of meat as shin of beef which when they are simmered enrich the cooking liquid and give it a gelatinous thickness. For this reason conger eel is a more or less essential ingredient to a good fish soup (though other fish like dogfish or ray have similar qualities). On its own, conger eel is a bit overpowering in flavour unless accompanied with something quite strong. In Brittany it is often served in a bordelaise sauce with button mushrooms and onions. The recipe for char-grilled conger eel with a rich red wine sauce (pp. 198–9) is the same sort of idea. A special treatment would be the *poêle* of conger eel (pp. 203–4), where a thick cut of conger, taken from the thickest part, is skinned, wrapped in caul fat and pot-roasted with various root vegetables.

## Crab: the common brown crab and the spider crab

Both crabs weigh up to 6 lb. (2.7 kg).

The vast difference in price between crabs and lobsters seems to me more a matter of the difficulty of extracting crab meat than any great superiority in flavour on the part of lobsters. Crabs are fiddly to dress, and the meat doesn't come out in firm chunks which can be sliced like lobster. But as far as flavour is concerned, crabs are almost as nice. To me a freshly boiled crab with fresh bread and plenty of mayonnaise is a perfect pleasure. Because the flesh falls to pieces when you extract it, crab is not an easy dish to present out of the shell. It is better used in conjunction with other fish or else made into a terrine. The spider crab terrine on pp. 140–41 can be made just as easily with brown crab, and in either form is extremely popular at our restaurant.

If anything, spider crabs have an even nicer flavour than brown crabs, and they are more highly esteemed in France and Spain, which is where most of our catch goes. But they are even more fiddly to dress, since they don't have the large claws of the brown crab; so the meat-to-shell ratio is lower, and you have to dress more crabs to get the same amount of meat.

Some advice about buying crabs. Large crabs are just as nice to eat as small ones and are less labour-intensive to dress. As with lobsters, it is always best to buy live ones if you can and don't mind cooking them, since the sooner you can eat a crab after cooking it, the better it will taste. It is a good idea to hold a crab when buying it to check that it feels heavy for its size; light ones tend to be watery. Cock crabs, identifiable by larger claws and a thin tail flap, fetch more money because their claws produce more white meat. Hen crabs, on the other hand, identifiable by having a wide tail flap, are a good buy from late August to October, when they are full of delicious red roe.

## Crawfish, crayfish, langouste, spiny lobster

Similar in taste and general appearance to a lobster, though orange-red where the lobster is blue, and without the lobster's impressive set of claws.

We have some difficulty explaining on our menu exactly what we mean by crawfish and crayfish. People often think we are referring to the small freshwater clawed shellfish, and they would have a shock to be presented with a creature that can easily weigh as much as 8 lb. (3.6 kg). If you intend to buy a crawfish, I would allow about 1¼ lb. to 1½ lb. (600–720 g) per person, live weight. If it is already cooked, remember that all shellfish lose about 15 per cent in weight through boiling; I should allow 1½ lb. (720 g) per person. This might seem a lot, but bear in mind that crabs, lobsters and crawfish are only about one-third usable meat. Crawfish are in fact better value than lobsters in that the meat-to-shell ratio is slightly higher.

And the taste? Some people prefer them to lobsters. They are less sweet, less positively flavoured. They, of all shellfish, should be eaten as soon as possible after cooking since they lose much of their flavour by being chilled in a fridge. The recipe for sliced crawfish salad with tomato, chervil and fish *fumet* (pp. 239–40) should show you how splendid a crawfish can be.

## Cuttlefish: see Squid

## Dab

Weight up to 1½ lb. (720 g).

A similar fish to plaice and flounder, distinguishable from them by its rough skin with small tooth-edged scales.

## Dogfish, lesser spotted dogfish or rough hound or murgy or huss, smooth hound or sweet william, spurdog, tope or sweet william

Weight up to 20 lb. (9 kg).

To the lobster fishermen of Padstow, dogfish represents one of the only catches available in the winter, when it is generally too rough to leave pots in the sea long enough to catch lobsters or crabs, and their boats are too small to go trawling for the abundant Dover sole which are to be found off Trevose Head in January and February. So they go long-lining. They bait up to 5000 hooks with mackerel and go out for eighteen-hour stretches. I remember one cold night last January opening our back door to let the cat out with a biting north-easterly wind and wondering with some awe about the comfort of two fishermen who I knew to be out there in a small boat in the snow flurries. When I asked them how they coped in a lobster boat not really equipped for being out at night; how they kept warm in the wheel house with no door one of them said 'Oh, it wasn't too bad really, we had an oil stove to warm our hands over when we got really cold.' I suppose I'm soft.

When they returned next morning, these dogfishermen, they dumped their dogfish in a cold heap on the wind-whipped quayside. They looked quite unprepossessing, red and bloody and with sandpaper skins that the Cornish would describe as 'barky'. They have huge and unpleasant intestines, more like an animal's, and are hard work to skin, but oh, they make good fish soup!

Spurdogs are the best eating and are what you would normally buy at your fish shop. They are identifiable by having one sharp spine in the dorsal fin, which fishermen are often unlucky enough to step on. Tope are quite good cut into steaks and grilled; they are identifiable by their sandpaper skin. The recipe for grilled marinated dogfish with a garlic sauce (pp. 199–200) would be well suited to tope. For the other dogfish – soup, I think.

*Dublin Bay prawns:* see *Langoustine*

## Eel

Weight up to 8 lb. (3.6 kg).

Eels are normally classed as freshwater fish, but I include them because we find them in the Padstow estuary and they spend a large part of their lives migrating to and from the Sargasso Sea; like salmon, I regard them as at home in both environments. We put eels on the menu as *Anguilles au vert* (see pp. 159–60 for the recipe and some enthusiasm about eels).

On the subject of smoked eel I am something of an authority; I once 'worked my passage', as they used to say, on a German freighter from New Zealand to New York as a greaser in the engine room. The Germans are inordinately fond of smoked eel, and the smoked eel from New Zealand is fat, thick and sweetly smoky. These German seamen had cleaned Auckland out of it, and I soon realized why.

## Flounder

Weight up to 5 lb. (2.3 kg).

Very similar in appearance to plaice, being a deep browny-green, and often having orange-yellow spots like a plaice, but these are always faint. It is a good idea to be able to tell plaice from flounder, since flounder is by no means as good. Plaice has a number of bony nodules on the head; flounder doesn't. At the restaurant we only use flounder as part of the raw material for a fish terrine. Other than that, I would suggest simply filleting, dusting with flour and frying in clarified butter.

## Garfish

Weight up to 2 lb. (960 g).

I've never seen a garfish at a fish shop and never had one brought to the back door of the kitchen. I used to catch them on mackerel feathers when I was on holiday in the Scilly Isles, and my mother used to grill them like mackerel. I remember them as being very nice but odd, with their curious greeny-blue bones. George Lassalle, in his highly enthusiastic book *The Adventurous Fish Cook* (published by Macmillan), says they can be used in any recipes where brill, sole or turbot is called for. So go ahead.

## Grey mullet

Weight up to 5 lb. (2.3 kg).

Grey mullet is much under-rated. If you ask a fisherman in Padstow where the greatest concentrations of these fish are to be found, he will say round a sewage outlet, but I have certainly never found any sign of sewage when removing the guts from a mullet. Mud, yes, and small crabs too. I find grey mullet well flavoured, with firm but quite soft flesh. It is similar in texture to bass, and any recipe for the latter will suit grey mullet well. We use it a lot in bouillabaisse, and it cooks well on our charcoal grill.

A summer fish appearing round our coasts in May and disappearing into deeper waters towards the end of October.

## Gurnard (red and grey)

Weight up to 6 lb. (2.7 kg).

Like grey mullet, this is an undervalued fish, mostly going as bait for lobster pots in the south-west. The red gurnard is excellent in stews like bouillabaisse (pp. 224–6) or retsina fish stew (pp. 226–8), because its delightful colour adds excitement to the dish. Firm in texture, it is ideal for serving in filleted form with a sauce, and any recipe for fillet of sole, turbot, brill or John Dory would suit gurnard. With its large bony head, there is quite a lot of wastage, but at the price of gurnard this is not a problem. We usually include a gurnard or two in our fish soups (see pp. 132–3).

## Haddock

Weight up to 6 lb. (2.7 kg).

Easily identified by having a black smudge on either side just behind the gills, haddock belongs to the same family as the cod (*Gadidae*), and opinions vary as to which has the better flavour. I think haddock is marginally better than cod; I particularly like small ones, which are good just filleted and fried in butter with some *beurre noisette*.

Many cookery books skim over the cod family because they are a bit on the dull side, but I don't think this is always a drawback; it gives one a chance to produce some well-flavoured dishes without the nagging fear that one may be masking the true flavour of some expensive fish.

We serve haddock with a fennel and pastis hot butter sauce (p. 96), which has proved very popular, and it could well be used as the main ingredient in seafood Thermidor (pp. 201–2).

Just as salting cod seems to transform it into something rich and strange, so smoking makes haddock something special, and Finnan haddock is the most special of all. Try the recipe for mousseline of Finnan haddock with a horseradish sauce (pp. 143–4).

## Hake

Weight up to 15 lb. (6.8 kg).

As one of my catering college textbooks, *The Larder Chef* by M. J. Leto and W. K. Bode (published by Heinemann) put it, the hake is identifiable by having a 'pleased expression', and it does indeed seem to flash its fine set of pin teeth with satisfaction. A sleek, eel-like fish, dull silver-grey in colour, it quickly shows signs of going stale, soon becoming washed-out and squashy-looking.

Hake is a member of the cod family, and I think the best (an opinion shared by the Spanish and Portuguese). I am particularly fond of the hake and potato pie with garlic and parsley (p. 209); it's not the sort of dish we sell in the restaurant, it's best consumed with relish around a kitchen table.

Hake has a denser flesh than the other cod-type fish, and is also rather soft. When it is not fresh, it becomes very soft indeed and extremely difficult to fillet without falling apart.

## Halibut and Greenland halibut

Since the halibut can easily weigh over 450 lb. (200 kg), it is unlikely that you would ever come across a whole one. It is normally sold in fillet or steak form. The Greenland halibut is much smaller, weighing up to 30 lb. (13.5 kg).

I have fond memories of eating a large fillet of halibut in an exemplary batter at Harry Ramsden's famous fish and chip shop at Guiseley in Yorkshire. Everyone should go there at least once to see how perfectly possible it is to do something in restaurant terms which is naturally English, where no concessions are made to the cuisine of any other country, and where the most obvious and delightful thing to drink with your fish is tea.

It is a source of regret to me that halibut is not caught in the south of

England; we do not use it at the restaurant, because we can very rarely get it. If I could feature it regularly on our menu, I would braise it with vegetables and some herbs (in the same way as the turbot on pp. 263–4), which would be an ideal way of counteracting its slight dryness. I made up the recipe for poached halibut with dill (pp. 247–8) without the ingredients in front of me, thinking of a Scandinavian set of accompaniments for a northern fish. I have since found with pleasure that it works well. The aquavit is not essential but a pleasant addition if you can get it.

## Herring

Weight up to 1½ lb. (720 g).

A highly versatile fish for cooking fresh, salting, smoking or pickling. The herring is one of the finest fish in the sea, yet who would believe that from its price? How extraordinary that a fish of such character, which cannot fail to delight with its positive, slightly oily flavour, is so difficult for us to sell in the restaurant! It is a somewhat irritating fact that when people eat out they want expensive foods that they would not normally have at home. If I were to buy perfectly fresh herrings and serve them fried in oatmeal with bacon, a small one as a first course, I doubt if I would sell two on a busy night. People should trust me more, if I said herrings are the best thing today, they would be. Not long ago, during a fortnight of the most foul weather, a regular customer wrote to me complaining about the poor selection on our menu. I suppose he wanted lobster and turbot and sole. I had managed to buy gurnard and John Dory, and the merchant who sold them said I was probably buying the last decent fresh fish in Europe until the gales died down. People want the fresh fish but don't accept what that implies when the weather closes in.

## Huss: see Dogfish

## John Dory

Weight up to 4 lb. (1.8 kg). You should allow about 1½ lb. (720 g) of unfilleted John Dory to give you an 8-oz. (240-g) fillet as a main course.

A fish of excellent quality, with firm well-flavoured flesh. You can cook John Dory in any way you like. I like to send them out to the restaurant cooked whole, because their extraordinary appearance creates a stir; my wife disagrees with me on this point, saying that people don't want to be messing around with bones. A fundamental disagreement which I feel we shall never resolve until we can employ enough waiting staff to fillet everything at the table.

*Langoustine, Dublin Bay prawns, scampi*

Average weight about 1½ oz. (45 g); large ones weigh up to 8 oz. (240 g).

Dublin Bay prawns, which we usually call langoustine, are generally sold only in their breaded and frozen form for deep frying. Still in their shell and freshly boiled, they are unbelievably good. Slightly to the north of us here at Padstow, out west in the Irish Sea, is a fishing ground where langoustine abound. Most of the langoustine you buy in Brittany come from there. A few years ago trawlers from Newlyn started to fish there regularly and we were able to get any amount of fresh langoustine, a raw material which is pretty much *de rigueur* in seafood restaurants; but unfortunately for us the trawlermen found that though they were earning the same money for langoustine as for other fish, they were losing more trawling nets, so they went back to fishing for hake. We now buy our langoustine from Scotland. They are caught in small creel pots off the coast of Argyllshire, landed at Crinan every night (if the weather permits), cooked, packed in ice and dispatched by train. They reach us in the afternoon of the next day. They are of excellent quality; the firm that markets them, Loch Fynne Oysters, sends them all over Europe. You could order some from them if you would take 14 lb., which is not a great deal when you consider how much of that is shell (which you can turn into an excellent bisque). Of course, Loch Fynne also sell oysters, smoked salmon and exquisite kippers; their telephone number is Ardkinglas (04996) 264.

We generally serve langoustine simply with mayonnaise or grilled with some herb butter. But if you fancy something a bit special, try the recipe on pp. 241–2 for braised Dublin Bay prawns with asparagus and a shellfish cream; the particularly interesting thing about this recipe is that the sauce is made, not with a base of fish or shellfish stock, but with a *fumet* of vegetables.

*Lemon sole*

Weight up to 4 lb. (1.8 kg).

One of the best-flavoured flat fish, but under-rated and therefore always good value for money.

*Ling*

Weight up to 30 lb. (13.5 kg).

Another member of the cod family, ling is easy to identify since it looks more like an eel than a cod and has a dark spot on its first dorsal fin.

It has a good flavour and is cheap. My *tourte* of ling and prawns (pp. 215–16) will I think impress you with how a relatively humble fish, backed up by some cheap shellfish, can produce a dish tasting as though it must have cost a great deal of money.

## Lobster

Weight up to 10 lb. (4.5 kg).

Lobsters are usually bought ready-cooked, which I don't think is a good idea unless you have a thoroughly understanding fishmonger. The problem is that opinions differ on cooking times, and more often than not lobsters and crabs are boiled without salt. Some people boil them with quite a lot of malt vinegar added; the reason for this is not known to me. The other problem with buying pre-cooked lobsters is that you don't know how long they have been cooked for; and although lobsters can be eaten days after cooking, the quality deteriorates even after one day. Indeed some people say that lobster should never be put in the fridge, and I think if you can eat them as soon as they have cooled down, there is no better way of appreciating their flavour.

Having decided that you are going to cook your own lobsters, here are some suggestions on buying them. There is no reason why you shouldn't be able to get them. Hotels and restaurants throughout England can, so I'm sure it should be perfectly easy for your fishmonger to order them for you. The best size to choose is from 1¼ lb. (600 g) to 2½ lb. (just over a kilo). The 1¼-lb. lobster would be a reasonable size for one person, the 2½-lb. one for two. Larger lobsters tend to have much thicker shells, and unless the price is reduced they are not good value for money. Furthermore, I don't think the bigger lobsters have such a sweet, intense flavour as the 'prime' sizes.

I tend to favour hen lobsters because they have a slightly higher meat-to-shell ratio owing to their coral. Some people feel that hen lobsters also have a better flavour, but I haven't noticed this. It's a small point, and it would probably be asking a bit much of your fishmonger to demand hen lobsters only.

The lobsters that you buy should be quite plainly still alive, and the tail should spring back when you move it. Many people seem to think that a dead lobster spells instant food poisoning. This is not so; the reason for using live lobsters is that as soon as they die, their flesh deteriorates astonishingly quickly by going very soft and mushy.

If you are ever in a position to buy lobsters straight from a fishing boat, as we are, remember that the trauma of being caught actually affects their flesh, and it is best to leave them in the bottom of the fridge (covered with a damp cloth or seaweed) for a few hours or even overnight, to allow them to calm down. Life is tough, isn't it?

## Mackerel

Weight up to 1½ lb. (720 g).

Almost too well-flavoured, I think – a fish to be eaten in moderation. If you ask anyone who knows a bit about fish for a comment on mackerel, they will invariably say that it's not worth eating unless cooked just after being caught. While I would not deny that mackerel doesn't keep for very long, I don't think one needs to be quite so doctrinaire. Once gutted it seems to keep perfectly well in our fish fridge for two or three days. Since mackerel in the summer is landed daily from small boats it's going to be very fresh anyway. Winter mackerel, which are trawled from deep water, tend to be bigger and plumper and keep better than the inshore summer mackerel; it is these that mackerel smokers use since they have a higher oil content than the summer fish, which tend to dry out too quickly. On the other hand, summer fish are nicer to eat fresh, since they are more likely to have been recently caught and have a more agreeable flavour through being less oily.

We sell small mackerel cooked on our charcoal grill with a gooseberry sauce made in exactly the same way as the sorrel sauce on p. 235 but using gooseberries instead of sorrel. Like herring, mackerel are well suited to pickling, salting or smoking, and are particularly good in an *escabèche* (pp. 147–8).

Smoked mackerel is normally hot-smoked, that is, cooked in hot smoke; but sometimes you can buy it cold-smoked in the same way as smoked salmon. In this form, it is something of a delicacy when thinly sliced and served with lemon and brown bread and butter, or as part of a combination of cured fish, as in the Baltic salad (pp. 141–3). Like all smoked produce, it freezes well. I recommend the cold-smoked mackerel of the Cornish Smoked Fish Company at Charlestown near St Austell who – like most suppliers in Cornwall, so far away from population centres – will send small boxes by train. The telephone number is St Austell (0726) 72356. Cornish Smoked Fish also produce smoked salmon, smoked trout, both hot- and cold-smoked, smoked pollack, kippers and bloaters (whole herring lightly hot-smoked with the guts left in, giving them a gamey flavour).

## Megrim sole, *whiff*

Weight up to 5 lb. (2.3 kg).

Though they look a bit anaemic, megrim sole are not a bad buy, being cheap and well-flavoured, if a little dry. We have served them with *beurre blanc* (pp. 96–7) to quite good response.

## Monkfish

Weight of the tail up to 8 lb. (3.6 kg).

A very useful fish, since it has a firm texture and no bones, and the tail is very low in wastage (about 65 per cent is fillet). It is a pity the heads aren't sold as well as the tails, since the cheeks are something of a delicacy and the heads make quite good fish stock; but the mouths of these fierce fish are so stuffed with large, razor-sharp teeth as to be positively hazardous to handle.

I don't think the monkfish is quite as well-flavoured as some people claim, but if roughly treated – for instance cooked on a charcoal grill, having been marinaded with olive oil and strong herbs such as thyme, bay and fennel, and really well charred on the outside – it is superb. Similarly I have no qualms about stuffing it full of garlic and roasting it in the oven like a leg of lamb, and many other cooks treat it in the same way.

If it is to be cooked delicately, then it must be absolutely fresh and should be thinly sliced. The common mistake is to cut it into chunks; and monkfish a few days old, cooked in a sauce, is no different from eating India rubber.

Fresh monkfish should be a glistening pearly white, and the dark skin on the top side should feel loose. Occasionally monkfish are sold when they have recently spawned; in this condition they are thin and their flesh is like white jelly. Known as 'slinkfish' in this state, they are absolutely tasteless; I have been caught out more than once.

## Moonfish: see *Sunfish*

## Mussels

If your fishmonger doesn't sell mussels, tell him he ought to! They are easily our most abundant and cheap shellfish and are so good, sweetly tasting of the sea and not tough. And not only are the meats delicious, but the liquor which runs out of them when they are steamed is a crucial ingredient, a *fond de cuisine*, at the Seafood Restaurant, for adding to most fish stews and a variety of fish sauces as well as for making mussel soups.

Mussels can be picked anywhere round the coast, but you should be aware that they can present a health risk if taken from a polluted area. Mussels from beaches facing the open sea are safer than those from estuaries and harbours, because any pollution is likely to be far more diluted by the open sea. Mussels from the bays around Padstow are all quite safe but I advise people to steer clear of the ones in the estuary. Similar information should be fairly easy to get hold of by asking on the spot wherever you are. I think people worry too much about the danger of eating mussels. If you buy them from a fishmonger, you should have nothing to fear from pollution, as he is prohibited from selling them unless they come from a recognized pollution-free area or have been put through a purification process. The modern way of purifying mussels and other bivalves like oysters and clams is to set them in trays for thirty-six hours, during which time well-aerated water is pumped through the system. This water is also sterilized by passing through a quartz sleeve, which has an ultraviolet light of a particular frequency shining through it.

All bivalves feed by sucking in water, extracting vegetable plankton from it, and expelling water and digested material. Held in these tanks the mussels excrete any harmful bacteria, which are then destroyed by the ultraviolet light.

Even if you are going to pick your own and are still uneasy about the mussels on an ocean beach, do remember that you will be cooking them and it is reasonably certain that the heat which kills the mussels will also kill any germs in them.

When buying mussels, don't accept any from a batch in which some are gaping open: it is a sign that they have been out of the sea too long and are not fresh. Sometimes, however, mussels are cleaned mechanically in a machine like a commercial potato peeler, where they are rumbled around against abrasive surfaces in order to remove seaweed and barnacles. The cleaned mussels, while ready to be used, have to be cooked no more than a day after cleaning since the process will cause many of them to die. I imagine this method of treating mussels will become more popular, since there is none of the labour-intensive work of hand-cleaning them, but turnover would need to be very brisk. If you come across clean-looking mussels that are beginning to open, this is what has been done; you will need an honest answer from your fishmonger as to how recently they were processed.

*Octopus:* see *Squid*

*Opah:* see *Sunfish*

*Oyster*

There are two types of oysters on sale in Great Britain, the European (*ostrea edulis*) and the Pacific (*ostrea gigas*). The European oyster, often called a native, usually costs about twice as much as the Pacific. The native oyster is relatively smooth, round and flat. The Pacific oyster (which originally came from British Columbia) is deeper, longer and narrower, with a gnarled, many-leaved shell, and it is far more readily available. It is cheaper than the native oyster because it can be grown very much more quickly and so is the variety favoured by commercial shellfish farmers. Pacific oysters are normally grown in plastic mesh bags attached to steel trestles below the mean low-water mark in tidal estuaries or lochs. This means that they are uncovered only at low spring tides and thus benefit from being able to feed for the maximum time, but it also allows the oyster-grower to clean and salt them for three or four days every fortnight. They are also grown in boxes suspended from floating rafts where they can be winched up and down. They are bought by the grower from a oyster hatchery when they are about the size of your thumbnail and are then grown on to a commercial size, which takes about three years (two if the summers are particularly warm). Having sold every type of oyster available over the last twelve years, I can't help feeling there is too much snobbery towards the Pacific oyster. People who seem to know a thing or two about oysters don't rate it very highly and claim that the native, flat oyster is far superior in taste. I agree that the local variety is a degree more subtle in flavour, but to me what counts more is where they were grown, how old they are and how fresh they are.

I used to have oyster beds in an old sea mill on the Camel Estuary, and to me no oyster ever tasted as good as the ones I opened there and then, in the mud and the seaweed – and they were Pacific oysters. Sadly I had to give up the beds and sell all the oysters because most of the work of grading them and keeping them free from mud had to be done in the summer, when the restaurant was at its busiest. A great shame, because it was the most peaceful and satisfying work.

Having spoken up for the Pacific oyster, I would add that Helford oysters are something quite special. They seem to have a slightly metallic bitterness on first tasting which gives way to a salty freshness; it is difficult to describe a flavour, but I would say that the Pacific oyster is all fresh sweet delight, whereas the Helford is made of sterner stuff, which would indeed satisfy the aficionado more than the novice – but there is certainly an element of 'It must be better if it's twice the cost.'

Our customers are often somewhat uneasy about eating raw shellfish; and it is true that the Chinese would not consider it – in China, that is: they are the first to order up a dozen or two when they come to my

restaurant. Shellfish poisoning is comparatively rare, and, though unpleasant, it is not usually serious. Modern ultraviolet purification techniques make shellfish quite safe to eat raw. A lot of people still think that oysters shouldn't be eaten when there is no 'r' in the month, i.e. in summer. The reasons for this rule were (a) that it was more dangerous to eat them in summer, because the water was warmer and bacteriological activity was higher, and (b) that because the oysters were reproducing in the summer they were full of roe. Nowadays they are as safe to eat in summer as in winter, but sometimes the roe content is too high and they become rather bland and milky.

People have the curious idea that oysters should be swallowed whole, which seems rather a waste for something that's likely to cost £1 a time. They are best served on crushed ice with plenty of lemon and perhaps decorated with a little seaweed if you can get it. Americans are very fond of tomato ketchup and horseradish sauce to go with them, and some people like tabasco or red pepper. I just like lemon. And to drink: a Muscadet, Gros Plant or Sauvignon. Sometimes Chablis in a bad year, when it is green and a bit acid, goes well, but the trend these days is to produce a fuller rounder Chablis, and this won't bring out the best in an oyster.

## Pilchard, sardine

Weights: up to 10 oz. (300 g) for pilchards, up to 4 oz. (120 g) for sardines.

The pilchard, which is an adult sardine, used to be a very important catch in Cornwall, with many coves up and down the coast having their own 'fish cellar' where the pilchards were gutted and salted down in barrels or salted and smoked. The curing process is described in *Hevva!* by K. Harris, one of those delightful local interest books you find in country bookshops. 'Hevva!' was the cry shouted through a long tin trumpet by a lookout man on the clifftop telling the seine-netters in the boats below he had seen a shoal of pilchards.

The process of bulking or balking pilchards was done by first putting a heavy layer of salt on the floor of the fish cellar or palace, then on that a layer of fish, then a layer of salt, then a layer of fish and so on, until the stack was five or six feet high, a catch of 200 hogsheads would take 24 hours to stack. After a month's salting the balk was broken into and the fish taken out and washed before being packed in barrels. The fish were laid in barrels by fish maidens, tails towards the centre. The barrels then had a small lid called a buckler placed on top. A large weight or stone was placed on the buckler and this, in the period of ten days, would press out the train oil, which would run away to drain into tanks for later sale. During the pressing process the barrels were periodically opened and topped up with more fish.

Harris goes on to say that pilchard oil or train oil was sold throughout Britain as a cheap alternative to candles. In addition to salting and smoking, pilchard were also canned and sold as 'fairmaids' or 'fumados' baked with spice and vinegar.

One firm in Newlyn still cures pilchards in this way and sends them off to Italy in wooden barrels at the rate of 120 tonnes a year. We are planning to buy one, so if you come to the restaurant, you may find pilchards served with your apéritif marinated in olive oil with garlic, bayleaf, thyme and some lemon juice.

Fresh pilchards are difficult to get, since virtually the whole catch goes to the salting sheds or the canning factory in Newlyn. But to give you an idea of the extent of the shoals off the south-west, in 1978 a number of deep-sea Scottish trawlers came to Cornwall to catch mackerel (which they sold to Russian factory ships, the latter not being allowed to fish in our waters). But then a quota was imposed on the mackerel, because of the alarming rate at which they were being removed from the sea, so for one month the Scottish ships went over to pilchard fishing. They landed 25,000 tonnes, all of which was turned into fish meal. Today about 600 tonnes of pilchard are caught each year, mostly from boats out of Mevagissey and Looe.

We occasionally get a stone or two, and I have seen pilchards on sale in the fish shop in Truro, so you might be lucky enough to find some. If not, you have the consolation that sardines, which are, of course, exactly the same thing, only younger, are fairly easy to get. Either way, a fresh pilchard or sardine is a delight, best grilled, I feel, or scrowled (see pp. 216–17).

Frozen pilchards or sardines are not worth buying. Oily fish like mackerel and members of the clupeoid family, such as pilchards, herrings and sprats, freeze well enough for a short time, but after a while the oil in them turns rancid.

## Plaice

Weight up to 5 lb. (2.3 kg).

I grow ever more fond of this flat fish with its almost fluorescent orange and red spots on a deep shining green skin. It has a watery, fresh delicacy very soon lost as it stales. Plaice are best avoided in spring, when they spawn and can then (like all fish after spawning) be of poor quality, thin, tasteless, with the flesh unusually soft. Like dabs and flounders, plaice feed on bivalves, particularly cockles and mussels. If you have difficulty telling a flounder from a plaice, remember that the plaice has bony nodules on its head, and the flounder doesn't.

## Pollack

Weight up to 20 lb. (9 kg).

A rather dull member of the cod family, similar in shape to haddock, but browner and without the haddock's black smudge on either side behind the head. Smoked pollack is quite pleasant as a lesser but cheaper alternative to smoked haddock. I might buy pollack as the bulk for a large fish stew for enthusiastic and not too critical consumption, for example the fish stew with cream and saffron on pp. 228–9. But try my battered and marinated pollack with raita and kachumber (pp. 218–20) for an idea on what to do with a dull but cheap fish.

## Pout or pouting or bib

Weight up to 5 lb. (2.3 kg).

A small and rather bony member of the cod family which is often caught in lobster pots. We sometimes get them as part of a box of assorted varieties from Plymouth fish market, and usually just put them in with the fish stock bones. Not a great fish, but very cheap; they are occasionally used in fish and chip shops.

### Porbeagle: see Shark

### Prawns (the North Atlantic prawn, the common prawn)

Average 20 to a lb. (480 g).

It is very difficult to get fresh prawns in Great Britain. The ones you normally buy are from the cold North Atlantic waters around Greenland, Norway and Iceland; they have a pleasant-sounding Latin name, *pandalus borealis*. These are boiled in seawater and frozen at sea. They are very good and a far better buy than the same prawns which have been removed from the shell, given an ice glaze and are sold in packets. If you have the time to remove prawns from the shell, you will have a far better-tasting raw material and also the bonus of a pile of heads and shells which can be turned into delicious soups or sauces (see the recipe for shellfish reduction on pp. 92–3).

Very occasionally we are given small quantities of common prawns that are accidentally caught in lobster pots. I have been trying to persuade a local lobster fisherman to lay down some creel pots for them, but without success. One day I'll get my own fishing boat.

### Queen, queen scallop, quin

Average diameter 2½ inches (6 cm).

These look like small scallops, but they are more rounded and both their shells are the same shape, rather flatter than the deep shell of the scallop. They are best stuffed with the garlic butter, breadcrumb and cheese stuffing given for the stuffed grilled mussels on p. 186.

### Ray: see Skate

### Red fish

Weight up to 6 lb. (2.7 kg).

Red fish is often confused with red bream and red mullet, but is inferior in flavour to them both. Nonetheless, it is quite a nice ordinary fish, which like gurnard adds a dash of brilliant red to a fish stew. An oily fish, it is related to the Mediterranean rascasse, which is held to be the indispensable ingredient in bouillabaisse.

## Red mullet

With its beautiful pink colour, tinged with yellow, mullet is one of my favourite fishes. The taste is somewhere between fish and lobster, and they have a marvellous texture, coming apart in thick firm flakes. The smell of mullet grilling brings back memories of pine and charcoal evenings in the Mediterranean. But though the Mediterranean association is so strong, they are, in fact, reasonably common, at least in the south of England. They are always very expensive, so are something to serve in quite small portions. They don't grow very big; a 3-lb. (1.4-kg) fish is probably the largest you will see, and they normally weigh under 1 lb. (480 g). At the restaurant we serve a single fish of about 6–7 oz. (180–200 g) as a first course with a tomato and tarragon dressing (p. 173). We grill them but leave the liver inside, because, naturally for a fish liver, it is pleasant to eat (mullet seems to have no gall bladder, which is what makes most fish liver very bitter). If you value aroma as an important part of the enjoyment of eating, try the recipe for red mullet cooked over seaweed (pp. 172–3); the combination of the red mullet and the ozone smell of the seaweed is most agreeable.

## Rock turbot: see Wolf fish

## Saithe: see Coley

## Salmon

It is a good idea to ask at your fishmonger whether the salmon you are buying is wild or farmed. Price is the best initial guideline: you can pay twice as much for the wild variety. I would have to lie if I said we never sold farmed salmon; out of the salmon-fishing season, we do. The fish we get from Loch Fynne in Scotland are really quite good, with a definite loch-watery taste, but there is no doubt that the local wild salmon from the Camel River are far nicer. Firm and sleek of shape, their flesh is much paler than the farmed variety and tastes, as one of my sons says, of wildness.

Such an expensive and, alas, always dwindling wild food is too often ruined by unsympathetic treatment. It has to be treated with the utmost simplicity, and it must be undercooked or not cooked at all. When cooked too far, as it so often is, it just tastes dry. All the recipes in this book call for the fish to be undercooked; even the salmon in puff pastry (pp. 261–3) has a cooking time which ensures that the centre will still be quite moist and deep pink. There is something to be salvaged from a Dover sole which has been cooked too far, but nothing from an overdone salmon.

When buying salmon, you may find grilse, salmon which return to spawn when only a year old and which are normally under 6 lb. (2.7 kg) in weight; they are usually at least £1 a lb. (about 500 g) less than adult salmon. If you are able to specify what part of a whole fish you want, a cut from the middle is best; the flesh around the gut cavity is not as nice, and the tail piece has slightly less flavour than the thicker parts.

## Salmon trout, salmon peel, sea trout, sewin

This is the most wonderful fish, a brown trout which has exchanged its habitat of rivers for the open sea and has developed a pink flesh less deep-coloured than salmon. I sometimes find it quite hard to tell a large salmon trout from a salmon until I fillet them, when the orange pink of the salmon shows up. There are two other ways to distinguish them. A salmon has a slight bulge in its shape just before the tail fin, which allows a salmon to be held up by the tail when wet, impossible to do with a salmon trout. Second, the eyes on a salmon trout are slightly higher up the head than on a salmon; if you take an imaginary line from the mouth through to the centre of the gill cover, it will bisect the eye of a salmon but the salmon trout's eye will be above it.

In early summer we get stone after stone of salmon peel delivered to the back door by our salmon fisherman, small ones just big enough for a single portion. We serve them in only two ways, either raw and thinly sliced with a marinade of fresh lime juice and ginger (see p. 151) or cooked *en papillote* with vanilla grass. This last may seem too esoteric, but try opening a parcel of fresh salmon peel cooked simply with butter, salt, pepper, and vanilla grass, which according to the seed catalogue recalls 'the smell of old hay meadows'! Perhaps an over-statement, but grow some and see for yourself.

## Sand eel, sand lance

Up to 8 inches (20 cm) long. About 40 to the lb. (480 g).

My father used to catch these thin, silvery fish at low water wading in the river outside the harbour walls at Padstow. With a small steel hook he would rake through the sand, catching the sand eels in his hand as he displaced them from under the sand where they hide from predators. He used to say that occasionally one could be unlucky and pick up a weever instead, and as they have decidedly poisonous spines, I have always been a bit wary of doing it myself. Sand eels are fried like whitebait, and very nice they are too.

### Sand smelt: see Silverside

### Sardine: see Pilchard

### Scad, horse mackerel

Weight up to 2 lb. (960 g).

Generally go for bait for lobster pots and are rarely seen in fish shops. We buy them occasionally as part of an odd box of fish from the market. They are not the best, but are perfectly acceptable filleted, skinned and fried. Scad, like gurnard, weever or red fish, may lack interest in their own right but can be given much more weight in dishes which contain a number of varieties, including some that are well thought of – maybe adding fillets of scad to a dish of mixed fried fish with tempura batter (see p. 244) which also contained monkfish, langoustine and squid.

### Scaldfish

Weight up to 1 lb. (480 g).

A less common flat fish, closely related to the megrim. Not particularly good; treat it in the same way as sole or plaice, fried or grilled.

### Scallops

One of the most commonly available bivalves (living in two hinged shells), scallops are also one of the most abused in processing plants. Just as peas are given a lurid green colour to appeal (supposedly) to the eye, scallops are generally cut out of their shells and then soaked for twenty-four hours to make them swell to twice their original size. They are then given an ice glaze and frozen. When you get the scallops you are (apparently) impressed by their size and fail to notice that in the cooking they shrink to their original size, losing all the soaking water and all their flavour. A fish processor interviewed by Derek Cooper on BBC Radio 4's *Food Programme* explained that soaking scallops kept the price per pound attractively low – but at what real cost! Most of the scallops you can buy are simply tasteless when compared to fresh. For this reason, it is always sensible to ask for scallops in the shell and cut them out yourself or at least ask for scallops that haven't been soaked. I wouldn't bother to buy frozen scallops until this practice is abandoned, which is a pity because unsoaked scallops freeze very well.

*Scampi:* see *Langoustine*

*Sea bass:* see *Bass*

## Sea scorpion, sculpin

Weight up to 1½ lb. (720 g).

Not a fish you are likely to come across very often, but a worthy ingredient for fish soup. One day, when I manage to get enough sea scorpions, red fish, scads, gurnards, garfish, and smelts, I'm going to produce a dish that the French might call a *Mélange de poissons étranges*, a large plate of unusual fish, some grilled, some fried, some steamed, with maybe two sauces, a light butter sauce with *fines herbes* and a shallot dressing. I know that it will sell well and that those who try it will be pleasantly surprised by the variety and interest of the flavours.

*Sea trout:* see *Salmon trout*

## Sea urchin

There is very little to eat inside a sea urchin, just a few strips of roe which are in fact deliciously sweet eaten raw. We put sea urchins in our *fruits de mer*; the roes can also be used like lobster coral or the coral of scallops to thicken sauces.

*Sewin:* see *Salmon trout*

## Shad, or allis shad or twaite shad

Weight up to 3 lb. (1.4 kg).

A similar fish to the herring but larger; from the same family as pilchards and sprats, the clupeoids. The problem with shad is its bones; there are three lines of them in each fillet, which make it rather tricky to eat (see p. 59 for a suggestion on removing these bones). The custom in south-west France is to eat shad stuffed with sorrel, which some say has a softening effect on the bones, though I've never noticed it (the bones are quite soft anyway).

The best time to eat shad is in May, when they appear in estuaries before going up river to spawn. After spawning they are not great. In my part of the country they are not common, but I have sometimes grilled them and made a very simple sorrel sauce as follows: I remove the stalks from a large handful of sorrel and soften it in some butter. When it has turned into a purée, I pour in a little water, then whisk in enough butter to thicken it. I season the sauce with salt and ground black pepper, and that is all.

## Shark, porbeagle

I predict that shark will become much more widely available as interest in the more unusual types of fish grows. People who try it always find it agreeable, full of lemony flavour and without bones; it is more like veal, say, than fish, but, of course, it is far cheaper. We buy small porbeagles at about 25 lb. (11 kg), but they come much bigger, up to 200 lb. (95 kg). The small ones tend to be a better buy, being more tender, but all shark can be improved by marinading in oil with herbs. You would normally expect to buy shark in steaks (a slice across the fish) or cutlets (half a steak).

Although shark is excellent in small quantities, like many of the other members of the shark family (particularly dogfish), its insistent flavour becomes a little overpowering if it is the only fish in a main course. For this reason, we sell it as part of a selection of fish, for example, raw fish with horseradish and a soya sauce (pp. 150–51), *grillade* (pp. 242–3), or mixed deep-fried fish in tempura batter (p. 244).

## Shrimp, brown shrimp

I used to have oyster beds in the bottom of an old sea mill at Little Petherick, up the estuary from Padstow. Sea mills worked by trapping a large volume of tidal water behind an extensive dam, and then letting it run out through a mill race, so turning the wheel. The original gates for trapping the water had long since gone, but I built a small wooden door big enough to keep my bags of oysters permanently covered with water. I used sometimes to open this door and let the water out through it, having first slung a net across the opening, which allowed me to catch large numbers of shrimps, together with a lot of tiny grey mullet no bigger than whitebait. The shrimps I would boil, the mullet were deep-fried like whitebait. Some of the shrimps went into a most excellent, fresh-tasting bisque (pp. 127–8); so much labour is involved in removing the shells from shrimps that I think a soup is as good a way as any of dealing with them. The French eat shrimps whole and often serve them with drinks. I find eating shrimps whole a bit like eating small ears of barley.

## Silverside, sand smelt

Usually sold commercially as whitebait, though it is a different species. Dip in milk and deep-fry, as for whitebait; serve with plenty of lemon. A pleasant alternative is to dip the fish in beaten egg then pass them through a mixture of seasoned flour and sesame seeds for deep frying.

## Skate, thornback ray, starry ray, spotted ray

Any of the above are likely to be sold to you as 'skate' or 'ray', but if possible choose thornback ray, which is the best-tasting and slowest to smell of ammonia. The wings of skate are the only part sold and are normally skinned before sale. We prefer to buy wings weighing about 1–2 lb. (480–960 g) each. Bigger than that, the flesh becomes a bit coarse; smaller, they are rather fiddly.

A puzzling feature of most information about skate (and dogfish) is that it is said to be quite in order for them to smell of ammonia. I can only say that if your skate smells particularly strongly of ammonia, you shouldn't buy it. Fish are less salty than the sea around them, so, to avoid dehydration, they have to counteract osmosis (the tendency of salt to attract water). Sharks do this by producing urea, which after death gradually breaks down into ammonia, hence the smell. It doesn't set in strongly for at least a week after death, but once it does, no amount of cooking will drive it off; it will still be there in the cooked fish, and it is most unpleasant. Skate is tough and tasteless when totally fresh; it needs to be refrigerated for two or three days, after which it will be quite tender. For three days it will then be in perfect condition; after that, it will start to smell faintly and then distinctly of ammonia. A faint smell is acceptable; a strong smell is not.

Skate in black butter is one of my favourite dishes, a perfect combination of fish and sauce. You will find the recipe on pp. 223–4.

## Slip sole: see Sole

## Smelt

Weight up to 12 oz. (350 g).

I must admit to never having eaten a smelt, mainly because they are not caught locally. They sound delicious, being related to salmon and trout. The normal suggestion for cooking small ones is to dip them in milk and seasoned flour, skewer four or five of them through the eyes and deep-fry them. They are said to smell of cucumber when fresh. If I could get larger ones, I would cook them *en papillote* with vanilla grass like salmon trout (see p. 86).

## Sole, Dover sole

Weight up to 2½ lb. (1.2 kg).

I rarely serve sole at the restaurant in any other way than grilled (p. 240) or *à la meunière* (p. 73). No other fish is so ideally suited to being cooked and served on the bone. The fillets are so firm and the bone structure so intact after cooking (unlike lemon sole), that it is perfectly easy to separate fillet from bone on the plate. Sole is so very expensive now that rolling it up into paupiettes stuffed with mousseline or smothering it in one of the hundreds of sauces and garnishes to be found in older cookery books is, I think, a waste. A simple rule of thumb with fish – and indeed any raw material in cookery – is that the more expensive it is, the less it needs to be embellished.

Perhaps nothing could illustrate our attitude towards cookery better than sole. I would far rather be known for serving the freshest sole simply cooked than for rolling it, stuffing it, pinning it, poaching it, masking it, glazing it, and turning it out looking like anything but what it is. For more thoughts on the same subject, see my recipe for Dover sole from Padstow (pp. 174–5).

Slip soles are small Dover soles weighing up to 8 oz. (240 g), and are normally much cheaper than full-grown soles. Two make a good portion for a main course.

## Spiny lobster: see Crawfish

## Sprat

A member of the herring family (the clupeoids). Never much longer than 5 inches (13 cm), they are best fried or grilled, as in the recipe for grilled sprats with a cobnut sauce (pp. 175–6). To fry them, just brush a frying pan with a tiny amount of oil and cook a few at a time, turning them over when they brown. Season with salt and freshly ground black pepper and serve with a sliced tomato and sliced onion salad well drenched in a good olive oil vinaigrette, with plenty of good bread and lemon.

See also the recipe on p. 120 for salted fillets of sprats preserved in olive oil, which makes a very pleasant *amuse-gueule*.

*Spurdog:* see *Dogfish*

*Squid, cuttlefish, octopus*

Good sizes to buy: squid anything up to 10 inches (25 cm) body length, excluding tentacles; cuttlefish or octopus 1 lb (500 g).

Not so long ago I was asked to give a cookery demonstration to a class at my sons' primary school who were doing a project on Padstow as a port. They went down to the docks to see how fish were caught and sold, and I was asked to cook a few fish to follow the idea through. I decided to take along some squid to show how much a strange-looking creature is not only edible but can be thoroughly enjoyed. Children of seven and eight are a good audience; predictably, when I held up a raw squid they howled with disgust, but they were delightfully appreciative of the taste when it had been cleaned, sliced, floured and fried in olive oil.

The knowledge that all the cephalopods can be caught in reasonable quantities around the British Isles is quite recent. I saw octopus, squid and cuttlefish in the fish shop in Truro the other day for the first time. With all three, the smaller they are, the tenderer they will be. Squid is the least tough, octopus the most. If you have not tried these varieties before, I advise you to start with squid as an introduction to their flavour; the other two, being tougher, are less immediately enjoyable.

*Sunfish, opah, moonfish*

Nick Howell, one of the main fish merchants in Newlyn and a constant source of information to me, says I'll be lucky ever to get a sunfish from the market, because fishermen don't like catching them. They flap lazily around lobster fishing boats, keeping the men company, and so they are held in some affection. They look so serene and sedate that it would seem wrong to lash out at them with a gaff. Nick had only ever seen two at the market. I at once ordered the third, though I had no idea what I would do with it all: they can be as much as 18 inches (45 cm) thick, and the ones Nick saw were as big as a pallet. Since then I have managed to buy some sunfish when I was in Australia. It was sold cut from a large fish in thick boneless fillets, pinkish-white in colour. It was extraordinarily good. I served it once thinly sliced with soya sauce, and also fried in olive oil on a fresh tomato salad. It was sweet and delicate, and could have been sliced and treated in the same way as scallops. If you ever see one for sale here, give me a ring.

*Tope:* see *Dogfish*

## Topknot

A rare flat fish which Alan Davidson in *North Atlantic Seafood* says is quite good.

## Trigger fish

Weight up to 3 lb. (1.4 kg).

Looks a bit like a John Dory but has a skin like thick leather. I have only ever been given one, brought in from a lobster pot. I skinned it, cooked it under the grill and ate it with a spoonful of hollandaise sauce. I've been trying to get some more ever since.

## Turbot

Weight up to 20 lb. (9 kg).

A prized flat fish. With its firm, sweet flesh, white and moist, turbot is in the same class of luxury as lobster. Fortunately for us it is abundant off the north Cornish coast during summer, and the price, though never agreeable, is not too bad.

There is a lot to be said for letting the taste of turbot speak for itself and serving it simply grilled with hollandaise sauce or steamed with *beurre blanc*. But it is also very successful when braised with small vegetables. We put turbot and sliced scallops on a bed of root vegetables previously sweated in butter and Vouvray with some fresh basil and a drop of fish stock. We cover with a butter paper and cook either on top of the stove or in the oven, then add a little cream (recipe on pp. 263–4).

## Weever

A very good fish, firm and good-tasting but not common; I wouldn't expect to come across it at a fish shop because of its poisonous spines. They are on the first dorsal fin and the gill cover; I cut them off very warily and have never had any trouble with them. I've never been able to buy enough to put weever on as a special course in the restaurant, but if I could I would steam them and add a sauce made with reduced fish *fumet*, only enough butter to turn the *fumet* yellow, a dash of vermouth and a couple of sprigs of broad-leaved parsley chopped at the last minute.

## Whelks

*The Good Food Guide* once described our restaurant as 'within a whelk's throw of the harbour'. We buy in whelks occasionally, and when freshly boiled in salt water they can taste almost like lobster, albeit a bit tough.

But the flavour is variable: sometimes they taste frightful, and they exude a disgusting kind of goo! Our whelks come from areas of muddy seabed off Bude; perhaps there are better fishing grounds. When we put them on the *fruits de mer*, we are sometimes asked for more; but I can't say I am an enthusiast for whelks.

### Whiff: see Megrim sole

### Whitebait

Normally the young of herrings and sprats, though other species such as sand eels and sand smelts are commonly called whitebait too. Dip them in milk then seasoned flour and deep-fry; serve with plenty of lemon.

### Whiting

Weight up to 4 lb. (1.8 kg).

A member of the cod family. Small whiting have a fine watery flavour when fresh, but that is a very transient state which, when over, leaves a very dull-tasting fish; so haste in eating is essential. The clear whiting soup (pp. 135–6) would be made with the freshest of fish. Like hake, whiting becomes progressively softer and more difficult to fillet as it stales.

### Winkles

I rarely see people on our seashores picking winkles or mussels, or for that matter anything else, whereas the coasts of Brittany are practically stripped clean. There's something to be said for our current lack of interest in eating marine life, I must say. Winkles are easy to gather on rocky shores, usually underneath seaweed or in crevices in the rock. They are washed in cold water, brought to the boil in well-salted water and boiled for two minutes only, which will be quite long enough to cook them through without overcooking them. They are eaten cold by being unwound from the shell with a small pin – a winkle-picker, no less. Dip them in shallot vinegar (see p. 106).

### Wolf fish, catfish, rock turbot

Weight up to 20 lb. (9 kg).

These are unknown in my part of the world. Well-flavoured, firm-fleshed varieties with a single bone, like a monkfish, allowing the fish to be cut easily into two bone-free fillets. Like monkfish, too, they are sold without the head, which is rather severe-looking, with a set of impressive teeth designed to bite through sea urchins.

A simple recipe for wolf fish is to cut some good-sized fillets crossways, about ½ inch (15 mm) thick, pass these through seasoned flour and fry them in clarified butter. Remove them from the pan and place a thin slice of tomato on top of each; add a little salted butter to the pan and heat till the butter smells nutty, then add a little red wine vinegar. Finally, just before pouring the butter over the fish, throw in some very finely chopped shallots and some parsley and pour over the fish.

## Wrasse

Weight up to 6 lb. (2.7 kg).

The dazzling colours of the wrasse, red, yellow or greeny brown, and its plump rounded shape suggest a fish worthy of note; but in my experience they are rather watery and excessively flaky. We use them in fish stews, where their yellow flesh looks fine.

# Three

# PREPARING FISH

The instructions which follow on preparing fish for cooking are very detailed. It is true that drawings and photographs may seem easier to follow when trying to grasp the intricacies of cutting up fish, but in the end I think a written description is the best way to explain the finer details I have learnt over twelve years of doing the same thing day after day. People often ask me whether I get bored repeating the same jobs over and over again. I don't. Cleaning and filleting fish is a perfect relaxation to me. A job like filleting, where your hands and brain are working in complete agreement because you have done it so often before, is a pleasure, a feeling that you're doing something right.

## · WET FISH ·

### Storing fish

Domestic refrigerators are not well suited to storing fish, being too warm and not damp enough. Commercial fish fridges work at 32°F (0°C); domestic fridges work at about 39°F (4°C). The answer is to eat what you buy the day you buy it. If you have to store fish for any time, place it on a plate or tray and wrap clingfilm over both plate and fish; don't wrap the actual fish itself. Place it in the coldest part of the refrigerator. If you have to store fish, a whole fish will keep much better than a fillet.

Fish that you intend to store any longer than a couple of days is better frozen, but it is only worth freezing fish that you know to have been freshly caught. I wouldn't advise freezing anything that you bought from a fish shop, since you can't know whether it has been frozen once already. I find that fish frozen whole, guts and all, keeps better than fish filleted or cut into steaks. I believe most advisers on freezing would disagree, but the fact that the fish is not broken into in any way seems to keep it in much better condition through the process of freezing and defrosting.

I can't help but add that to me freezing is the lesser of two evils – stale fish or frozen fish. I am not an enthusiast of frozen fish (or frozen anything, for that matter, except ice cream and *eau de vie*), but we live in an imperfect world; sometimes I buy too much and have to freeze, but normally what I freeze goes to making fish soup, along with fresh fish too.

## Cleaning and filleting fish

If you intend to fillet and skin your fish, you need not remove fins or scales, but you must if you are serving it whole. If your fish is bought ungutted, you should remove the guts as soon as possible; if you leave them in, they will taint the flesh. If you are removing scales, do it as soon as possible, since if you leave them on and let the skin dry, they are very hard to remove. You remove fins and scales as follows.

### ROUND FISH WITH SCALES

Place several sheets of newspaper over a chopping board and around the work-top. Put the fish on the paper and snip off the fins with a good pair of kitchen scissors (we use orange-handled scissors made in Finland for Wilkinson Sword). Now scrape the scales away, working from tail to head and using a blunt, thick-bladed knife or the back of a knife, or a special fish scraper, or even a scallop shell. The scales will fly everywhere, which is why the newspaper is such a good idea. When the fish is de-scaled, you can wrap the paper up and throw it away.

In the restaurant kitchen, we have a special sink with a very large, flat but slightly tilted draining board and a high tiled wall behind sealed to the sink. As we work scaling and then filleting fish, we constantly spray water over this area, washing the scales down into the sink (which has a perforated guard round the drain allowing the water to run away but trapping the scales).

Having de-scaled the fish, remove the intestines by slitting the fish along the belly from the head to the anal fin. Pull most of the guts out with your hand, then use scissors to cut away any pieces of entrail left. If you like, you can also remove the gills by cutting them away from the two places where they join the fish, at the back of the head and just under the mouth.

Having removed the insides of the fish, give the cavity a good wash. Hold the fish under running water and run the point of a knife along both sides of the backbone to remove any blood left inside; this is quite an operation with salmon and salmon trout, which have a lot. Having washed out the cavity, dry it with kitchen paper or a clean cloth, and the fish is ready for cooking.

### CLEANING FLAT FISH FOR SERVING WHOLE

Snip off the side fins with scissors as close to the flesh as possible and trim the tail fin. The only flat fish with scales which flake off is the Dover sole, and that is skinned before cooking; so no de-scaling is required with flat fish.

Flat fish are normally gutted at sea, but if you happen to catch your own or buy one fished from inshore waters, make a small incision on one side of the fish just behind the gills and, as they say in the best circles, eviscerate it.

## REMOVING THE BONES
### FROM A ROUND FISH FOR SUBSEQUENT STUFFING

If you intend to stuff a whole fish, you can use the gut cavity as a natural container for the stuffing by removing the guts through the gills. You do this by reaching your finger through the gills and pulling out the insides. Pull out the gills at the same time and snip each side off with scissors. When you have removed the insides, it is a good idea to cut a small opening just in front of the anal fin and wash the cavity through from the gills.

## BONING ROUND FISH FOR SERVING WHOLE

It is possible to remove most of the internal bones so that when the fish is stuffed it can be eaten without the bones getting in the way. To do this, gut the fish as normal, but slit it right along the belly from the head to the tail, cutting through to the backbone beyond the gut cavity, so that the backbone is exposed all the way down. Remove the rib bones in the gut cavity by pulling them out one by one with a pair of pliers and cutting them off where they join the backbone. Cut into the flesh on either side of the backbone with the point of a knife and run right down either side of the bone. Snip the backbone through near the head and tail, and carefully pull it out.

## TO DO THE SAME FOR A FLAT FISH

Cut a flat fish down the centre of its back, and free the top two fillets from the underlying rib bones without cutting through to the sides. Free the backbone by snipping it near the head and tail, then break it by bending the fish double in two or three places, and lift out the broken sections of backbone and ribs. You have to leave the bones which join on to the fins in place, but this method gives a more or less bone-free fillet to stuff through the back.

## Skinning a flat fish

Dover sole and its relatives, the sand or French sole or the thickback sole, are the only flat fish which can be skinned if eaten whole. It is impossible to skin any of the others whole, but the skins on all but turbot are quite pleasant to eat. Turbot has small shell-like knobs on its top side like tiny limpets; the top skin should therefore be scraped off after cooking and before serving.

### To skin a sole

Remove the side fins. With a thin-bladed filleting knife, make a small incision at the point where the tail joins the body. Push the flat of the knifepoint into this incision and run it across the fish, lifting a flap of skin away from the flesh to give yourself a bit of purchase. Pour out a little salt and get a teatowel. Dip the fingers of your left hand in the salt, and hold the tail (the salt helps you to grip). Grasp the flap of skin with the towel in your right hand, and pull the skin away from the tail right over the head. Repeat with the other side.

The fresher the sole, the more tenaciously the skin will stick to the flesh. If it sticks so firmly that pulling it away is starting to tear it, stop, run your finger between one side of the fish and the skin from the point where you have stopped tearing up towards the head; you will find that a half-inch flap comes away easily at the side. Put more salt on your fingers and hold the flesh at the side near the top and pull the skin with the cloth across the fish and down towards the point where the flesh caught; by approaching this point from a different direction, you will avoid badly tearing into the flesh.

## Filleting fish

### Filleting round fish
(like the cod family, bass, salmon, red bream, gurnards and any other with a similar bone structure)

The larger the fish, the more tricky the filleting becomes. Small fish like mackerel and herring can be done with one easy sweep of the knife; large fish like bass and salmon require calm concentration, mostly because they are heavy and bulky and so it is more difficult to keep what you have already cut out of your way as you continue cutting.

Fillet small fish like salmon trout, herrings, mackerel and whiting as follows:

Lay the fish on a chopping board with its back towards you. Cut across the fish through to the backbone just behind the head.

Turn the cutting edge of the knife towards the tail and cut the fillet away from the backbone right down to the tail, using the flat of the knife against the backbone as a guide.

Turn the fish over and repeat on the other side. Trim the rib bones away from the fillets.

Any fish over about 12 oz. (350 g) will need to be filleted more carefully. The quick way of filleting small fish is quite wasteful, in that it leaves some fillet along the backbone. On a small fish, this is hardly worth saving, but on larger fish it is.

## ——— A simple way to fillet small fish ———
### (e.g. mackerel or herring)

Slit the fish from head to tail. Put the fish on a chopping board belly side down; press the back firmly with the flat of your hand and gradually flatten the fish out on the board. Now lift out the backbone and remove any bones left in the fillet with a pair of tweezers.

## ——— How to fillet larger round fish ———

Lay the fish on a chopping board and cut off the head just behind the gills and pectoral fin. Use a good heavy kitchen knife to make it easy to cut through the backbone. Don't cut straight through but rather follow the line of the gills in a V-shape to make sure that you don't lose any of the fillet. Lay the fish with its back towards you and make an incision in the middle of the back with a filleting knife about one third of the way up the fish from the tail.

Easing the knife under the flesh, make sure that the blade glides over the backbone. Turn the blade towards the tail and cut right down to the tail with a bold sweep against the backbone.

Follow the original incision up towards the thick end of the fish, carefully cutting away with the knife against the backbone. As you cut lift the flap of fillet up with your fingers to make it easier to see what you are doing; don't cut further through the fish than the spine or you will find that you are cutting through the ribs, and you want to glide over them.

Now turn the fish so that the thick end faces you, and ease your filleting knife over the rib bones towards the belly, again lifting the fillet up off the bone so that you can see what you are doing (much easier with the head removed).

Gradually work down the fish till you meet the point where you cut the tail section free. Remove the fillet.

Turn the fish over with the back facing you and do the same with this side. This is slightly harder, as you don't have the other fillet to cushion the operation and keep all the bones firmly in place. I always find that I leave more fish on the bone on this side (but not much).

This method of filleting will produce two good clean-looking fillets with all the rib bones and the flesh round them removed. This is desirable because the flesh immediately surrounding the stomach tends to be the least pleasant-tasting part of the fish.

Remove any bones left in the fillet with a pair of tweezers.

## Skinning fillets of fish

Place a fillet on a chopping board, skin side down. Put your fingertips on the extreme tail end of the fillet and work your filleting knife up the fillet against the skin, working away from your fingers in a series of short, jerky cuts.

## Filleting a flat fish

Lay the fish on the chopping board with the top (dark) side uppermost and the tail facing you. Make an incision with a filleting knife in the centre of the back, just behind the head. Cut down to the backbone, then open the fish up from the head down to the tail, working along the backbone with your knife.

Using the bone structure as a guide, cut away the left-hand-side fillet from the head towards the side fins, with the filleting knife at a very shallow angle. Cut with a series of short, gentle, scything motions. Lift up the flap of fillet as you cut to make it easier to see what you are doing. Continue down to the tail and remove the fillet. Do the same with the other side, then turn over and repeat the operation.

## Eels and dogfish

### SKINNING EELS AND DOGFISH

It is not possible or necessary to skin most round fish, since the skin without the scales is neither an impediment to cooking nor inedible. However, conger eel and members of the shark family have skins so tough and inedible that they are best removed where possible. Conger eel and all dogfish, including tope and freshwater eel as well, are skinned as follows. You will need strong string, pliers and somewhere to hang the fish. Slit right along the belly and remove the guts. Cut off the fins and tail. Cut through the skin just behind the neck, and continue this cut right round at the back of the head so that the skin is parted from the head all the way round, like ring barking. With the point of a filleting knife ease about half an inch of skin away from the flesh all the way round to gain some purchase when pulling away the skin. Tie a piece of string round this cut with a long enough loose end to attach to some anchorage point like a window catch, a hook on a wall, a shelf bracket, or even a strong doorhandle. Attach the fish. Grip the flap of skin with the pliers and pull the skin towards the tail. Some of the flesh will start to come away with the skin. Keep moving the pliers around to different parts of the skin and pulling; you will find that the skin soon starts to pull away cleanly. Firmly and steadily pull the skin off the body. As you approach the tail it will get harder. Grasp the skinned body with your other hand and with a final smooth tug the whole skin will peel off. It is a most satisfying task.

### TO FILLET AN EEL

Cut down to the backbone just behind the head. Turn the knife towards the tail and cut down to the tail against the backbone, lifting the fillet off as you go. Turn the eel over and do the same thing on the other side.

### HOW TO FILLET A DOGFISH

Cut off the head. Starting at the top, cut in from the centre of the back to the cartilaginous spine with a filleting knife. Cut over the spine towards the belly, lifting the fillet away as you do. As you get towards the tail, where the fish becomes thinner, you can free the whole fillet by cutting at a shallow angle towards the tail against the backbone.

## Skinning a skate

Unfortunately, the skin on a skate does not readily pull off, so it has to be cut off. This is a bit tricky, but not more so than, say, skinning a rack of lamb. Use a thin-bladed filleting knife and ease the skin away from the flesh along the edge that was joined to the body; with a gentle sweeping motion cut through the join of flesh and skin while pulling the skin away from the flesh. Imagine you are shearing a sheep.

## How to skin and fillet monkfish

### SKINNING

Skinning a monkfish is very easy; just grasp the thick end in one hand and the skin in the other, and pull away the skin.

### FILLETING

Again very easy, since monkfish has only one central bone. Cut the tail into two large fillets by running your filleting knife against the spine from where it obtrudes at the thick end down to the tail.

Monkfish has a thick membrane under the skin which is inedible and has to be removed. The best way to deal with this is to treat it like a second skin and remove it from the fillets as you would skin any fillet of fish (see above).

Lay the fillet on a chopping board membrane side down, hold the fillet at the very end of the tail with your left hand and cut into the fillet just in front of your fingers with a filleting knife. With a series of little jagged cuts, force the knife up the fillet against the membrane.

## Filleting and skinning John Dory

Lay the fish on a chopping board with its head facing you. Insert the point of your filleting knife into the right-hand side of the fish next to the tail, just above the bony fins which run all round the body. Gradually work the point of the knife up the fish against these bony fins, cutting away a little flap of fillet. Repeat on the left-hand side.

Lift up the flap you have created and gradually work your way right across one side of the fish, with your filleting knife against the central bones radiating out from the spine. Lift the fillet off the bones as you cut. Remove the whole side as one fillet.

Turn the fish over and do the same thing on the other side.
Skin in the same way as any other fillet of fish (see above).

### How to fillet and remove the bones from shad

Remove the fillets from the shad in the same way as you would for a herring (see p. 55).

There are three lines of bones running down each fillet. Run your filleting knife down each side of the bone lines then gripping one end of the line of bones between the thumb and the blade of the knife peel it away from the fillet. Unfortunately this bone removal is slightly complicated by the fact that the bones do not run straight up and down through the flesh; but you will see which way they lean and can angle the knife accordingly. You should be left with four strips of fillet on each side, which should be cooked with the skin left on.

## · CRUSTACEANS ·

### Storing crabs, lobsters and crawfish

All will stay alive for at least two days, even three or four if they were lively when you bought them. Keep them in the bottom of a refrigerator, covered with damp seaweed or a damp cloth.

### Preparing crabs, lobsters and crawfish

#### CRABS

One of the most disconcerting experiences I had when writing a fish column for *Woman's Realm* magazine was to receive a vehement letter from a reader who ran a cats' home in Kent ('a haven for cats in need'). She called me a pervert because I had written that crabs should be plunged into boiling water to kill them instantly. She suggested that I actually enjoyed inflicting pain on these poor creatures, and she said that her local fishmonger, a very humane man, killed crabs by piercing them with a sharp instrument in exactly the right place between the eyes, so that they died instantly.

This is indeed the way crabs are killed commercially, but it is not done for humanitarian reasons. If you plunge a crab into boiling water it will shed both its claws and all its legs and so won't be any good to sell. I'm not suggesting that the fishmonger was not humane, only that there are practical arguments too for this method of killing – which I have since adopted. Take a small knife or screwdriver, turn the crab over and pierce it through the mouth straight up to strike the underside of the back shell right behind the eyes. Now pierce it again right in the middle of the undershell, underneath the flap which folds over the shell. This is small in the male crab and large on the female (and is incidentally one way to tell the sex, the other being the size of the claws, which are larger on the male).

Crabs should be cooked in water salted at the rate of 5½ oz. (165 g) to the gallon (5 litres). This is roughly the salinity of seawater, in which we usually cook our shellfish. The cooking times recommended in many books are too long; I would suggest 15 minutes from coming to the boil for anything up to 1¼ lb. (600 g); 20 minutes for anything up to 2 lb. (960 g); 25 minutes up to 3½ lb. (1.6 kg); and 30 minutes for anything larger.

## LOBSTERS

Unlike crabs, lobsters cannot be easily killed by stabbing them or giving them a sharp blow on the back of the head. For the reason why, I quote from *The Cook's Encyclopaedia* by Tom Stobard (Papermac):

Lobsters are not vertebrates, and their main nerve cord runs down the under side and not the back, so exhortations to kill a lobster by severing its spinal cord are way off . . . The lobster is a very primitive creature, more so than the crab, for instance, and it has no brain, only a long nerve cord with various swellings (ganglia) along its course, and it cannot be killed by a knife thrust. Only those who can split a lobster in two down the middle line in one blow can claim to kill it instantly.

Lobsters have to be boiled alive, and there is no point in worrying too much about it. I hate killing lobsters but love eating them. All I can say about that is to quote from *The Walrus and the Carpenter*:

> 'I weep for you,' the Walrus said:
> 'I deeply sympathize.'
> With sobs and tears he sorted out
> Those of the largest size . . .

In order to kill the lobsters quickly you need plenty of boiling water in a large pan, so that the time taken for the water to come back to the boil once you have put the lobster in is minimized. I suggest a large pan too because nothing seems more cruel than forcing a live lobster into a small pan. The water should be salted at the rate of about 5½ oz. (165 g) to the gallon (5 litres), which is the same strength as seawater.

Lobsters should be cooked for 15 minutes for anything up to 1½ lb. (720 g); 20 minutes up to 2½ lb. (1.2 kg); and an extra 5 minutes for each 1 lb. (500 g) after that. These times start when the lobster comes back to the boil. Don't boil hard during the cooking; a gentle simmer is enough.

When the lobsters are cooked, cut them open and serve as described on p. 251 for grilled or cold lobster, and on pp. 252–4 for lobster with vanilla sauce. The method for splitting live lobsters cleanly in half is also given in the recipe for grilled lobsters (p. 251).

## CRAWFISH

Boil in the same way as lobsters. Allow 20 minutes for anything up to 2½ lb. (1.2 kg), and an extra 5 minutes for each 1 lb. (500 g) after that.

### Extracting the meat from a crawfish

Leave to cool and slice in half as follows. Place on a chopping board and drive a large knife through the middle of the carapace (the body section) and cut down towards and between the eyes. Turn the knife round, place it in the original cut and bring it down right through the tail to split it in half. Remove the meat from the tail, taking care to extract the pieces tucked into the extreme tail section. Pull off all the claws and legs, and take the meat out of these. The best way to do this is to cut off one end of each section near a joint and push the meat through from the other joint with the thin end of a lobster pick. Remove the meat from the head and first joints of the feelers. Then remove all the meat from the body cavity; on a crawfish this is most simply done with your fingers, as you can push and pull it out quite easily. The rather soft sponge-like material just inside the carapace is quite edible; it is in fact the next shell forming. The dark brown, soft and runny substance in the head is not usually worth keeping, being rather bitter. The bright orange coral, on the other hand, is excellent.

## · CEPHALOPODS ·

### Preparing squid for cooking

If you intend to stuff squid or cut it into rings, reach into the body with your fingers and pull out the insides, which will be attached to the head. Pull out the plastic-like quill from inside the body and any of the soft white material which is often found inside.

Pull the purple-coloured skin off the body (it comes away very easily). Remove the two fins and skin them too. Wash the body. Cut off the tentacles from the head and insides, just in front of the eyes. Squeeze the beak-like mouth out of the centre of the tentacles and throw it away.

If you intend to slice the squid into strips, pull the head and insides away from the body as before, but open the body up with your knife from top to bottom and flatten it out. Remove the quill and any soft white material on the inside and the skin on the outside. Deal with the head and tentacles in the same way as before.

If you need the ink to make a sauce, as in the recipe for squid with an ink sauce (p. 176), carefully remove the ink sac from the rest of the insides. It is easily identifiable, being pearly in colour with a blue tinge.

If you are parsimonious there are two pieces of muscle running down either side of the insides which can be detached and used; this is certainly worth considering if the squid is a large one.

## Preparing octopus for cooking

Cut the tentacles off just in front of the eyes.

Press the mouth, both beak and soft surround, out from the centre of the tentacles.

Cut the head section from the body sac at the openings into the body. Discard the head.

Turn the body inside out and pull away all the entrails. Pull off the small bone-like strips sticking to the sides of the body. Turn the body the right side round, and try to pull off the skin, which with small octopus is usually possible; similarly remove the skin from the tentacles. If you can't remove the skin, you will have to do so after it is cooked.

It is debatable whether it is a good idea to try to tenderize octopus, as for instance the Greeks do, by bashing it against a rock at least forty times before preparing it. Certainly large octopuses are extremely tough; we tenderize small ones (which we fry like squid) by laying them out on a chopping board after we have cleaned them and flattening them repeatedly with blows from a cutlet bat. You could do the same with a rolling pin. We cook large octopuses in a little oil in a low oven (300°F; 150°C; gas mark 2) for an hour or two till they are so tender that a knife will easily pierce the tentacle. In this case, you don't need to tenderize them at all. The body section will soften more quickly and should be removed from the oven some time before the tentacles.

## Preparing cuttlefish for cooking

Cut the tentacles off just in front of the eyes and remove the beak-like mouth from the centre of the tentacles.

Cut the head section from the body and discard it. (The head sections in all of the cephalopods, though not inedible, seem to me so gristly as to be not worth saving.) Cut open the body section from top to bottom along the dark-coloured back; remove the white cuttlebone and the entrails. Scrape clean and wash it out, then skin the body and the tentacles. Cuttlefish can be cooked in exactly the same ways as squid.

## · MOLLUSCS ·

### Opening oysters

I have never yet found an oyster knife that was any good for opening oysters. The blades are too short and too blunt. If you watch oyster shuckers in Parisian seafood restaurants, you will see that they use an ordinary knife. They hold the oyster in one hand and the knife in the other, insert the tip of the knife in the hinge of the oystershell and worry away at it till it opens. They don't seem to exert any particular pressure, and the speed they work at can only be described as astonishing.

Following their techniques, here is how to open an oyster. Take a tea towel and a small thick-bladed knife with a reasonably sharp point. Fold the tea towel two or three times and put it in your left hand. Place the oyster on top of the towel and grip it. Place your left hand on your knee and push the tip of the knife into the hinge of the oyster. Using firm but not excessive pressure, work the knife backwards and forwards into the shell. When the oyster gives up, slide the blade into the centre against the top shell, cutting the muscle that joins the oyster to its shell as close to the flat top shell as possible. Lift off the top shell, keeping the bottom shell upright at all times to avoid losing any of the juice. Pick out any little pieces of shell that might have broken off.

### How to prepare scallops for cooking

Place the scallop on a chopping board, flat shell uppermost. Slide the blade of a filleting knife between the two shells (they don't close particularly tightly). Keeping the blade of the knife flat against the flat shell, find the muscle that joins the shell to the body of the scallop and cut through it. Remove the top shell.

Cut the scallop away from its bottom shell by severing the joining muscle which lies underneath the scallop. A flexible knife is essential for this, so that you can follow the curve of the shell and thus avoid cutting into the scallop itself. There is actually a knife with a curved blade designed specifically to cut out scallops.

Take the scallop out of the shell and carefully pull the skirts away from the scallop meat. Cut the dark stomach section away from the point where it joins the coral, and you are left with the yellow, marble-coloured meat and the coral. Wash this thoroughly to remove any sand

and finally cut away any traces of the white sinew which joined the body to the round undershell.

## Preparing mussels for cooking

Disregard any information about leaving mussels in a bucket of cold water to let them cleanse themselves (with or without a handful of oatmeal). Mussels are extremely particular about the type of water they find themselves in. A bucket of cold tap water will cause them to stay firmly closed, since they very quickly sense that there is no air in the water and that it is not salty. They will not self-cleanse unless they are in seawater or brackish water which is well aerated. Furthermore, leaving them for any length of time in a bucket of still water will soon kill them. There is in any case no need to clean mussels like this, because unlike cockles, which live under sand, they are not gritty.

Wash mussels in the sink with plenty of changes of cold water, swirling them round and round each time until the water is clear. Scrape the mussels with a short thick-bladed knife to remove any barnacles or seaweed, and pull out the beards if you are going to serve them as *moules marinière* or in any other dish where they are cooked and served immediately. (If you are going on to stuff them, it is easier to remove the beards after you have cooked them and let them cool down.)

## Preparing cockles for cooking

Cockles present a bit more of a problem in cleaning than mussels because they are apt to be gritty internally. Proceed as follows. Wash the cockles in a large colander in a sink of cold water swirling them round the colander. Change the water two or three times and continue washing until no more sand can be seen dropping down out of the colander. You can then go on to cook the cockles, though they will still be a little gritty. This can be dealt with by straining the cooked cockles through a colander, leaving the cooking liquor to settle. Pour the liquor off the settled sediment, then use this liquor to wash out the last of the grit. (Keep the cooking liquor; it's as good as mussel juice.)

If you want to get rid of the last traces from the live cockles you can make them self-cleanse in a bucket, but the water must be seawater or at least tap water made up to the same salinity as seawater (5½ oz. salt to the gallon or 165 g to 5 litres). There must be plenty of it, at least three times as much water as cockles, and it must be well aerated; you can do this by scooping the water up with a jug and pouring it back into the bucket about ten times. You should change the water after 20 minutes and aerate once more. The cockles will take about 45 minutes to clean. You can tell if they are cleansing; they will open, tubes will appear, and little blobs of mucus and grit will puff up out of them.

## Clams

Clams, particularly the soft-shelled variety which lives under sand, can be cleaned in the same way as cockles; they can be steamed open like cockles or mussels, and they can also be opened and eaten raw, but should have been purified or taken from a known pollutant-free area. Clams and cockles that you buy ready purified should be sand-free since they will have been left in clean running seawater to self-cleanse for some hours. To clean your own live clams follow the directions for cockles above.

To open a clam, carefully insert the blade of a small thick-bladed knife between the two shells, not at the hinge as with an oyster, but on the opposite side. Twist slightly to force the shells open and cut through the two pieces of sinewy tissue which join the top and bottom shells at either end. Remove the top shell and cut under the meat to free it from the bottom shell, keeping the shell upright to avoid spilling the juice. As with oysters, wrapping your hand in a tea towel before holding the clam will help to avoid injuries if the knife slips.

# Four

# COOKING FISH

I often rent a house in another part of the British Isles or France or even this winter Australia. One of my fascinations is to try to cook well without all the *batterie de cuisine* of the restaurant, the steamers, fish kettles, copper sauté pans, generous thick steel frying pans, solid French and German steel knives, and plenty of stainless steel work-tops, with sinks all over the place, as well as fridges, grills and stoves.

On the whole, I don't seem to do too well. Rather arrogantly, I am amazed at the sort of kitchen equipment other people consider useful. More often than not, it all seems designed to make it hard to cook well. Wafer-thin frying pans, tiny sources of heat, no work space, saucepans that would burn anything, grills with handles that fall off, and terrible knives designed to cut *you*. But it all serves to remind me how many people manage to produce creditable meals with equipment far less sophisticated than ours.

It leads me to wonder if good cooking is not more a matter of good equipment than of skill. Perhaps it would be an interesting test of a good cook to take away all the props, give him a kitchen equipped from the local ironmonger's shop and raw materials bought at the corner shop, and tell him to see what he could do. That would be a more challenging test of culinary skill than the Chef of the Year Competition.

Good, solid, simple equipment is so important if you are to cook well, and most domestic equipment is money wasted. Eschew the local tin-pan shops; go somewhere like the French Kitchen and Tableware Supply Company, 42 Westbourne Grove, London W2 (telephone 01 221 2112).

But I mention this only in passing. This book is intended for those with a degree of sophistication in their kitchens; I assume you have some good equipment and I feel it necessary only to describe some pieces of kitchen equipment needed particularly for fish cookery which you may not have.

### Special equipment for cooking fish

1. A fish filleting knife, with a blade that is about 7 inches (18 cm) and flexible, made either of carbon steel, which is easy to sharpen but hard to keep clean, or good stainless steel, such as a Victorinox or Gustav Ern.

2. An extra large cook's knife with a 10-inch (25-cm) blade for cutting lobsters and crawfish in half.

3. A fish scaler. A blunt knife or even a scallop shell will do, but a fish scaler, with a blunt serrated blade turned round on itself and fastened, will remove scales quicker and will deal with tough scaled varieties like bass or fish where the skin has dried and the scales have stuck.

4. A good pair of kitchen scissors for cutting off fins. We use Wilkinson Sword (we don't buy fish scissors because they rust).

5. A small pair of long-nosed pliers or tweezers for extracting bones from fillets of fish.

6. Some crab and lobster picks.

7. A couple of lobster claw crackers.

8. An extra large 12-inch (30-cm) diameter saucepan into which a standard 10-inch (25-cm) dinner plate will fit with ample space to lift it in and out. This makes a simple basic steamer. The plate is set on some sort of stand (an upturned soufflé dish, say). Water is put in the bottom; fillets of fish are steamed on the plate.

Also useful for boiling shellfish.

9. A flower-petal-shaped perforated steamer (available at most iron-mongers), which expands to fit the pan it is put in. This is for steaming whole small fish and is much more versatile than the steamer pans you can buy.

10. A fish kettle for poaching whole salmon and salmon trout. To decide on a size, bear in mind that a grilse (young salmon) or salmon trout weighing 5 lb. (2.3 kg) and about 25 inches (63 cm) long would serve six

or seven people and would fit into a size 1, 24-inch (61-cm) aluminium fish kettle. But you can also cook salmon or salmon trout very slowly in the oven wrapped in foil brushed with oil (275°F; 135°C; gas mark 1): allow about 12 minutes to each 1 lb. (500 g).

11. Some sort of grill arrangement where the heat comes from underneath rather than overhead. This could be a portable barbecue, a thick ribbed fish grilling pan, a chargrill (using pumice-stone rather than charcoal), a simple mild steel grill stand for setting over an open fire or a fish grill, a fish-shaped wire grill. A whole fish is placed on one half of this and the other half is closed over the fish and fastened. The fish can then be easily turned over the fire.

12. A conical strainer and small ladle – essential for passing soups, particularly bisques. You push as much soup as you can through the strainer with the back of the ladle.

13. A pepper grinder for white peppercorns. White peppercorns, which the French call mignonette pepper (meaning dainty), are used a great deal in fish cookery for delicate dishes where black pepper would be too harsh.

Finally, back to the subject of knives. Mr Tom Chivers, a chef of the old school who taught me at Cornwall Catering College and made it completely enjoyable, once said 'You can cook an awful lot better with a sharp knife' – to which I would add that the obvious things in life are those which we most often forget!

## · THE MAIN WAYS OF COOKING FISH ·

### Baking

By 'baking' I mean the process of cooking a fish in a reasonably deep dish without a lid with accompanying flavouring elements such as tomatoes, olives and anchovies with fennel (see p. 211 for mullet cooked in this way). The temperature should be lower than for roasting – about 325°F;

170°C; gas mark 3 – because the idea here is for the fish to assimilate the flavours of its accompaniments without burning. The accompanying vegetables also protect the fish and moisten it.

## BAKING EN PAPILLOTE

The fish is wrapped in buttered greaseproof paper or foil with vegetables and herbs and baked in the oven. No flavour or aroma is lost in this method, and the parcel can be taken to the table and snipped open – with dramatic effect, because the smell is always so good. We cook *en papillote* in a hot oven (450°F; 230°C; gas mark 8): since the fish is sealed, there is no danger of even a fillet drying out.

## BAKING IN A BAIN-MARIE

Fish terrines and various moulded mousselines are cooked in a moderate oven (325°F; 170°C; gas mark 3) with the dish in a bath of boiling water which comes halfway up it. The terrine will cook slowly surrounded with moisture.

## Braising

Quite hefty steaks or even whole fish are placed on a bed of well-buttered root vegetables in a fairly shallow pan to fit quite tightly. A liquid, half fish stock and half wine (with us always a specific wine, often Vouvray), is poured on to come about halfway up the fish. Herbs are sprinkled over and a loose-fitting lid or a butter paper is placed on top. The pan is then put in the oven or on the stove until the fish is almost cooked. The lid is then removed and the cooking juices reduced to a glaze by rapid boiling. The fish is served coated with the sauce, which is often given a little cream to give it more body.

## Boiling

As a general rule if you find yourself boiling a piece of fish, even for the cat, you are ruining it. Not so, however, when making a fish stew, where the purpose of boiling is precisely to take all the flavour out of the fish to flavour the *bouillon*. In pure terms the point of a fish stew is the *bouillon* or soup and not the pieces of fish which are included with the accompanying flavouring vegetables. But we actually make our fish stew *bouillon* with fish stock rather than water, so that there is plenty of flavour to go round. The other purpose of boiling a fish stew hard is to amalgamate oil or butter and water into an emulsion.

## Frying

### SHALLOW FRYING

We use clarified butter, the purpose of clarification being to remove the water and solids which burn and discolour when the butter is heated up.

When shallow frying, don't overcrowd the frying pan, particularly if you haven't got a strong source of heat. This is because you need to seal the fish first to prevent the oil from saturating the inside. If you cook at too low a temperature (and overcrowding the pan on an inadequate source of heat will reduce the temperature) the fish becomes soggy with oil or fat rather than crisp on the outside and juicy on the inside. After sealing the fish over a high heat, lower the heat to finish the cooking, otherwise the outside will burn.

When cooking fillets of fish, particularly flaky fish, it is usual to pass the fish through seasoned flour first. This forms a coating which prevents the oil from getting inside the fish (just like the batter in deep-frying). Sometimes, however, if you are using a particularly well-flavoured oil with a close-textured fish, like monkfish or squid, it is nice not to use any flour and so allow more of the oil to flavour the fish.

Shallow frying is probably the most common way of cooking fish at home; certainly it is for me, simply because it is so quick and convenient. It always transforms a meal if, having cooked the fish, you season it with salt and, if possible, freshly ground white pepper, sprinkle it with lemon juice and freshly chopped parsley; then discard the cooking butter from the frying pan, put in a fresh knob and cook it till it is going brown and smelling nutty, and pour this right over the fish, cooking *à la meunière*. If you are cooking with olive oil in a more Mediterranean style, a small quantity of warmed olive oil dressing poured round the fish at the last minute is rather good. We often have a simply fried fillet of fish with a herb dressing on as a first course in the restaurant.

### DEEP FRYING

Provided you have some excellent cooking oil (we use groundnut) and don't let it become too dirty before throwing it away, and also that the coating you use for whatever you are frying is light and crisp, then deep frying is a marvellous way of cooking, and it is always popular. These are the essential points to remember.

Getting the right temperature for the food you are cooking is crucial, so if you haven't got a thermostatically controlled deep fryer, you should use a frying thermometer. Fish should be cooked at 360–375°F (185–190°C); the higher temperature is for very small fish like whitebait.

If the temperature is too high the oil will burn the coating of batter or breadcrumbs before the inside is cooked. If it is too low, a crust will not be formed on the outside and the oil will get into the fish.

Don't deep-fry any fillets of fish more than about one inch (2.5 cm) thick, or the outside will dry out before the middle is cooked through.

Don't put too much in at one time because, as with shallow frying, you will lower the temperature and cause the oil to permeate the whole of the fish.

For the same reason, use plenty of oil; the fish should be able to float quite freely in it.

Strain the oil after each use.

## STIR FRYING

Stir frying is the Chinese method of cookery where vegetables, meat or fish cut into small pieces are cooked very quickly in hot oil. It is a highly agreeable method of cookery, because very little flavour is lost and the textures of the food are preserved.

I'm sure most people now possess a wok. Unfortunately, with a wok should come a wok stove, where the wok is fiercely heated by a nest of large gas jets. Trying to re-create this in the home is not easy; for a start the wok won't sit on the cooker properly and soon runs out of residual heat when anything but a small amount of food is added. I've got two types of wok, one with a pointed bottom and one with a shallow bottom. Neither is particularly satisfactory, but as long as I'm cooking for no more than four and get both pans very hot before I start, and fry in small quantities, I can just about get away with it.

### Cooking under a grill

In the restaurant our overhead grill, or salamander, as it is called in the trade, is the most used piece of equipment in the kitchen.

We have one about a yard or metre long and use it for cooking whole fish and fillets as well as 'flashing' dishes: giving them a last burst of heat just before they are sent out to the restaurant. We also use the grill for gratinating dishes: giving them a pleasing lightly burnt top. Many dishes in the book call for fish, particularly fillets, to be grilled under a salamander. I find it an excellent way of cooking fillets without losing flavour, since the intense heat of the grill has cooked the fillet before any of its juices have leached out and dried away.

Make sure you turn on your overhead grill well in advance, and if cooking fillets set the grilling tray as close as possible to the source of heat so that the fillet cooks quickly and doesn't 'sweat'. Whole fish should be grilled further away from the heat to avoid burning. Their skins will protect them from drying out. Larger fish can be slashed a few times on each side to speed up their cooking, though you will of course lose some moistness by doing this.

### Cooking on a grill

This is, aromatically, the most pleasing way of cooking but also the most smoke-producing. At the restaurant we have a piece of equipment called a charcoal grill, which is a bit of a misnomer, since the heat is produced by gas underneath a bed of pumice-stone rock; but though purists (myself among them) would claim that nothing is as good as grilling over real charcoal, here as with so many aspects of commercial cookery, life is a constant battle between expediency and the ideal. Our charcoal grill is as near to the real thing as space will allow (we would need over a tonne of charcoal a season). We make things even better by throwing on handfuls of charcoal dust, dried herbs, or sawdust. If you have an open fire, you should consider having a gridiron made for you so that you can cook over it occasionally. You can buy them in France with a long handle, and you can also get a solid ribbed steel pan especially for grilling fish on top of the cooker.

But by far the most enjoyable way of cooking on a grill at home is barbecue cooking. Countless books have been written on this subject dear to many people's hearts, so what can I add? Only a couple of points: most people are too mean with charcoal. You must build a really good fire, with plenty of residual heat, to achieve the right results. The whole barbecue must be really very hot, but, as has been said many times before, the charcoal should not be in flames; it should be able to burn down to a white mass. We find that it is best, even when cooking delicate pieces of fish, to have the grill bars extremely hot; as long as the fillets are well oiled they won't stick to the bars as long as you don't try to move them too quickly. The flesh needs to be seared and then carbonized on the surface before you turn them over.

If the charcoal grill is not hot enough, the fish will not be sealed on the outside and it will cook by sweating away all its juices, becoming dry and rather dull. Don't salt anything cooked on a grill until it is served, because salt leaches juice out. It is always nice to throw herbs on to the coals for additional flavour; I am very fond of using twigs of partly dried fennel for this purpose.

### Poaching, shallow poaching

Few of the recipes in this book call for poaching. This is because I think it is better to cook fillets of fish under the salamander, since they retain their natural juices better this way. The sauce is then made from the trimmings of the fish.

But poaching fillets allows you to make a sauce from the juices of the fish you are actually cooking and thereby save a great deal of time. In this case, shallow poaching is the answer. Fillets of fish or perhaps whole flat fish are laid in a shallow buttered dish, perhaps on some chopped shallots or other finely chopped vegetables such as leek, fennel or celery. A little water and dry white wine is poured over; the fish is covered with a butter paper and poached in the oven or on top of the stove until it has barely turned white. The fillets are then removed, the cooking liquor is reduced, a little cream or butter added, with a few chopped herbs or some chopped tomato, and that's it!

## POACHING IN A *COURT BOUILLON*

A good *court bouillon* made with carrots, onion, celery, bayleaf, pepper-corns, white wine, sometimes red, and sometimes vinegar, is a pleasure to cook since it smells so good simmering away on the stove. The ingredients should be simmered for 30 to 40 minutes before cooking the fish. If you are going to poach whole fish, let it go cold before immersing your fish in it, then if you are going to serve the fish cold, bring it carefully to the boil, let it bubble a couple of times, take it off the boil and leave it to go quite cold in the liquid. If cooking in *court bouillon* for serving warm cook at 'tremble' (about 175°F; 80°C) and test the centre of the fish with a trussing needle on your top lip: when it feels warm it is done.

Cuts of fish such as steaks should be lowered into boiling *court bouillon* and the pan should then be pushed to the side of the stove to allow the heat to spread through the fish most gently.

If cooking whole salmon, I often use salted water only, and I never cook lobsters and crabs in *court bouillon*, since I feel that their flavour needs nothing added.

However, there is no better way of cooking skate before turning it into skate with black butter. A *court bouillon* is also a good way of cooking dull fish like pollack or coley which you are going to make into fish cakes.

Don't throw your *court bouillon* away after you have used it. You can add it to a fish soup, or reduce it down by rapid boiling and freeze it (in cubes in an ice-cube tray) to use on another occasion for adding flavour to a fish soup or stew.

Smoked fish like haddock are often poached in a milk and lemon *court bouillon*. This gives the fish a milky whiteness when cooked which looks most attractive in contrast to the brown smoked appearance of the surface of the fish.

## Roasting

Bass is particularly suitable for roasting in the oven; the skin is excellent when well basted with butter and seasoned in salt and freshly ground black pepper.

Roasting fish can be done at a high oven temperature (450°F; 230°C; gas mark 8) because there is nothing in a fish to toughen up by fierce heat, the object being to get a crisp skin while cooking the inside as quickly as possible.

### POÊLE OR POT ROASTING

With particularly firm fish like conger eel (see pp. 203–4) or monkfish, a good-sized 'joint' can be placed on a bed of root vegetables (carrots, celery, garlic) with plenty of melted butter and pot-roasted.

## Steaming

At the restaurant, we have two steamers, and this is a method of cookery which we use a great deal since the fish is cooked delicately and with minimum loss of internal juices (most of the flavour of fish is in its liquid content). For some suggestions on making a steamer, see p. 70.

When steaming, make sure the water level is not so high that it boils up over the fish.

I don't like pressure cookers for steaming fish because it is very difficult to get the timing right when you can't get inside and see what's going on.

# Five

# HERBS AND VEGETABLES FOR FISH COOKERY

I n the last chapter, I suggested that first-class equipment may have as much to do with cooking well as any special skill on the part of the cook. The same is certainly true of the raw materials that go into a dish, which must be as fresh as possible.

Unfortunately the selection of herbs and unusual vegetables available in greengrocers and supermarkets is not all it could be. Fresh basil, tarragon, broad-leaved, Italian and Hamburg parsley, rocket, red chicory, lambs' tongues, sorrel, lovage – these need some searching out unless you live in London.

Many of the recipes in this book which contain some unusual herb or vegetable also suggest a substitute, but the point of the dish often lies in the particular herb chosen; variety is so important in good cooking. So if you can't buy it, I suggest that like me you grow it.

Here is an A-to-Z of the more unusual herbs and vegetables in this book, with some suggestions on growing them and where to get the seeds.

On the subject of herbs and salad vegetables, Joy Larkom's book *The Salad Garden* (published by Windward) has been a great influence on me. It is full of inspiring photographs which make one eager to try the culinary possibilities of many unusual plants.

### Artichokes (globe)

Quite easy to buy but worth growing because they make a vegetable garden look so impressive. One or two in your garden seem to elevate the importance of a vegetable patch and turn it into more of a *potager*.

Allow at least 3 feet (90 cm) between plants. If you could acquire a plant in Brittany, you would get the best. You can split plants after a year's growth and replant the offshoots in spring.

### Basil

Quite easy to buy but basil doesn't keep well and it is a good idea therefore to grow your own supply of this ephemeral herb.

Grow it in a greenhouse, but it does quite well outside in good summers. If sown after the middle of May it will then last till about mid-September.

Of all herbs basil has the most transient fragrance and should never be chopped until just before adding to a dish.

## Borage

We grow borage for its pale blue flowers, which we use in salads. Sow March to May outdoors.

## Broad-leaved parsley

We grow broad-leaved parsley in preference to the more common curly-leaved variety because it has a better flavour, sweeter and not at all bitter. Because one is so used to the taste of parsley, one tends to overlook it as having a distinctive flavour. In fact if chopped at the last minute and added to a simple fish stock and butter sauce, it is just the thing. Because parsley takes a long time to germinate, by the time it has sprung up it is in a jungle of weeds. I find it better to sow in little pots and transplant. Sow in March.

## Caraway

A hardy biennial herb best sown in August for an early growth of lush green foliage the following year. We use caraway leaf as an alternative to dill in gravlax and gravad mackerel. The seeds can be used in our walnut bread (pp. 141–3) to go with the Baltic salad.

## Chervil

An easy herb to grow. Sow regularly from February through to September. Doesn't do well in the warm summer months, but is one of the first herbs to appear in spring and one of the last to go in autumn.

## Chicory

We grow three types of chicory, two red and a green: Red Verona, and Red Treviso, and green Sugar Loaf. The red chicory which is now quite common and sold as 'radicchio' is normally a blanched Red Verona. Chicories do not flourish in the summer months and are best sown in July or August for autumn use; they can then be protected by cloches or transplanting into a greenhouse for use in early spring, but even if left in the open ground, they will normally re-sprout early in the year.

## Coriander

A herb which you have to become accustomed to; you then become an addict. Described variously on first tasting as 'like bleach' or 'like burnt sheets'. I use it with grilled fish and would draw your attention to the recipe for mussels and a coriander dressing on p. 118.

Sow from February to early September. A useful herb in that it starts early in the year and finishes late.

## Cress

If the seed that is normally grown in little plastic punnets is sown in the open ground, cress grows into a large feathery plant which is excellent in salads, as a substitute for watercress in a watercress sauce, or as one of the ingredients in the green herb terrine on pp. 264–6. Sow February to July.

## Dandelions

Best collected before they have flowered; afterwards they become too bitter for salads, though you can still blanch them for the smoked mackerel and dandelion salad on p. 147.

## Dill

An essential herb for fish cookery. I find it quite difficult to grow well, maybe because my soil is very sandy. Sow from March to August at regular intervals. The best herb for the Scandinavian gravlax, though fennel or caraway can be used too.

## Endive

Curly-leaved endive and Batavian endive, also known as scarole, which has broader leaves, are essential plants for good, well-varied salads. Sow in early spring for a summer crop, but be prepared for bolting in hot dry weather. Sow again in July for a late September crop which will last through to the first frosts. We transplant some of these to a greenhouse for an early crop the following year.

## Fennel

Another essential herb in fish cookery. We not only use the green foliage in sauces and marinades but also dry the stalks and use them strewn on to a charcoal grill. Sow in February–March, after which they will last perennially, providing the flowering heads are cut off. We also grow a bronze fennel, which is useful for garnishing dishes with fennel in them.

## Florence fennel

Florence fennel, called *finocchio* in Italy, is a variety of fennel which has thick bulbous leaves, like celery, and is grown as a vegetable. We use this in fish stews and soups. The frond tops can be finely chopped and used like fennel herb.

Sow in early summer for a crop in late summer or early autumn. When they are ready for use, they are best cut just above ground level, so that what is left will re-sprout, providing herb leaves into the late autumn and early winter.

## Good King Henry or Fat Hen

Normally classed as a weed, Good King Henry, with its dark green, arrow-shaped leaves, is a plant we often add to our salads. When cooked it is similar to spinach. We also grow orache, which is very similar, only red.

## Hamburg parsley

Useful both for the foliage and the root, which can be peeled and cooked like celeriac. Sow as for ordinary parsley.

## Horseradish

It is well worth having a patch of horseradish in the garden. You can easily grow it from a root bought from a greengrocer. Even the most dried-out-looking root will sprout. The jars of horseradish sauce you buy have rather a lot of extra ingredients like acetic acid which won't bring out the best in your cooking. Dried horseradish powder or flakes tend to be rather bitter and often gritty, but the Japanese green horseradish powder called wasabi is excellent.

## Hyssop

A perennial bush herb. We grow it for the pretty purple foliage, which we put in salads, and the pungently aromatic leaves, which we use sparingly in the marinade for our *grillade* (see p. 243). On hot summer afternoons, the scent of a bush of hyssop in the herb garden is a pleasure, reminiscent of baking Greek islands.

## Italian parsley

Like broad-leaved parsley but grows quite tall and has long feathery top growth which looks stylish draped over a fish. Sow like broad-leaved parsley (above).

### Japanese greens, mizuna

An oriental member of the brassica family, Japanese greens have dark green feathery leaves. They are very easy to grow; sow regularly from February to October. We use them in salads and also as an accompaniment to our steamed fish with garlic, ginger and spring onions (pp. 166–7), where, dropped briefly in boiling water, drained and splashed with a sauce made simply with fish stock and soya sauce, it sets off the fillet of fish extremely well.

### Lettuce:
### Lollo Red, Salad Bowl, Red Salad Bowl

The essence of good salad making is variety. There is no point in growing the well-known types such as Cos, Webbs Wonderful, Suttons Windermere, or Iceberg, since you can buy all you need of them. Reserve your patch of ground for the red varieties, Lollo Red or Red Salad Bowl, or even ordinary green Salad Bowl, which is not easy to get hold of.

### Lovage

Every garden should have a lovage plant somewhere. A member of the same family as celery, celeriac and even parsley (and hemlock!), the umbellifers, lovage is a broad-leaved herb of exceptional pungency, but used with discretion its curry-like flavour enhances some fish dishes, particularly the mussel, lovage and chervil soup with green vegetables on pp. 133–4.

### Parsley:
see Broad-leaved; Hamburg; Italian

### Rocket

A salad vegetable which people often comment on at the restaurant; it has a peppery, nutty flavour of the same kind as watercress. Rocket can be cooked like a vegetable (see p. 265). An easy plant to grow; make sowings from February through to late September. We use the white flowers in salads.

### Samphire

Marsh samphire, which grows on sandy mud in salt marshes and on muddy seashores all round the British Isles, is a highly fitting vegetable to serve with fish. With a delicious fresh salty taste and firm texture, it is easy to identify, having unusual fleshy, light green joined branches rather than leaves and growing little more than 9 inches (22 cm) off the mud.

## Seakale

Seakale is grown for the leaf stalks, which are blanched and eaten raw or lightly cooked and treated in the same way as asparagus. I have never tasted it, but we have a row of one-year-old plants which will be usable in two years' time. It will be on the menu from 1988 onwards!

## Sea spinach

A member of the beet family, sea spinach grows by the sea everywhere. It is very similar in appearance to spinach beet, but the leaves are shinier and slightly thicker. Cook like spinach (see pp. 273–4).

## Sorrel

An essential plant for fish cookery and one which grows with no problems anywhere. There are several marginally different varieties: French sorrel, for example, has larger leaves shaped like a shield, whereas the common sorrel has spear-shaped leaves. All have a distinctive tart flavour. Sorrel is of great use to us very early in the season since it appears before anything else at a time when other greenery is still coming from southern Spain. Sow the seeds in February or March for a perennial crop.

## Tarragon, French tarragon

A difficult plant to get hold of; it is all too common to be sold Russian tarragon as French and very difficult to tell which is which until you taste. Russian tarragon is not worth bothering with, except perhaps as decoration. You cannot buy French tarragon seeds. I bought my plants from Thompson & Morgan about eight years ago, and they are still going strong.

## Vanilla grass

Suffolk Herbs, who sell the seeds for vanilla grass (and from whom I buy most of my seeds), describe it as recalling 'the smell of old hay meadows'. I was captivated by this and recalled reading somewhere of a recipe for ham cooked in hay; so why not fish cooked in grass? I filleted two 2-lb. (900-g) salmon trout and prepared four *papillotes* exactly as described on p. 203. I brushed the fillets with melted butter, sprinkled them with a little white wine and some salt and ground white pepper, laid about ten blades of vanilla grass across each fillet, and baked them in a hot oven (400°F; 200°C; gas mark 6) for ten minutes: a very simple recipe and very, very nice – salmon trout *en papillote* with vanilla grass.

Vanilla grass, like any other grass, can be easily grown, and once established will go on for ever.

## · SOME SEED SUPPLIERS ·

Suttons Seeds Ltd, Hele Road, Torquay, Devon, TQ2 7QJ
Suffolk Herbs, Sawyers Farm, Little Cornard, Sudbury, Suffolk, CO10 0PF
Thompson & Morgan, London Road, Ipswich, IP2 0BA

# BASIC PREPARATIONS

(STOCKS, SAUCES, BUTTERS, DRESSINGS,
BATTERS, PASTRY AND SALTING)

## Fish stock

Fish stock is absolutely essential to the production of good fish dishes. Even if I were to cook only one fish dish in a week and then were only frying the fillets and not making a sauce, I would still use the trimmings for a stock which I would use the next day to make a small amount of fish soup (see pp. 132–3).

I always start the work on any dish by filling the bottom of a saucepan with chopped root vegetables ready to throw in any filleting scraps. Because it is such a fundamental part of fish cookery, I insist that it should be absolutely the most simple thing to prepare. You can read the most elaborate recipes for making fish stock (and indeed I used to go through a much more lengthy procedure). All you really need is a quantity of chopped vegetables, fish bones and cold water.

I never now add herbs or wine. This is because I always reduce my fish stock when making a sauce or a soup, and it is then that I add whichever particular herb or wine or prominent vegetable I need for the individual taste of the finished dish.

I shall give a precise recipe for fish stock, but in fact the quantities are not important. Use enough cold water to cover the fish bones and vegetables, and use whatever vegetables you have to hand from the following: leeks, celery, onions, carrots, Florence fennel, celeriac, parsley stalks.

### TYPES OF FISH TO USE

At the Seafood Restaurant, we make two types of fish stock. First, a large quantity of general-purpose stock for fish soups, stews and strong sauces, which we make with trimmings from every type of fish except oily fish like mackerel or herring. Second, we reserve some of the trimmings of turbot, sole and John Dory for a smaller volume of stock for the finer delicate sauces. In addition to these two stocks, we also keep a bowl of the juice from cooking mussels and other molluscs like cockles and clams, which is a marvellous addition to many sauces and soups.

# BASIC FISH STOCK

1 large onion
1 large carrot
1 stick of celery, including the top

3 lb. (1.4 kg) fish bones, including heads
3 pints (1.7 litres) water

Clean and peel the vegetables, then chop them into pieces roughly a quarter inch (6 mm) cube. The stock takes only 15 minutes to cook, so the vegetables must be cut small to extract the maximum flavour in so short a cooking time. Place the vegetables in a large saucepan (holding at least 6 pints or 3 litres) and put the fish trimmings on top. Pour on the water and bring slowly to the boil. As soon as the stock comes to the boil, turn the heat right down and leave at a very slow simmer for 15 minutes. Take the pan off the heat and leave the stock to go quite cold before straining. Making stock this way keeps the liquor clear and clean-tasting.

# SHELLFISH REDUCTION

In addition to fish stock, we make a basic preparation called shellfish reduction, which we use all the time. We sell a lot of shellfish removed from the shell, and it would be an enormous shame to throw away the shells, because in addition to the odd pieces of fish left behind in them, they are themselves filled with flavour and colour. We therefore use them to make a strong essence to flavour sauces, terrines and mousses.

You are unlikely to have access to the amount of raw material for this reduction that we have, but this is not a problem because the unshelled North Atlantic prawns you can buy from all fishmongers make an excellent base for a shellfish reduction.

The shells from 1 lb. (450 g) prawns, plus half a dozen whole prawns
2 oz. (60 g) carrot, peeled and chopped
2 oz. (60 g) onion, peeled and chopped
2 oz. (60 g) celery, chopped
½ oz. (15 g) butter
1 fl. oz. (30 ml) white wine
1 teaspoon (5 ml) chopped tarragon
3 oz. (90 g) tomato, roughly chopped
15 fl. oz. (450 ml) fish stock (see p. 92)
Pinch of cayenne pepper

Cook the shells and whole prawns with the carrot, onion and celery in the butter without colour. Add the wine, tarragon and tomato and boil to reduce for a couple of minutes. Add the fish stock, bring to the boil and simmer for 40 minutes. Liquidize everything and pass through a conical strainer then through a fine mesh sieve. Return the strained liquid to the heat, bring to the boil and reduce the volume by three-quarters. Season with cayenne. Now taste that!

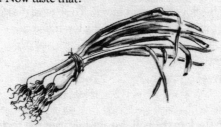

## COURT BOUILLON

A general-purpose poaching liquid for skate, salmon, and for any occasion where you want cooked fish with plenty of flavour. You can use the *bouillon* for fish soup afterwards (include the flavouring vegetables) or strain it and use it as fish stock (though not where a reduction is called for, because it is already salted and would thereby become too salty).

10 fl. oz. (300 ml) dry cider
40 fl. oz. (1.2 litres) water
3 fl. oz. (120 ml) white wine vinegar
2 bayleaves
12 peppercorns
1 onion, peeled and roughly chopped
2 carrots, peeled and roughly chopped
2 sticks celery, roughly chopped
2 teaspoons (10 ml) salt

Bring all the *court bouillon* ingredients to the boil and simmer for 30 minutes. To complete the infusion of flavours, leave to cool before using.

## · SAUCES ·

# VELOUTÉ

In the best culinary circles, flour-based sauces are frowned on nowadays as belonging to the old stodgy school of cookery rather than the *nouvelle*, or perhaps *moderne*, lighter approach. The new method is to thicken a sauce with a lot of butter and cream and air rather than a roux, and at their best these sauces are excellent balancing acts between lightness and extreme richness; at their worst, the excess of fat blankets any taste.

A well-made *velouté*-based sauce certainly shouldn't taste heavy or floury. As its name implies, it should taste velvety and carry no suggestion of the flour that went into it. To achieve the right texture the flour must be thoroughly cooked by long low simmering.

*To make one pint (600 ml)*

| | |
|---|---|
| 1 pint (600 ml) of fish stock (see p. 92) | 2 oz. (60 g) butter |
| | 1½ oz. (45 g) flour |

Bring the fish stock to the boil. Meanwhile melt the butter in a second, thick-bottomed pan, add the flour and cook for about 2 minutes, stirring constantly. Don't let the roux colour too much. When it starts to smell nutty, remove from the heat and cool a little. Gradually add the hot stock, stirring all the time until smooth, then return to the heat. Turn the heat right down and simmer for about 40 minutes, stirring occasionally to prevent the bottom sticking. Pass the sauce through a conical strainer into a bowl, cover with a butter paper to prevent a skin forming, and if not using immediately, chill when cooled.

# A QUICK WAY
# TO MAKE HOLLANDAISE

| | |
|---|---|
| 2 eggs | 8 oz. (250 g) unsalted butter |
| Lemon juice | Cayenne pepper |
| 1 tablespoon (15 ml) water | Salt to taste |

If you've got a liquidizer, hollandaise is extremely easy to make. You just separate the eggs and put the yolks in the liquidizer with a squeeze of lemon juice and the tablespoon of water. You melt the butter in a saucepan, whiz the yolks and add the hot butter through the small hole in the lid of the goblet, keeping the liquidizer turned on all the time. This makes a nice light sauce, lighter still if you add some of the egg white with the yolks. Season with cayenne, salt and more lemon juice to your taste.

# THE LIGHTEST HOLLANDAISE

Hollandaise and similar hot butter sauces are really very rich, and made in the usual way they are a bit heavy. By incorporating more water in the sauce and increasing the amount of egg yolk, an altogether lighter and more agreeable sauce is made.

| | |
|---|---|
| 6 oz. (90 g) unsalted butter | 3 egg yolks |
| 3 tablespoons (45 ml) water | Salt, lemon juice and cayenne pepper |

You will need a stainless steel bowl, a saucepan into which it will fit, and a wire whisk.

Clarify the butter by heating it in a small saucepan until the solids fall to the bottom.

Half fill the large saucepan with water and bring to the boil. Turn the heat down so that the water simmers, and place the bowl on top. Pour in the 3 tablespoons of water, add the egg yolks, and whisk the mixture over the heat to form a voluminous, creamy *sabayon*.

The egg yolks should 'cook out', that is to say, the temperature of the egg should be raised to 140°F (60°C), but no higher. The simple test for the right temperature is to use your little finger. If the *sabayon* is hot enough it will feel uncomfortably hot to your finger, but not so hot that you would immediately have to remove it. If you let it get any hotter you will start to produce scrambled egg as the protein in the egg coagulates. Remove the pan from the heat, whisk in the butter a ladleful at a time, and season to produce a wonderfully light sauce.

# A PASTIS AND FENNEL
# HOT BUTTER SAUCE

This is very good with any grilled fillet of fish. We serve it with hake or haddock.

1 tablespoon (15 ml) chopped fennel
4 fl. oz. (120 ml) fish stock

2 tablespoons (30 ml) Ricard or Pernod
The light hollandaise sauce above

Put the fennel, fish stock and all but a teaspoon of the pastis in a small pan and reduce down to a couple of tablespoons (30 ml) of liquid by rapid boiling. Stir into the hollandaise and add the reserved teaspoon of pastis.

# *BEURRE BLANC*

*Beurre blanc* is often held to be difficult to make, but there is absolutely nothing complicated about it, nor is it particularly unstable; and if it does separate, it is much easier to reconstitute than an egg-based sauce like hollandaise. All you do is add a bit more water and boil it vigorously to emulsify butter and water. You may lose some lightness if you have to do this, but you are spared the embarrassment of producing a split and greasy sauce.

2 oz. (60 g) finely chopped shallots (not red ones) or onions
2 tablespoons (30 ml) white wine vinegar
4 tablespoons (60 ml) dry white wine

6 tablespoons (90 ml) water
2 tablespoons (30 ml) double cream
6 oz. (180 g) unsalted butter, cut into pieces

Put shallots, vinegar, wine and water in a small pan, bring to the boil and simmer till nearly all the liquid has evaporated. Add the cream and reduce a little, then remove the pan from the heat and whisk in the butter, a little at a time, till it has all amalgamated.

Another method is to reduce down and add the cream as above, then add a couple of tablespoons (30 ml) of water, bring the sauce to a rapid boil, and whisk in the butter while boiling. This will produce a perfectly acceptable sauce which is not quite so light as with the normal method. This second procedure is also the way to reconstitute a sauce which has got too hot and split.

## BEURRE ROUGE

2 oz. (60 g) finely chopped shallots
10 fl. oz. (300 ml) Beaujolais or other fresh red wine

A pinch of sugar
6 oz. (180 g) unsalted butter

Put the shallots, wine and sugar in a pan and simmer till all but a couple of tablespoons (30 ml) of the wine have boiled away. Take off the heat and whisk in the butter, a little at a time, till it has all been amalgamated.

## MAYONNAISE

The best mayonnaise is made by hand. For years we used to make bulk mayonnaise at the restaurant in a Kenwood mixer, which produces much better mayonnaise than a food processor does; but both seem to a greater or lesser degree to toughen up the protein in the egg yolk, giving the mayonnaise an imperfect stiffness and starchiness. This is even worse if you use egg white (as you can in a food processor). Making mayonnaise by hand produces a soft melting texture which seems to taste better too.

I have two recipes for mayonnaise, one of the utmost simplicity, using best virgin olive oil, and a second one, using groundnut or sunflower oil, which is strongly flavoured with mustard and is very pleasant with fresh crab. An observation worth passing on is that we prefer to use Colman's English mustard powder for most cooking, as it seems to produce a flavour that is exclusively of mustard.

---

### THE BEST MAYONNAISE

2 egg yolks
2 teaspoons (10 ml) white wine vinegar

⅓ of a teaspoon (2 ml) salt
10 fl. oz. (300 ml) best olive oil

See that all the ingredients are at room temperature. Put the egg yolks, vinegar and salt into a mixing bowl which you have placed on a tea towel (to stop it slipping). Using a wire hand whisk, beat the oil into the egg mixture a little at a time till you have incorporated it all. Once you have carefully added about the same volume of oil as the original mixture of egg yolks and vinegar, you can add the rest more quickly.

The science of all cold and hot butter sauces is as follows. Oil or hot butter likes to stay in one large puddle. Beating separates it into millions of tiny droplets which would reform into one large puddle as soon as you stopped; but if you add oil to egg yolk and whisk it, the egg coats each droplet of oil and prevents it from joining the rest. A little egg yolk will go a very long way provided you add the oil in small quantities and beat well. For the scientific discussion of this and every other culinary process, I recommend *On Food and Cooking, the Science and Lore of the Kitchen* by Harold McGee (Allen & Unwin).

---

### MUSTARD MAYONNAISE

2½ teaspoons (12.5 ml) Colman's
  mustard powder
2 egg yolks
1 tablespoon (15 ml) white wine
  vinegar

½ teaspoon (2.5 ml) salt
A few turns of the white peppermill
10 fl. oz. (300 ml) groundnut or
  sunflower oil

Mix the mustard powder with a little water, then combine it with all the other ingredients except the oil in a mixing bowl. Proceed as above.

## AÏOLI

8 cloves of garlic
2 egg yolks
Juice of a quarter lemon
A pinch of salt

12 fl. oz. (360 ml) of a good
  first-pressing olive oil (usually
  called 'virgin')

*If making with a mortar and pestle:* Reduce the garlic to a purée with the pestle, add the salt, egg yolks and lemon juice, and beat in the oil in a steady drizzle.

*If making in a food processor:* Put the garlic, egg yolks and lemon juice in the food processor. Turn it on and blend for about 10 seconds, then add the oil slowly to build up a thick mayonnaise.

# ROUILLE

The fiery accompaniment to fish soup and *bouillabaisse*. If you are in a hurry, you can just mix mayonnaise with garlic and cayenne pepper. But here is the recipe we use in the restaurant, which needs *harissa*, a chilli, red pepper and coriander sauce from North Africa. It is available in small tins from good continental food shops, but we have evolved our own recipe, which seems about right.

—————————— *HARISSA* ——————————

1 tablespoon (15 ml) tomato purée
1 tablespoon (15 ml) ground coriander
1 teaspoon (5 ml) powdered saffron

3 red peppers, deseeded, roasted and skinned
15 green chillies (small hot)
1 teaspoon (5 ml) salt
1 teaspoon (5 ml) cayenne pepper

Put all the ingredients in a liquidizer and blend.

—————————— *ROUILLE* ——————————

2 oz. (60 g) dry bread, soaked in fish stock
6 cloves garlic
1 egg yolk

6 tablespoons (90 ml) *harissa*
½ teaspoon (2.5 ml) salt
¾ pint (450 ml) olive oil

Put all the ingredients except the olive oil in a food processor and blend. Then pour in the oil as for making mayonnaise.

# SKORTHALIA

3 cloves of garlic
1 fl. oz. (30 ml) water
¼ teaspoon (1 ml) salt
2 oz. (60 g) mashed potato

1 oz. (30 g) ground almonds
1 fl. oz. (30 ml) white wine vinegar
5 fl. oz. (150 ml) good olive oil
    (preferably, of course, Greek)

Blend everything in a food processor and chill.

# TARTARE SAUCE

The mustard mayonnaise above
  (p. 98)
1 teaspoon (5 ml) green olives, finely
  chopped
1 teaspoon (5 ml) gherkins, finely
  chopped

1 teaspoon (5 ml) capers, finely
  chopped
1 teaspoon (5 ml) chopped chives
1 teaspoon (5 ml) chopped parsley

Add the last five ingredients to the mustard mayonnaise. Use for deep-fried breaded fish.

# MONTPELIER BUTTER

Use this sauce for cold poached fish.

Tarragon
Parsley
Chives    altogether about 3 oz.
Chervil      (90 g)
Watercress
1 oz. (30 g) spinach
1 oz. (30 g) shallots, finely chopped
3 small gherkins

9 capers
1 small clove of garlic
6 anchovy fillets
1 raw egg yolk
3 hard-boiled egg yolks
4 oz. (120 g) butter
3 fl. oz. (90 ml) olive oil

Blanch the tarragon, parsley, chives, chervil, watercress, and spinach in boiling water for about 30 seconds. Plunge them into cold water, drain and squeeze out as much water as you can. Blanch the shallots and squeeze dry, then put everything but the oil in a food processor and turn on till all is smooth. Finally add the olive oil.

## · FLAVOURED BUTTERS ·

These butters are used sliced into rounds and arranged down the centre of grilled fish. They are also used for flavouring sauces and for stuffing fillets of fish.

All of them can be most easily made by simply putting all the flavouring ingredients and the butter (which should be soft) into a food processor and switching on till all is smooth. The butter is then turned out on to a sheet of clingfilm or greaseproof paper, rolled up into a sausage shape, and chilled. It is then sliced into rounds when required.

## MUSTARD BUTTER

Good with grilled oily fish like herrings, mackerel or sardines.

4 oz. (100 g) unsalted butter
1 tablespoon (15 ml) French mustard

Salt and ground black pepper

## TARRAGON BUTTER

The stuffing for the salmon in puff pastry on pp. 261–3; good with grilled fish.

6 oz. (180 g) unsalted butter
1 tablespoon (15 ml) fresh tarragon
½ teaspoon (2.5 ml) salt

4 turns of the black peppermill
Juice of a quarter lemon

# GARLIC BUTTER

8 oz. (240 g) unsalted butter
4 large cloves of garlic
1 oz. (30 g) parsley

1 teaspoon (5 ml) brandy
1 teaspoon (5 ml) lemon juice
Good pinch of salt

# GARLIC
# AND ROASTED HAZELNUT BUTTER

The ingredients for garlic butter
(see above)

3 oz. (90 g) hazelnuts

Turn on your grill. Roast the hazelnuts under the grill, turning them over to ensure even colouring. When the skins are dark brown, tip them on to one half of a teatowel, fold over the other half and roll off the skins. Open the teatowel and roll the nuts to one side, leaving the skins behind. Blend the nuts with the other ingredients in a food processor.

# CORIANDER AND PARSLEY BUTTER

3 oz. (90 g) roasted hazelnuts
(prepared as in the previous recipe)
8 oz. (240 g) unsalted butter
1 oz. (30 g) fresh coriander

½ oz. (15 g) parsley
1 oz. (30 g) shallot, peeled
Juice of half a lemon
16 turns of a peppermill

# PINK PEPPERCORN BUTTER

Try grilling small dabs and serving this with them.

3 oz. (90 g) unsalted butter
2 teaspoons (10 ml) chopped pink
peppercorns

5 turns of the black peppermill
½ teaspoon (2.5 ml) salt
1 teaspoon (5 ml) brandy

# PARSLEY BUTTER

4 oz. (120 g) unsalted butter
A small bunch of parsley
Juice of a quarter lemon

5 turns of the black peppermill
½ teaspoon (2.5 ml) salt

# PRAWN BUTTER

4 oz. (120 g) butter
3 oz. (90 g) unshelled prawns

1 teaspoon (5 ml) lemon juice
Pinch of cayenne pepper

After amalgamating these ingredients in a food processor, pass the butter through a sieve, pushing it through with the back of a ladle or wooden spoon.

## · DRESSINGS FOR SALADS ·

There is not much point in preparing an exciting salad – say young spinach leaves with Lollo Red and Salad Bowl lettuce – if you then add a dressing spoiled by wrong proportions or indifferent ingredients.

Some French wine vinegars are much better than others, and some vegetable oils are unsuitable for making a vinaigrette. Two vinegars which I particularly like for my dressings are one by Martin-Pouret from Orléans and one from Bordeaux, made by Menier and imported into this country by Bouchard Aîné of London. Both are produced by the Orléans method, which makes them more expensive (because it takes time, and good-quality wine is used) but well worth the price for use with salads. In the Orléans process, wine is poured into barrels with some vinegar and a vinegar culture; the barrels are left open to let in air, and the culture slowly turns the alcohol in the wine into vinegar. Cheaper wine vinegar is made much more quickly by mechanically oxygenating wine with a vinegar culture in a tank kept at blood heat. This promotes rapid conversion of alcohol into vinegar but the result is harsher and lacks many of the subtle flavours of the Orléans variety.

Cider vinegar is good for salads, malt vinegar is not. Sherry vinegar I think is too strong, and fruit-flavoured vinegars in salads are not my cup of tea.

The best vegetable oils to use for dressings are olive oil, walnut oil, groundnut oil, sunflower oil and soya oil. It is best to avoid blended oils, since, more often than not they have a slight fishy flavour which comes through more strongly in a dressing. Sesame oil has a strongly nutty flavour which you might occasionally like in a salad, but if you want a robustly flavoured oil I think walnut is more satisfactory.

My recipes for a walnut oil dressing and an olive oil dressing include a certain amount of neutral-tasting groundnut oil, which, as cooks say, 'lengthens' the dressing. As long as you buy the first-pressing, unrefined olive oil and a similar good-quality walnut oil, you don't need to use 100 per cent of either in the dressing, and indeed I suggest that a first-pressing walnut or olive oil on its own is too strong. It is preferable to buy the best and tone it down yourself rather than to use a more refined oil, since with cheaper walnut and olive oils the refining process involves heat and chemicals rather than purely mechanical pressing.

I prefer dressings highly biased in favour of the oil; a ratio of 5 to 1 is normal.

## BASIC DRESSING

1 fl. oz. (30 ml) red wine vinegar
5 fl. oz. (150 ml) groundnut oil, soya oil or sunflower oil

½ teaspoon (3 ml) salt
3 twists of the black peppermill

## OLIVE OIL DRESSING

The essential accompaniment to a tomato and basil salad.

2½ fl. oz. (75 ml) olive oil
2½ fl. oz. (75 ml) groundnut oil

1 fl. oz. (30 ml) red wine vinegar
½ teaspoon (3 ml) salt

# WALNUT DRESSING

Best used with bitter salads like chicory, endive and scarole.

2½ fl. oz. (75 ml) walnut oil
5 fl. oz. (150 ml) groundnut oil
1½ fl. oz. (45 ml) red wine vinegar
¾ teaspoon (4 ml) salt

¾ teaspoon (4 ml) Colman's English
   mustard powder
6 turns of the peppermill

Mix the mustard with a little water, then combine all the ingredients
with a whisk.

# A LIGHT WHITE WINE DRESSING

If you mix wine with vinegar you can create a dressing which is less oily
and therefore less fattening but is still not too vinegary.

2 fl. oz. (60 ml) olive oil
2 fl. oz. (60 ml) groundnut oil
2 fl. oz. (60 ml) dry white wine

1 fl. oz. (30 ml) white wine vinegar
½ teaspoon (3 ml) salt

# SAUCE RAVIGOTE

Very nice with grilled fish.

The basic dressing above (p. 104)
2 teaspoons (10 ml) Colman's English
   mustard powder
1 tablespoon (15 ml) chopped capers
1 tablespoon (15 ml) gherkins, cut
   into fine matchsticks

1 tablespoon (15 ml) chopped fresh
   *fines herbes* (parsley, chervil,
   chives, tarragon) or in winter just
   parsley and watercress

Mix the mustard with a little water, then combine all the ingredients.

# SHALLOT VINEGAR

Use for raw shellfish such as oysters or mussels.

2 fl. oz. (60 ml) red wine vinegar      1 oz. (30 g) finely chopped shallots
2 fl. oz. (60 ml) red wine

Combine all the ingredients (the shallots should be freshly chopped).

## · BATTERS FOR DEEP FRYING ·

I don't think there is a nicer batter than yeast batter for a combination of lightness, crispness and flavour. In addition to producing carbon dioxide, which makes the batter light, yeast also matures the dough and gives the batter a flavour of yeast, beer and bread. The only drawback is that it needs to be made some time in advance, so I also give a batter recipe using baking powder as the aerating agent which can be used at once and is also very good.

You can flavour your batter with whatever you like – even monosodium glutamate, like the food industry. I think batter should stay simple, though what you put inside can be highly flavoured (for an example, see battered marinated pollack, pp. 218–20).

The last of the batters below, tempura, is the one we are currently using at the Seafood Restaurant for our deep-fried fish and shellfish in tempura batter recipe (see p. 244). This is a very light thin batter which barely coats the food. The secret of making good tempura batter is to leave mixing it to the very last minute and to have the ingredients really cold.

# YEAST BATTER

½ oz. (15 g) fresh yeast      8 oz. (240 g) flour
10 fl. oz. (300 ml) tepid water (it      1 teaspoon (5 ml) salt
    should feel neither warm nor cold)

Dissolve the yeast with a little of the water. Sieve the flour and salt into a bowl and make a well in the centre. Pour in the water and dissolved yeast and whisk into a batter. Leave covered for 2 hours before using at room temperature.

# BAKING POWDER BATTER

8 oz. (240 g) flour
1 teaspoon (5 ml) salt

1 teaspoon (5 ml) baking powder
10 fl. oz. (300 ml) water

Sieve the flour, salt and baking powder into a bowl. Make a well in the centre, add the water and whisk into a batter.

# TEMPURA BATTER

7 fl. oz. (210 ml) water
1 egg
4 oz. (120 g) flour

2 oz. (60 g) cornflour
½ teaspoon (2.5 ml) salt

Chill the water and egg. Whisk all the ingredients together just before dipping the food. The batter should be only just amalgamated, so that a few small lumps of flour are still apparent.

## · PASTRY RECIPES ·

# PUFF PASTRY

Frozen puff pastry is all right, but you can't beat the real thing made with butter. The recipe we use at the restaurant makes superb pastry with a good lift and a delicate texture, achieved by using all plain rather than strong flour and a certain amount of butter crumbed into the dough. If you haven't made puff pastry before, it's the most satisfying task in the kitchen.

The most common mistake in making puff pastry is to let it become too warm. This causes the butter to ooze out between the layers, so destroying the lift. But if the butter is too cold and therefore hard, it will break through the thin layers of dough and destroy the lift. The dough and the butter should be of similar consistency, neither too hot nor too cold. If you can work on a cold surface like marble or slate you will find it easier. Once you have the knack it's a delight to be getting it right. The recipe below is for quite a large quantity since it freezes well and it is very useful to have some constantly on hand.

| | |
|---|---|
| Five 250 g blocks of butter, i.e. 1.25 kg (2¾ lb.) | 4 teaspoons of salt |
| | 24 fl. oz. (700 ml) water |
| A 1.5 kg bag of plain flour | 1 teaspoon (5 ml) fresh lemon juice |

Unwrap the butter and leave on a tray to soften at room temperature.

If you have a Kenwood mixer or something similar, put on the paddle mixer, cut up one of the blocks of butter into small chunks and put it in the mixing bowl with the flour and salt. Turn on low and mix until the butter has gone into crumbs as if you were making shortcrust pastry. Add the water and lemon juice and knead for 3 minutes.

If making by hand, put the flour and salt in a bowl and crumb one block of butter into it, make a well in the centre, add the water and mix and hand-knead the dough on a floured surface.

Put the dough in the refrigerator for 25 minutes to relax, covered with clingfilm or a damp cloth. Form the dough into a ball and cut a cross in it halfway through the dough. Pull out the four corners of the cross to form a star shape, lightly roll the centre of the star into a square, keeping it thick, and roll out the points of the star evenly so that the extreme points of the star joined together would form a square. The square of pastry at the centre should be 4 times thicker than the rolled out points of the star.

Form the remaining butter into a rough square and wrap it in clingfilm. With a rolling pin, shape it into a square, slightly smaller than the square of pastry in the middle of the star. Unwrap the butter and place it on the square centre of the star. Fold the flaps over it and roll the square into a rectangle about 30 inches (75 cm) by 12 inches (30 cm) keeping the edges as straight as possible by nudging any parts that are bulging out back in line with the rolling pin.

Now mark the length of the pastry into three thirds. Fold one of the end thirds over the centre third, then fold the other third over those two. Turn the pastry so that the folded edges are at the sides, roll the pastry out again as before – i.e. 30 inches (75 cm) by 12 inches (30 cm) – and fold it in the same way again.

Cover the pastry and chill for 25 minutes to relax the dough. If you are working in a cool environment, you can leave it where it is. Turn the pastry again so that the folded edges are at the side and roll out as before. Fold as before, turn the pastry to bring the folded edges to the sides again and roll out once more. Fold again and leave covered for 25 minutes.

Repeat the same sequence, rolling twice and folding twice, to make 6 rolls and 6 folds in all. Leave the pastry for a further 25 minutes after the last fold before using. I suggest cutting the pastry into about five sections and wrapping and freezing those that you don't want immediately.

# A GOOD SHORTCRUST PASTRY

8 oz. (240 g) flour
Just under ½ teaspoon (2.5 ml) salt

5 oz. (150 g) cold unsalted butter
4 tablespoons (60 ml) ice-cold water

Put the flour and salt in a mixing bowl. Cut the butter up into small pieces and crumb it quickly in the flour with your fingertips, trying to avoid warming up the butter. When the lumps are beginning to disappear but there are still a few, add some of the cold water and stir the flour round your fingers into a ball. Don't add all the water at once; as soon as you have a dough that sticks together fairly easily, that is enough. The more water you add the tougher the pastry will be, the ideal is a compromise between too little water, where rolling out and moulding up of the dough will be difficult, and too much, where rolling and moulding will be easy but the pastry will not crumble away in your mouth in the way that good short pastry does.

Having obtained a ball of dough, flatten it out on a floured surface in one long push with the palm of your hand. This is called *fraiser* in French; there is no translation. This action smears any last lumps of butter into the dough. Wrap the dough in clingfilm and refrigerate for at least an hour to give it time to relax and become more pliable for pinning out.

## · TO SALT YOUR OWN COD ·

Buy good thick cod fillets. Put them in a plastic bowl or ice-cream container, completely cover with a thick layer of salt, and refrigerate for 24 hours.

After a day, most of the salt will have turned to brine with the water it has drawn out of the cod. The fish will now be sufficiently preserved to keep for up to a week; if you want to keep it indefinitely you will need to add more salt and a little water to cover the fish.

To prepare the salt cod for cooking, simply soak it in plenty of cold water for at least 24 hours, changing the water once or twice.

To salt herrings, proceed as for salt cod.

# Seven

# FOR SERVING WITH APÉRITIFS

The correct name in the catering trade for the small pre-dinner morsels in this chapter is *amuse-gueule*, which means 'an amusement for the palate'. We regard these as a very important part of the meal, since the first thing one eats when one is hungriest is likely to be remembered above all else.

# ANCHOVY ICE CREAM
# IN PUFF PASTRY

I am fond of putting ice cream in warm puff pastry for a sweet, and we have adapted that idea for a savoury *amuse-gueule*. It is very good indeed.

| | |
|---|---|
| 2 small tins anchovy fillets (total weight 3½ oz. [105 g]) | Pinch of cayenne |
| | 2½ oz. (75 g) double cream |
| 1 egg yolk | 1 lb. (450 g) puff pastry (see pp. 107–9) |
| 2 teaspoons (10 ml) olive oil | 1 egg (for egg wash) |

Put the anchovy fillets, egg yolk, olive oil and cayenne in a food processor and blend till smooth. Now pour in the cream, keeping the blender on for no more than 15 seconds. Pour out and freeze.

Roll out the puff pastry so that it is ⅛ inch (3 mm) thick. Cut into little parallelogram shapes with sides 2 inches and 1 inch (5 cm and 2.5 cm). Lay on a baking tray and chill them till you need them.

Set the oven at 450°F (230°C; gas mark 8).

Brush the tops of the pastry cutouts with beaten egg and bake in the oven for 6 to 8 minutes.

Leave to cool a little on a wire rack, then slice each one in half horizontally.

Sandwich a teaspoon of the anchovy ice cream between the two layers of puff pastry and serve at once.

# ANCHOÏADE

2 small tins of anchovies
4 cloves of garlic
1 tablespoon (15 ml) olive oil
1 teaspoon (5 ml) red wine vinegar

Pinch of cayenne pepper
1 teaspoon (5 ml) tomato purée
Black pepper from the peppermill

Pound the anchovies and garlic in a mortar, then work in the rest of the ingredients; or blend everything in a food processor. Serve on toasted French bread.

# BRANDADE

1 lb. (450 g) cooked salt cod fillet, soaked before cooking (see p. 110)

1 large clove of garlic
3 fl. oz. (90 ml) good olive oil
2 fl. oz. (60 ml) double cream

Put the salt cod in a food processor with the garlic, turn it on and pour in the olive oil.

Bring the double cream to the boil, then take it off the heat. Put the salt cod and garlic mixture in a second saucepan and stir the warm cream into it. Keep this pan warm till you need the *brandade*, which should be liberally spread on thin slices of fresh French bread (if you cut these slices diagonally rather than straight across, they look better).

# BRANDADE
# IN PUFF PASTRY

4 oz. (120 g) salt cod, soaked and skinned (see p. 110)
½ oz. (15 g) onion
2 cloves of garlic

1 egg white
4 fl. oz. (120 ml) double cream
12 oz. (360 g) puff pastry

Before making the filling, chill all the ingredients in the refrigerator. This lessens the risk of the mousseline mixture curdling when you blend the ingredients.

Place the salt cod, onion, garlic, and egg white in a food processor and blend until smooth. Pour in the double cream and mix for 15 seconds, no longer, or the mixture will separate. Chill until needed.

Set the oven at 450°F (230°C; gas mark 8).

Roll out the puff pastry thinly and trim into a square 15 by 15 inches (38 by 38 cm). Cut the square into two identical rectangles. Spread one of the rectangles with the *brandade* and lay the other on top. Trim the edges and cut the rectangle into four strips lengthways. Cut the strips into 1-inch (2.5-cm) rectangles or similar-sized triangles. Place on a baking tray, brush with egg wash (made from egg yolk and a little milk) and bake for 8 to 10 minutes.

# CRAB IN FILO PASTRY WITH GINGER AND LIME

Frozen leaves of filo pastry in packets are quite easy to get hold of now. Filo pastry is ideal for wrapping round small morsels of meat or seafood for a cocktail canapé. In addition to this recipe with crab, we have one which uses finely chopped lamb, coriander and a pinch of curry.

These quantities will make 24 canapés.

3 oz. (90 g) white crab meat
½ teaspoon (2.5 ml) finely chopped fresh ginger
Zest and juice of half a lime
½ oz. (15 g) butter
Tiny pinch of cayenne
2 leaves of filo pastry about 12 by 16 inches (30 by 40 cm)
Melted butter for brushing the filo leaves

Mix the crab meat with the ginger, lime, butter and cayenne. Lay out the first leaf of filo and brush it with melted butter. Lay the second leaf on top and brush that with butter. Cut the leaves into squares with sides of 2½ inches (6.2 cm).

Set the oven at 425°F (220°C; gas mark 7).

Place a teaspoon of the crab mixture at the centre of each square and fold one corner over to the opposite corner to form a triangle. Squeeze the edges together. Put on a baking tray and bake in the oven for 6 to 8 minutes.

# HERRING ROE CREAM

This has a delicate flavour, carefully enhanced by small amounts of garlic and onion.

½ oz. (15 g) butter
4 oz. (120 g) herring roe
An eighth of a clove of garlic (i.e. a
  very small piece)

An eighth of an oz. (4 g) onion
Small pinch salt
6 drops lemon juice

Melt the butter in a frying pan and lightly fry the roes so that they are just – but only just – cooked. Place in a food processor with all the other ingredients and turn it on till the mixture is beginning to thicken. Chill and serve with raw vegetables or small rounds of lightly toasted French bread.

# PICKLED SALT HERRING
# WITH RED ONIONS

2 pints (1.2 litres) water
5 oz. (150 g) salt
2 herrings, each weighing 8–10 oz.
  (240–300 g)
6 fl. oz. (180 ml) white wine
6 fl. oz. (180 ml) white wine vinegar

6 juniper berries, crushed
12 peppercorns, crushed
½ teaspoon (2.5 ml) coriander seeds
1 bayleaf
1½ tablespoons (23 ml) sugar
1 red onion

Put the water and salt in a pan and bring to the boil to dissolve the salt. Leave to go cold. Fillet the herrings using the method for filleting small round fish described on pp. 54–5. Put the herring fillets in the brine and leave them there for just 30 minutes.

Cut the herrings into ½-inch (15-mm) slices. Put the white wine, white wine vinegar, crushed juniper berries, crushed peppercorns, coriander seeds, bayleaf and sugar in a pan, bring to the boil and simmer for 5 minutes.

Leave to cool, then pour through a sieve over the herrings and leave them in the refrigerator till the evening (or next day, when they will be just as good).

An hour before serving, peel the onion and cut it in half. Thinly slice the halves and mix with the herring pieces. Serve impaled on cocktail sticks.

## MACKEREL WITH TARRAGON

Slices of mackerel cooked quickly in oil and left to marinate in the cooking oil flavoured with tarragon and white wine vinegar.

| | |
|---|---|
| 4 decent-sized fillets of mackerel | ½ fl. oz. (15 ml) white wine vinegar |
| 2 fl. oz. (60 ml) groundnut oil | Salt and freshly ground black pepper |
| 1 teaspoon (5 ml) chopped tarragon | |

Cut the mackerel into slices about as big as your little finger. Fry quickly in a little of the oil. Throw in the tarragon and remove fish and tarragon to a serving dish. Add vinegar to frying pan, bubble for a couple of seconds, add the rest of the oil and pour over the fish. Season with salt and pepper and serve hot or cold with cocktail sticks.

## SMALL ROLLS OF BROWN BREAD AND SMOKED MACKEREL WITH HORSERADISH

The Cornish Smoked Fish Company at Charlestown near St Austell (address on p. 29) produces excellent thin-sliced cold-smoked mackerel as well as the more common hot-smoked mackerel (which is actually cooked in the smoke). If you can't get cold-smoked mackerel you can substitute smoked salmon, gravlax or gravad mackerel, prepared in the same way as gravlax (see the recipe on p. 142).

| | |
|---|---|
| About 4 inches (10 cm) of brown bread | 3 oz. (90 g) horseradish sauce |
| 3 oz. (90 g) soft butter | 8 oz. (240 g) thinly sliced cold-smoked mackerel |

Put the brown bread in the freezer till it has firmed up all the way through; this makes it very much easier to slice it very thinly. Cut it as thin as you can and remove the crusts.

Mix the soft butter with the horseradish sauce and spread the bread thinly with it. Lay slices of mackerel on top, roll up like a Swiss roll, and chill for half an hour in the refrigerator. Remove from the fridge and cut into thin rounds with a sharp, thin-bladed knife. Impale on cocktail sticks and set on a serving plate.

# MUSSELS
# WITH A CORIANDER DRESSING

Mussels in the shell are ideal for serving with drinks since they come in ready-made containers which can be easily picked up.

| | |
|---|---|
| 50 mussels | 1 tablespoon (15 ml) chopped shallot |
| Splash of white wine | 1 tablespoon (15 ml) chopped fresh coriander |
| 2 fl. oz. (30 ml) olive oil | |
| ½ fl. oz. (15 ml) red wine vinegar | Black pepper from the peppermill |
| 1 small clove of garlic, finely chopped | |

Refer to p. 65 for notes on cleaning mussels. Put them in a saucepan, splash on a little white wine and open the mussels over a high heat with the lid on. Remove, drain through a colander into a second saucepan, and put that on to boil in order to reduce the mussel juice down to a couple of tablespoons of liquor. Remove the beards from the mussels, and discard one half of each shell. Lay them out on a dish. Mix the rest of the ingredients with the reduced mussel liquor and pour over the mussels.

# PRAWN PROFITEROLES

I would always recommend buying prawns in the shell, if you have time to peel them, rather than packets of peeled prawns, as they have a much better flavour. Prawns are a very popular filling for what are rather vulgarly named 'finger buffets' in the trade. Instead of the usual *bouchées* with prawn fillings, these little choux buns the same size as profiteroles and filled with prawns and prawn-flavoured whipped cream are even lighter.

| | |
|---|---|
| 1 oz. (30 g) butter | 2 oz. (60 g) strong flour |
| A good pinch of salt | 2 eggs, size 4 |
| 5 tablespoons (75 ml) water | |

Set the oven at 400°F (200°C; gas mark 6). Lightly grease a baking sheet.

To make the choux pastry, place the butter and salt in a saucepan with water and bring to the boil. Remove the pan from the heat and stir in the flour with a wooden spoon; return to the heat and beat until the mixture leaves the sides of the pan. Remove from the heat, allow to cool slightly, add the eggs and beat until smooth. Spoon into a piping bag filled with a half-inch (1-cm) plain nozzle and pipe 20 walnut-sized balls on the baking sheet.

Bake for 15 to 20 minutes until light brown (don't open the oven door for the first 10 minutes). Remove and cool on a wire rack.

## THE FILLING

| | |
|---|---|
| Half the shellfish reduction ingredients on p. 93, using the prawn shells | 1 teaspoon (5 ml) fresh lemon juice |
| | ½ lb. (225 g) (20–22) prawns in the shell |
| 4 fl. oz. (120 ml) double cream | |

Make the shellfish reduction but reduce the liquid right down to a thick purée. Leave to cool. When cold, add the cream and lemon juice and whip till quite stiff.

Spoon into a piping bag fitted with a half-inch (1-cm) nozzle.

Make a hole in the base of each bun with your little finger. Place one peeled prawn inside each and fill the rest of the cavity with the prawn cream.

# CHOPPED SALMON
# WITH GINGER AND SPRING ONIONS

A 4-oz. (120-g) skinned fillet of salmon, free from bones

2 spring onions

Zest and juice of half a lime (or a quarter lemon)

1 teaspoon (5 ml) finely chopped fresh ginger

½ fl. oz. (15 ml) soya sauce

3–4 slices of brown bread

Chop the salmon up into dice about ¼ by ¼ inch (6 by 6 mm). Finely chop the spring onions. Mix them with the salmon, the lime juice and zest, the ginger and the soya sauce. Chill for 30 minutes.

Cut the slices of brown bread into 30 1-inch (2.5-cm) rounds with a pastry cutter. Put a teaspoon of the salmon mixture on each piece and serve.

# SALTED SPRATS
# IN OLIVE OIL

We would serve these with drinks in the bar, as part of an hors d'œuvre with, maybe, some mussels in coriander dressing, cockles with shallot vinegar, peppered squid and salt cod with *aïoli*.

Take about 20 fresh sprats and fillet them using the method for filleting small round fish described on p. 55.

Prepare a brine of 6 oz. (180 g) salt to 2 pints (1 litre) of water by bringing the water to the boil with the salt and letting it go cold.

Put the fillets in the brine for 30 minutes, remove and leave them to dry out overnight on a wire rack in the refrigerator.

Place in a shallow dish, cover with olive oil and keep in the fridge.

# PEPPERED SQUID

❦❦❦❦❦❦

A very popular little *amuse-gueule* at the restaurant.

8 oz. (240 g) squid
2½ fl. oz. (75 ml) olive oil
1 tablespoon (15 ml) white wine
   vinegar

1 clove garlic
1 level teaspoon (5 ml) salt
A good pinch of cayenne pepper

See pp. 62–3 for notes on preparing squid. Cut the body of the squid into thin rounds and the tentacles and triangular fins into pieces. Dry it on kitchen paper.

Heat the oil in a frying pan and fry the squid in two batches, removing the first batch to a bowl with a perforated spoon. Fry it only till it turns completely white. Pour the cooking oil into the bowl with the squid. Pour the vinegar into the pan and stir it quickly around to 'deglaze' the pan, then pour the vinegar into the bowl. Add the garlic, salt and cayenne pepper, and stir everything round. Leave to go cold; it tastes better if you don't have to chill it.

Serve spiked with cocktail sticks.

# SQUID AND RED PEPPERS
## ON COCKTAIL STICKS

❦❦❦❦❦❦

1 squid
1 red pepper

Olive oil

Clean the squid following the instructions on p. 62. Cut it into strips ¼ by 2 inches (6 mm by 5 cm).

Cut the pepper in half, remove the seeds, and flatten it. Brush with oil and place under the grill or in the oven to blister the skin. Remove the skin and cut the pepper in pieces ¼ by ½ inch (6 mm by 1.25 cm).

Thread the squid on to cocktail sticks in an 'S' shape with two pieces of pepper, one in each bend of the S.

Chill till required, then brush with olive oil and cook quickly under the grill.

# SOUPS

# A LOBSTER SALAD
# AND A LOBSTER BISQUE

When one ruminates on the poor value for money of lobster because of its high proportion of shell to meat, one can console oneself that what isn't served to the customer makes exquisite soup. At the restaurant, we are able to make lobster bisque using fresh lobster because some of our lobster dishes are served out of the shell. This leaves us with a plentiful supply of raw materials which we turn rapidly into soup and sell quite inexpensively. If you were to go out and buy a live lobster just to turn it into soup, you might well wonder if there were better things to do with it; but with my recipe you need have no worries: you get the wonderful fresh flavour of a bisque made with a live lobster but you don't lose the lobster meat to the soup. It is served separately as a salad – the best of both worlds.

Live lobsters make an exceptionally pleasant soup, but any cooked shellfish – prawns, shrimps, crayfish, crawfish, crabs, even just the shells and body cavities – can be turned into nice everyday soups. In addition to this special recipe for lobster bisque, I give below a general recipe for shellfish bisque.

A 1½-lb. (700-g) live lobster

2 oz. (60 g) unsalted butter

2oz. (60 g) onion, peeled and chopped

2 oz. (60 g) carrot, peeled and chopped

2 oz. (60 g) celery, chopped

1 bayleaf

1 fl. oz. (30 ml) cognac

3 oz. (90 g) tomatoes

3 fl. oz. (90 ml) dry white wine

A good-sized sprig of fresh tarragon

2½ pints (1.4 litres) fish stock (see p. 92)

Salt and black pepper

2 fl. oz. (60 ml) double cream

Pinch of cayenne pepper

Juice of a quarter lemon

2 oz. (60 g) butter

---

### FOR THE SALAD

1 teaspoon (5 ml) chopped chives and chervil

Salad leaves for 4 small plated salads (say, Salad Bowl lettuce, spinach leaves, some Lollo Red lettuce, perhaps a few sorrel leaves)

1 fl. oz. (30 ml) olive oil dressing (see p. 104)

If you can't bring yourself to cut a live lobster in half, drop it into rapidly boiling water till it has turned red (this will take about 3 minutes).

Split the lobster in half as follows: place it on a chopping board and push the point of a large knife right through the carapace on the line that runs down the middle of the back of the body section. Bring the knife down on to the chopping board, cutting right through the tail. Turn the knife round and push it down through the carapace to sever the body

section in two. Twist off the claws. Remove the stomach sac from the body (just behind the mouth) and also remove the intestine, which runs down to the tail. Scrape out the tomalley from the body section into a small bowl and any dark blue coral. Collect all the liquid that has run out of the lobster as you cut it up. Pull the tails away from the body section. Crack the claws and chop them into three pieces at the joints. Cut the two small sections of claw in two. Pull the carapace away from the body section and cut the body into two or three pieces.

Mix the tomalley and any coral with the 2 oz. (60 g) of butter, which should be soft. This will be stirred into the soup right at the end to thicken it.

Melt the butter in a thick-bottomed pan and add the chopped onion, carrot, and celery, and the bayleaf. Cook these without browning too much; stir the pieces around once or twice, then add all the pieces of lobster and the liquid (blood, actually) from cutting the lobster up. Stir the pieces of lobster around in the vegetables and they will begin to turn red. As the lobster begins to colour, throw in the brandy and boil off the alcohol. Add the tomato, white wine, tarragon and a generous splash of the fish stock; bring to the boil and simmer for 10 minutes with the lid on. Remove the two tail sections of lobster and the two large claw sections. Add the rest of the fish stock to the pan and simmer for 20 minutes. Remove the meat from the tail sections and the claws and slice thinly. Cut the tail shell up and return it with the claw shells to the pan.

At the restaurant, while we are cooking the soup, we serve the lobster salad as a first course. You can do the same; once you have got the soup to this stage, you only need to liquidize it, pass it and finish it off with the tomalley butter, then you can be enjoying the salad with your guests while the soup is simmering. Toss the salad leaves in the dressing, arrange them on four plates, lay the lobster slices on top and sprinkle the plates with the chopped herbs.

After 20 minutes, liquidize the soup, first removing the tough claw shells, which will not break up easily in the liquidizer; everything else should cause no problem. Liquidize in two or three stages. Run the liquidizer only till the shell is reduced to small pieces, about the size of your fingernail; the object is not to produce powdered shell but rather to extract all possible flavour from any meat left sticking to it, particularly in the body section. Strain the soup through a conical strainer, pushing as much liquid as you can through with the back of a ladle, then pass it through a fine strainer, return to the heat and season.

Add the salt and black pepper, cream, cayenne pepper and lemon juice and stir the butter mixed with the tomalley and coral into the soup right at the end; don't reboil after you've done this. Think of coral and tomalley as similar to egg yolks, in that they thicken a sauce or soup at about 140–150°F (55–60°C); above this temperature the protein progressively hardens, like boiled egg.

## SHELLFISH BISQUE

Soups using the shells as well as the meat of lobsters, crabs and prawns, which give them a slightly grainy texture, are very satisfying to make. One of the most pleasurable things about cooking in a restaurant is that very little gets wasted. Because the job goes on day after day, something unwanted for one recipe can almost always be used elsewhere, leek tops in stock, dried cheese for a *gratin*, scraps of puff pastry for an apple tart, the parings from turned vegetables for a vegetable soup, leftover bread for croutons, and the shells of lobsters, crabs and prawns in a bisque.

The shells of 1½ lb. (700 g) of prawns, crabs etc. (including heads and body cavities)
3 oz. (90 g) butter
3 oz. (90 g) peeled and chopped onions
3 oz. (90 g) peeled and chopped carrots
3 oz. (90 g) chopped celery
1 bayleaf
1 fl. oz. (30 ml) brandy

4 oz. (120 g) tomatoes
1 tablespoon (15 ml) tomato purée
2 fl. oz. (60 ml) dry vermouth
2½ pints (1.4 litres) fish stock (see p. 92) or chicken stock (a stock cube is not totally inadmissible here)
2 oz. (60 g) rice
4 fl. oz. (120 ml) cream
Juice of a quarter lemon
A pinch of cayenne pepper, salt and ground black pepper

Remove any stomach sacs from the crustaceans and cut the shells up as much as possible with a heavy knife. Melt the butter in a thick-bottomed pan and add the onions, carrots, celery and bayleaf. Cook till just beginning to colour. Add the shells and tamp them down into the vegetables with the end of a rolling pin. Pour on the brandy and evaporate it away; then add the tomatoes, tomato purée, and dry vermouth. Reduce somewhat and add the fish stock (or chicken stock) and the rice.

Bring to the boil and simmer for 20 minutes, then liquidize in two or three stages, removing any particularly thick shells before you do this. You need only liquidize the shells to a point where the largest pieces are about the size of your little fingernail. Pass the soup through a conical strainer, pressing as much liquid as you can through with the back of a ladle. Now pass the soup through a fine strainer twice, and again if you find it too grainy, though I like a certain amount of texture to the bisque.

Add the cream and lemon juice and season with salt, ground black pepper and cayenne pepper to your taste.

# *BOURRIDE* OF SALT COD

A recipe using salt cod, with lots of garlic: a strong assertive fish soup. Remember that the cod needs to be soaked for 36 hours before using (less if it is home-salted).

4 cloves of garlic
2 fl. oz. (60 ml) olive oil
8 oz. (240 g) chopped onion
1 leek, roughly chopped
1 strip orange peel
1 oz. (30 g) tomato, sliced
1 pint (600 ml) fish stock
2 parsley stalks

1 bayleaf
1 sprig of thyme
12 oz. (360 g) salt cod, soaked for 24 to 36 hours
4 fl. oz. (120 ml) *aïoli* (see pp. 98–9)
A piece of French bread about 8 inches (23 cm) long

Chop up three of the garlic cloves and cook them gently in a saucepan with the olive oil, onions and leek. Add the orange peel and tomato, the stock and the herbs. Bring to the boil and simmer for 10 minutes, then add the fish and poach for 5 to 10 minutes, depending on the thickness of the fillet. Remove the fish and keep warm in a soup tureen or similar deep serving dish. Strain the cooking liquor through a sieve into a second saucepan, pressing the vegetables against the mesh of the sieve to extract as much flavour as possible. Pour a cupful or so of the hot stock on to the *aïoli* in a mixing bowl and whisk the two together. Now add this to the remainder of the strained fish stock. Return it to the heat and warm the sauce to the temperature of an egg custard (hot enough to be uncomfortable to your little finger), stirring with a wooden spoon. This will thicken the soup. Pour it over the fish and serve with the French bread cut into four slices, lightly toasted and rubbed with the remaining slightly crushed garlic clove. For a more substantial meal serve with some boiled potatoes.

# COD AND MUSSEL CHOWDER

The combination of fish, molluscs and salt pork in a cream-based soup is most agreeable. Fish stews made on this basis are as exciting in a Northern Atlantic way as the combination of fish, tomato, olive oil and garlic is in a Mediterranean stew like *bouillabaisse* (pp. 224–6).

20 mussels

2 oz. (60 g) salt pork, cut into small dice

1 oz. (30 g) butter

4 oz. (120 g) onions, diced

8 oz. (240 g) potatoes, diced and not washed (you need the starch to thicken the liquid)

10 fl. oz. (300 ml) milk

4 fl. oz. (120 ml) cream

1 bayleaf, sliced (preferably a fresh one)

The liquor from cooking the mussels

4 oz. (120 g) cod fillet, skinned

A small amount of freshly chopped parsley

2 water biscuits

Clean the mussels (see p. 65) and open them by placing them in a pan with a splash of water and steaming them over a high heat with a lid on the saucepan. As soon as the mussels open, take off the heat and drain them through a colander, saving the cooking liquor in a bowl underneath. When the mussels have cooled enough to handle, remove the meats from the shells and take out the beards.

Fry the diced pork in butter till beginning to brown, then add the onions and fry till soft.

At the same time, bring the potatoes to the boil in the milk and cream with the bayleaf. Slowly simmer till still firm but not raw. Add the pork and onions and the mussel juice and simmer for another five minutes. Season with salt if necessary and black pepper.

Add the cod fillet, cut into smallish pieces, and simmer till cooked, then add the mussels; do not continue to cook or you will toughen the mussels up. Pour the chowder into a serving tureen and finish with the chopped parsley and crushed water biscuits.

## CONGER EEL SOUP WITH ORANGE

Conger eel is an ideal fish for turning into soup because, in addition to being exceptionally cheap, it has a lot of flavour and a lot of body. The flavour, which some people find unpleasant on its own, is perfectly agreeable, I think, when combined with some other forceful flavours like orange and saffron.

1½ lb. (720 g) conger eel
2 pints (1.2 litres) water
8 oz. (240 g) onion, peeled and roughly chopped
2 oz. (60 g) celery, washed and sliced
3 oz. (90 g) carrot, peeled and roughly chopped
2 cloves of garlic, peeled and chopped

2 oz. (60 g) butter
4 oz. (120 g) tomatoes
The thinly peeled zest of a small orange
Juice of 2 oranges
½ teaspoon (2.5 ml) saffron
2 fl. oz. (60 ml) double cream
Salt and cayenne pepper

Fillet and skin the eel (see p. 57). Put the bones and skin in a saucepan with the water and 6 oz. (180 g) of the chopped onion. Bring to the boil and simmer for 20 minutes. Strain through a colander into a bowl.

Meanwhile soften the celery, carrot, garlic and the rest of the onion in the butter. Add the tomatoes, orange peel, orange juice, saffron and fish cut into chunks. Add the stock made from the bones, simmer for 20 minutes, then pass through a conical strainer. Pour in the cream and season with salt and cayenne pepper.

# VELVET CRAB
# AND CHILLI SOUP

Velvet or swimming crabs are not well known in the British Isles, though plenty are caught in lobster and crab pots here. Most are exported to France and Spain, where they are highly esteemed. They are small, just a little bigger than the green shore crab, and therefore best turned into soups. They have an exquisite sweet fresh flavour, so if you are on holiday on the coast and see signs of lobster and crab fishing, ask around.

2 lb. (900 g) velvet crabs
2 oz. (60 g) red peppers without seeds
½ oz. (15 g) green chillies without seeds
3 cloves of garlic, peeled and chopped
3 oz. (90 g) onion, peeled and sliced

2 fl. oz. (60 ml) olive oil
1 teaspoon (5 ml) tomato purée
2 pints (1.2 litres) fish stock (see p. 92)
1 oz. (30 g) broken pasta

Drop the crabs into fiercely boiling water. Boil for a couple of minutes till all are dead (see the notes on killing shellfish, pp. 59–61). Remove the back shell from the crabs. Also remove the stomach sac, which is situated at the front of the body shell below the eyes; in making any bisque-type soup where you are going to liquidize the shell as well as everything else, it is a good idea to remove the stomach. Otherwise, if the shellfish has been feeding in a sandy or muddy area, the grit thus ingested will find its way through to the finished soup. Everything else can go in, however. Cut the crabs into 5 or 6 pieces. Chop the red pepper and chillies and put them in a saucepan with the garlic, onion and olive oil. Fry over a medium heat to bring out the flavour. Stir in the crabs and add the tomato purée, sweat for a further couple of minutes, then pour on the fish stock. Bring to the boil and simmer for 20 minutes.

Liquidize everything (do it in small amounts if your liquidizer isn't particularly robust). Pass the liquidized soup through a conical strainer, pushing it through with the back of the ladle. After passing it once through the conical strainer, pass it twice more through a fine sieve. Reheat the soup and add the pasta. Simmer till the pasta is cooked, then serve.

# FISH SOUP

The sort of *soupe de poissons* that you find in virtually every coastal restaurant in France.

Now that almost everyone owns a liquidizer, a common error in making fish soup is to include the heads and bones of the fish when liquidizing. This gives the soup a bitter gluey flavour which one also notices too often in French restaurants.

In this recipe, the fish is filleted first, and the stock, made with the bones, is strained and added with the fillets of fish.

The quantities below make plenty of soup for four.

2–3 lb. (900 g–1.3 kg) fish*: conger eel, skate, cod, dogfish, shark – virtually any fish except oily ones like mackerel and herring
3 pints (1.7 litres) water
5 fl. oz. (150 ml) olive oil

6 oz. (180 g) onion, peeled and roughly chopped
6 oz. (180 g) celery, washed and roughly chopped
6 oz. (180 g) leek, washed and roughly chopped

* We always try to combine a mixture of fish with body, like conger or dogfish, with some cheap white fish like pollack or whiting, gurnard or grey mullet; and there is no reason why you shouldn't include in the initial fish stock any shellfish scraps you might have.

6 oz. (180 g) Florence fennel, roughly
  chopped
5 cloves of garlic
A 2-inch (5-cm) piece of orange peel
10 oz. (300 g) tomatoes
2 teaspoons (10 ml) tomato purée

A quarter of a large red pepper,
  blistered under the grill and peeled
1 bayleaf
A large pinch of saffron
Salt and ground black pepper
A large pinch of cayenne pepper

Fillet all the fish and use the heads and bones to make a fish stock with the
3 pints (1.7 litres) of water (as on p. 92, but using extra vegetables).

Heat the olive oil in a large pan and add the onion, celery, leek,
Florence fennel and garlic. Cook with a little colour till the vegetables
are very soft (about 45 minutes). Add the orange peel, tomatoes, tomato
purée, red pepper, bayleaf, saffron, and the fish fillets. Cook briskly,
turning everything over as you do. Now add the fish stock, bring to the
boil and simmer for 40 minutes.

Liquidize the soup and pass it through a conical strainer, pushing as
much as you can through with the back of a ladle. Put it back on the heat
and heat up. Season with salt, pepper and cayenne. The soup should be a
little on the salty side, with a subtle but noticeable heat about it from the
cayenne.

Serve the soup with some French bread, thinly sliced and fried in
olive oil, then rubbed with garlic, some grated cheese (Emmenthal or
Parmesan) and some *rouille* (recipe on p. 99). Spread the croutons with
*rouille* and float them on the soup scattered with the cheese.

# MUSSEL, LOVAGE AND CHERVIL SOUP
# WITH GREEN VEGETABLES

A dish of mussels in a soup, flavoured with lovage and with mange-tout
peas, spinach, thin slices of courgette, chervil and chives.

60 small mussels
2 fl. oz. (60 ml) dry white wine
1 pint (600 ml) fish stock (see p. 92)
2 small branches of lovage
2 sticks of celery
Half an onion roughly chopped
2-inch (50-mm) lemon peel without pith
The flesh of a quarter lemon, without pith
2 cloves of garlic
Pinch of curry powder
Good pinch of saffron
12 mange-tout peas
2 oz. (60 g) spinach, washed and with stalks removed
2 fl. oz. (60 ml) double cream
4 oz. (120 g) unsalted butter
2 oz. (60 g) courgettes, very thinly sliced
A large pinch of chopped chervil
A large pinch of chopped chives

Clean the mussels (see p. 65) and put them in a good-size saucepan with a splash of the white wine. With the lid on the saucepan, open the mussels over a high heat. As soon as they are open, take off the heat and drain through a colander, keeping the cooking liquid in a bowl. Pass the cooking liquid through a fine sieve into a saucepan and add the fish stock, lovage, celery, onion, lemon peel and flesh, garlic, the rest of the wine, curry powder and saffron. Bring to the boil and simmer for 30 minutes. While this is cooking remove the beards from all the mussels and the shells from all but eight of them.

Briefly blanch the mange-tout peas in boiling water and refresh them in cold water. Do the same with the spinach.

After 30 minutes, strain the *bouillon* and return to the heat. Add double cream and butter and reduce a little by rapid boiling. Add the courgettes, then the mange-tout peas and spinach. Finally, just before serving, add the mussels, including the eight still in the shell. These must be only just heated through or they will toughen up. Sprinkle with the chervil and chives and serve. Very nice it is, too.

## MUSSEL AND LEEK SOUP

Mussels and leeks go very well together to make, with saffron, a soup that smells and tastes quite exotic. Mussels are so abundant round our coastline that it is a pity they are not more readily available at fishmongers throughout Britain. It could be a question of demand creating a supply; so the more you ask for them, the better.

3 lb. (1.4 kg) or 3 pints (1.7 litres)
   mussels
1 fl. oz. (30 ml) white wine
8 oz. (240 g) leeks
1 small onion

3 oz. (90 g) butter
1½ oz. (45 g) plain flour
15 fl. oz. (450 ml) fish stock (see
   p. 92)
A good pinch of saffron
2 fl. oz. (60 ml) double cream

Thoroughly wash the mussels, scraping off barnacles and discarding any mussels that are gaping open and don't close up when given a good tap. Place the cleaned mussels in a pan. Add a dash of the wine, cover and cook over a high heat for about 5 minutes, shaking the pan until the mussels have opened. Strain the liquor through a colander into a bowl, shaking the colander well to drain off all the juice lodged in the shells.

Cut up the leeks and the onion. Melt the butter in a saucepan and soften the vegetables in it on a low heat for about 3 minutes. Add the remaining wine and let it reduce by half. Add the flour and stir until smooth. Mix the mussel liquor with the fish stock and gradually add it to the pan, stirring well. When the soup is smooth and simmering, add a good pinch of saffron and leave to cook for 25 minutes.

While it is simmering, pull all the beards out of the mussels and discard one half of each shell. Liquidize the soup and strain through a sieve into a clean saucepan. Reheat and stir in the cream and the mussels. Serve hot.

## CLEAR WHITING SOUP

Because whiting is one of the cheapest fish and, like many of the cod family, seems to lack flavour, it is often dismissed as uninteresting. But given the right delicate, clean flavours, small whiting can epitomize the excitement of fish cookery in that the difference between very boring and very subtle is often minute: there is a difference, and that's the point.

2 fillets from a small whiting, skin on
3 pints (1.7 litres) fish stock made
   with whiting bones
2 small egg whites

8 oz. (240 g) skinned whiting fillet,
   chopped up
Half an onion, finely chopped
1 small tomato, chopped
4 parsley stalks

## TO BE ADDED TO THE FINISHED SOUP

1 carrot
One quarter of a fennel bulb
A few chives

1 small spray of fennel
The juice of one quarter of a lemon
2 tablespoons (30 ml) soya sauce

Cut the two whiting fillets diagonally across into ½-inch (12.5-mm) 'lozenges'. Poach these in a little of the stock for one minute, drain, and pour the cooking liquor back with the rest of the stock. These little lozenges of whiting will be added to the soup at the end. Whisk the egg whites with a little of the fish stock, then add the rest together with the skinned and chopped whiting fillet, the onion, tomato and parsley stalks. Bring slowly to the boil, stirring occasionally as you do so. Give one final stir as it boils, then leave it, to allow the egg white to form a thick crust with all the cloudy elements in the stock. Simmer very gently for 20 minutes, then cool. Pass through a double thickness of muslin or a coffee filter paper.

Peel the carrot and cut into strips 1½ by ⅛ inches (4 cm by 3 mm). Cut the fennel bulb into strips of the same size. Blanch both these in boiling salted water for one minute, then refresh in cold water and drain. Cut the chives into similar lengths, and chop up the fennel herb. Heat up the consommé and add the lemon juice and soya sauce, the carrot, fennel bulb and herb, chives, and lastly the lozenges of poached whiting.

# Nine

# HORS D'ŒUVRES AND SALADS

# AÏOLI PROVENÇAL

T here are some dishes which one eats many times over and yet they never seem to lose their romance. I think it is because they are so exactly right. Some examples: skate with black butter, *moules marinière*, a *navarin* of lamb, and *aïoli provençal*.

I include *aïoli* only because I adore it and it goes very well in the restaurant. The ingredients must match the inherent romance of the dish: salt cod there must be, a thick fillet with large flakes peeling away; the fish and salt and biting garlic are the central point of the dish, but then some sweet boiled new potatoes cooked in their skins too, with some artichokes, preferably tiny ones which you can eat whole. Some thick slices of Florence fennel, dropped in boiling salted water and refreshed, some fine French beans cooked in the same way and hard-boiled eggs and some blanched and chilled carrots for a splash of colour.

Enough for four as a main course.

1 lb. (450 g) fillet of salt cod

---
### THE COURT BOUILLON
---

1 bayleaf
1 onion

2 cloves of garlic
2 pints (1.2 litres) water

1½ lb. (720 g) small new potatoes
8 small or 4 large artichokes
2 bulbs of Florence fennel, sliced
8 oz. (240 g) French beans

10 oz. (300 g) carrots, peeled and cut into sticks about ¼ inch (6 mm) thick
4 hard-boiled eggs
12 fl. oz. (360 ml) *aïoli* (see pp. 98–9)

For instructions on making your own salt cod, see p. 110. Soak the salt cod for 36 hours before cooking in plenty of cold water; change the water once during this time. Bring all the *court bouillon* ingredients to the boil and simmer for 10 minutes. Poach the cod but keep it slightly under-cooked; allow 10 minutes to the inch (2.5 cm) of thickness. Leave it to cool in the *bouillon*.

Boil the potatoes and leave them to cool. Cook the artichokes in salted water with a splash of wine vinegar added. When cooked, leave them to cool, then cut them into halves or quarters and remove the choke. Blanch the fennel, beans and carrots briefly in boiling salted water, then drop them into ice-cold water and drain them straightaway.

Lay all the vegetables with the eggs and salt cod around a large serving plate and put the *aïoli* in the middle.

Serve with plenty of bread and some chilled bottles of strong but unsubtle white wine from Provence or the Southern Rhône.

# SPIDER CRAB TERRINE
# WITH AVOCADO

This is made in the same way as a sweet *bavarois*. Spider crabs make the best terrine, but ordinary crabs are a very pleasant substitute.

A 1-lb. (450-g) spider crab

## INGREDIENTS FOR THE SHELLFISH REDUCTION

1 oz. (30 g) carrot, peeled and chopped

1 oz. (30 g) onion, peeled and chopped

1 oz. (30 g) celery, washed and chopped

The shells from the crab

2 oz. (60 g) tomato, roughly chopped

½ teaspoon (2.5 ml) tomato purée

1 fl. oz. (30 ml) dry white wine

12 fl. oz. (360 ml) water

## THE TERRINE

4 fl. oz. (120 ml) double cream

1 egg separated into yolk and white

1 leaf of gelatine or 1 level teaspoon of gelatine powder

Salt

1 teaspoon (5 ml) lemon juice

## ORDER OF WORK

1. Dress the crab.
2. Make the shellfish reduction.

3. Make the terrine.

Pick all the meat out of the crab.

## THE SHELLFISH REDUCTION

Melt the butter in a pan and cook the carrot, onion and celery in it till beginning to colour. Add the shells, tomato, tomato purée and white wine and stir over a high heat for 2 or 3 minutes. Add the water, bring to the boil and simmer for 40 minutes. Strain through a sieve into a second saucepan. Reduce this liquid to 2 tablespoons (30 ml) by rapid boiling.

## THE TERRINE

Bring half the cream to the boil, then take it off the heat. Whisk the egg yolk with the reduced shellfish reduction (which should have been cooled somewhat) and add the hot cream. Stir constantly with a wooden spoon over a moderate heat till the savoury custard starts to thicken. Take off the heat, add the gelatine and cool the pan by setting it in a bowl of ice and water. When it is quite cool, add the crab meat and season if necessary with salt and a pinch of cayenne pepper.

As the mixture gets colder it will begin to set. Both the whipped cream and the whipped egg white need to be folded into the mixture before it sets too hard. First whip the cream till it is thick and soft but not stiff and fold it in; then whip the egg white to soft peaks and fold that in. Pour the mixture into the terrine mould, which should be oiled with groundnut or sunflower oil. Leave to chill for at least 3 hours in the refrigerator. Turn the terrine out by turning the mould upside down and bringing it down on to a tray with a firm tap. Repeat until it slips out. The coating of oil should be enough to allow it to slide it out; if it fails to move, dip the mould briefly into hot water.

Slice the terrine with a thin-bladed knife dipped into very hot water. At the restaurant, we serve this with a quarter of an avocado pear for each person, peeled and sliced and dressed with an olive oil dressing and a couple of leaves of dressed frisé.

# CURED FISH WITH AQUAVIT IN THE BALTIC STYLE

Cold-smoked trout or mackerel, salmon cured with caraway and aquavit, and herrings with red onions and a mustard and dill mayonnaise, with thinly sliced wholewheat walnut bread and a glass of ice-cold aquavit, the caraway-flavoured spirit from Scandinavia. Because there is a lot of preparation involved in this dish and such parts as the cured salmon are not worth making for a few people, this recipe is for 12 people.

½ oz. (15 g) salt
½ oz. (15 g) sugar
1 teaspoon (5 ml) chopped caraway
    leaf or fennel
½ fl. oz. (15 ml) aquavit
12 oz. (360 g) salmon fillet

12 oz. (360 g) marinated salt herring
    with red onions (see pp. 116–17)
A 12-oz. (360-g) fillet of cold-smoked
    trout or the equivalent weight of
    cold-smoked mackerel fillets

### FOR THE WALNUT BREAD

A 1.5 kg bag of 100 per cent
    wholewheat flour
1½ oz. (45 g) salt
2 oz. (60 g) soft brown sugar

1 oz. (30 g) fresh yeast
2 pints (1.2 litres) water
2 oz. (60 g) butter
3 oz. (90 g) walnuts

### THE MUSTARD MAYONNAISE

1 pint mustard mayonnaise (see p. 98)
1 tablespoon (15 ml) caster sugar

1 teaspoon (5 ml) freshly chopped dill
1 fl. oz. (30 ml) double cream

### ORDER OF WORK

1. Make the gravlax.
2. Salt the herrings (as on p. 117).
3. Marinate the herrings.
4. Make the walnut bread.

5. Make the mustard
   mayonnaise.
6. Slice the fish and lay it out on
   the plates.

### THE GRAVLAX

Mix the salt and sugar with the caraway and aquavit and coat the fillet of salmon with it. Wrap it in clingfilm and leave in the refrigerator for at least 12 hours. You can scrape off the coating before you start to slice, but I think it is nice left on as an edge to each slice.

### THE WALNUT BREAD

Mix the wholewheat flour with the salt and brown sugar.

Dissolve the yeast in a quarter of a pint (150 ml) of the water, which should be at blood heat (i.e. should feel neither hot nor cold to the touch). Add the yeast mixture to the rest of the water, and mix it into the flour to form a loose moist dough.

Melt the butter and add. Knead for 3 minutes; add the walnuts towards the end. Then divide into 3 buttered bread tins (this amount makes 2½ standard bread loaves, so you will need two large and one small tin).

Place the tins in a black plastic dustbin bag and leave to prove in a warm place till doubled in size.

Set your oven to 450°F (230°C; gas mark 8) while the loaves are proving. Bake the bread for 35 minutes, then remove from the tin and bake for a further 5 minutes.

## THE MUSTARD MAYONNAISE

Follow the recipe on p. 98, then mix in the other mayonnaise ingredients.

## THE HERRINGS

Red onions should be thinly sliced and added to the herrings an hour before serving. (If you can't get red onions, use chopped spring onions.) Mix some chopped dill into the herrings just before serving.

## SERVING

Slice the trout or mackerel as thinly as possible and lay out on 12 chilled plates. Slice the salmon and lay out opposite; put the marinated herring between and a spoonful of the mayonnaise on the other side. Decorate each plate with a spray of dill, caraway or fennel. Everything must be cold, so if you find it easier to set everything out some time before serving, leave off the mayonnaise, wrap each plate in clingfilm and stack them in the refrigerator. The glasses for the aquavit must be ice-cold too and the aquavit itself should be put in the deep freeze for at least an hour before serving. Slice the walnut bread as thinly as possible and spread with unsalted butter.

# MOUSSELINE OF FINNAN HADDOCK WITH A HORSERADISH SAUCE

You can make this with lesser varieties of smoked haddock, but you can't beat the real thing.

12 oz. (350 g) Finnan haddock, weighed on the bone
6 oz. white fish fillet such as plaice, lemon sole, whiting, free from skin and bone

1 egg and 1 egg yolk
½ oz. (15 g) peeled onion
1 level teaspoon (5 ml) salt
Juice of a quarter lemon
12 fl. oz. (360 ml) double cream

———————— FOR THE HORSERADISH SAUCE ————————

2 teaspoons (10 ml) freshly grated
   horseradish (or horseradish sauce if
   you can't get fresh)
2 fl. oz. (60 ml) double cream

½ teaspoon (2.5 ml) white wine
   vinegar (leave this out if using
   horseradish sauce)
Pinch of salt

Ask your fishmonger to fillet and skin the Finnan haddock for you. Place the haddock and other white fish fillet, eggs, onion, salt and lemon juice in a food processor and blend until smooth. Pour in the cream, which must be well chilled, and continue to blend for 15 seconds only (don't go on any longer or you will curdle it). Chill the mixture for 30 minutes.

Set your oven to 300°F (150°C; gas mark 2).

Butter a suitable mould (I use a small bread tin about 9 by 4 by 2 inches, 23 by 10 by 5 cm), fill it with the mousseline and cover with buttered foil. Find a shallow tray in which you can fit your mould, place the mould in the tray and half fill the tray with water. Bring the water in the tray to the boil on top of the cooker and then transfer to the top shelf of the oven and cook for about 40 minutes. To test if the mousseline is cooked, insert a trussing needle or thin knife into the centre and test on your top lip; if it feels warm the mousseline is cooked enough. Remove from the oven, leave to cool and chill for at least 4 hours.

Turn out the mousseline by dipping the mould in a sink full of hot water while you count to six, then invert over a tray, bringing the mould down with a sharp tap. Make the horseradish sauce by mixing all the ingredients, and serve a slice of mousseline with a spoonful of sauce.

# MARINATED HERRING
# WITH CREAM

Somewhat similar to soused herring but far superior.

4 fl. oz. (120 g) white wine vinegar
½ pint (300 ml) water
2 teaspoons (10 ml) sugar
1 teaspoon (5 ml) salt
12 black peppercorns
2 bayleaves

Sprig of thyme
2 herrings, each weighing 6–8 oz.
   (180–240 g)
3 tablespoons (45 ml) cream
2 thin pieces of lemon peel
1 small onion, peeled and sliced

Put all the ingredients except the herrings, cream, lemon peel and onion in a saucepan. Boil, then simmer for 15 minutes and leave to cool.

Fillet the herrings (refer to the notes for filleting small round fish on p. 55).

Place the herring fillets in a shallow dish and just cover them with the marinade, topping up with a little water if necessary. Bring this up to the boil, let it bubble once, then immediately take it off the heat.

Mix the cream with 3 tablespoons (45 ml) of the cold marinade and pour on to 4 plates. Place a fillet on each. Cut the lemon peel into very fine strips and put two strips on each fillet with some onion. Serve cold with brown bread and butter.

## HOT KIPPER SALAD
## WITH WHISKY

Mixed salad leaves, enough to cover 4 plates (roughly 5 oz., 150 g)
5 oz. (150 g) kipper fillet
2 slices of wholemeal bread

2½ fl. oz. (75 ml) groundnut oil
1 fl. oz. (30 ml) whisky
½ fl. oz. (15 ml) white wine vinegar
Freshly ground black pepper

Arrange the salad leaves on 4 plates. Cut the kipper into strips about the size of your little finger. Cut the brown bread into small croutons and fry in a little of the oil until crisp. Remove from the pan with a perforated spoon and keep warm. Toss the kipper strips in the oil, adding the whisky and the rest of the oil and white wine vinegar at the same time. Season with black pepper. Only warm the kipper through in the dressing; don't fry it. Turn the kipper and dressing out on to the salad and serve.

## A SALAD OF LANGOUSTINE
## WITH CHICORY AND ENDIVE

In 1984 we won the *Sunday Times*/Taste of Britain Award for the best English restaurant. This increased our turnover by about 50 per cent overnight. This was by no means all fun; we found ourselves quite unprepared for the extra business and upset quite a few people with slow service. It took us six months to sort the problems out. This is the salad I devised for the R A C Club lunch to celebrate the award. It's rather nice – very simple, but none the worse for that.

24 langoustine
2 oz. (60 g) chicory
2 oz. (60 g) endive
3 fl. oz. (90 ml) walnut dressing (see p. 105)
6 oz. (180 g) tomatoes, peeled, deseeded and chopped
1 teaspoon (5 ml) fresh chopped tarragon
1 teaspoon (5 ml) fresh chopped parsley
Salt and freshly ground black pepper

Completely peel all but four of the langoustine. Carefully peel the last four langoustine, keeping the peeled tail attached to the head. Wash and dry the chicory and endive. Slice the chicory lengthways into ½-inch (1.25-cm) strips. Put two-thirds of the walnut dressing in a mixing bowl and turn the endive and chicory over in it, ensuring that all the leaves are coated. Arrange the salad neatly on four plates, leaving the centre of the plate empty. Mix the tomatoes, tarragon, parsley and the rest of the dressing together in the mixing bowl. Season well with salt and ground black pepper. Spoon out into the centre of each plate. Place five peeled langoustine and a single half-peeled langoustine equidistantly around on the salad.

# HOT POTATO SALAD
# WITH SMOKED MACKEREL AND
# DANDELIONS

The bitterness of the dandelions goes very well with the smoke in the mackerel. There is something very satisfying about using weeds to flavour a dish.

10 oz. (300 g) new potatoes
1 oz. (30 g) dandelion leaves
½ oz. (15 g) finely chopped onion

3 oz. (90 g) smoked mackerel
3 fl. oz. (90 ml) basic dressing (see p. 104)

Scrub the potatoes and boil them. Wash the dandelion leaves and pull away the stems. Blanch the leaves in boiling water for a few seconds, then refresh them in cold water. Drain them in a sieve. Chop the onion. Remove skin and bone from the mackerel and cut into slices 1 by ¼ inch (2.5 cm by 6 mm). Slice the potatoes into ¼-inch (6-mm) slices and place in a saucepan with the dandelion leaves and onions, add the dressing, and warm everything through. Put the salad into a bowl and serve with a few turns of your black peppermill.

# MACKEREL *ESCABÈCHE*

A pleasant way of serving mackerel cold as an hors d'œuvre. The mackerel is first floured and fried in olive oil, then marinated with olive oil, wine vinegar and herbs. The point of the dish to me is to feature one fresh herb most strongly. I use Greek oregano, a rather fiery herb which is more like thyme in taste than oregano. You can buy the seeds from Suffolk Herbs (address on p. 87). Other herbs I would suggest are coriander leaf, thyme, marjoram, oregano, or fennel with a dash of pastis in the marinade.

Two mackerel, each weighing 8–
  10 oz. (240–300 g)
6 fl. oz. (120 ml) olive oil
Seasoned flour
2 oz. (60 g) carrot, peeled and thinly
  sliced
2 oz. (60 g) onion, peeled and thinly
  sliced

2 cloves of garlic
4 tablespoons (60 ml) wine vinegar
4 tablespoons (60 ml) water
1 teaspoon (5 ml) chopped Greek
  oregano
Salt and ground black pepper

Fillet the mackerel. Pour half the oil into a large frying pan (preferably not a steel pan: aluminium or non-stick are better, since simmering liquids like water and vinegar in a steel pan imparts a metallic flavour). Heat the oil in the pan and dust the mackerel fillets with the seasoned flour. Pat off any excess.

Fry the fillets on both sides till golden brown, then transfer them to a shallow dish, which should be just large enough to take them side by side.

Pour the rest of the olive oil into the frying pan and fry the carrot, onion and garlic until they begin to colour. At this point add the wine vinegar, water, oregano and seasoning. Simmer until the vegetables are cooked, then pour the contents of the frying pan over the fish and leave to go cold.

# MONKFISH SALAD WITH MUSHROOMS AND PICKLED CHERRIES

The idea for this recipe comes from a refreshing and unusual cookery book, *Le Menu Gastronomique* (Macdonald), by a doctor who won the Mouton Cadet/Observer Dinner Party Menu Competition a few years ago. Dr Jack Gillon once worked in Lyon and wrote this book out of his enthusiasm for the cookery of the area. He includes no recipes as such, but instead describes the basic idea of the dishes and gives the ingredients without quantities. Each dish is part of a dinner menu, and each course has a particular wine specified, even down to the vintage. The relationship between food and wine is described sensibly, and the book as a whole rekindles my enthusiasm for the higher subtleties of food and wine in the long August days when the pressure of business, of endless meals over and over again, sometimes makes one falter! It is a most successful combination.

## PICKLING THE CHERRIES

20 cherries, fresh or tinned (morellos if you can get them)
4 fl. oz. (120 ml) white wine vinegar
1 oz. (30 g) sugar

4 allspice berries, crushed
4 black peppercorns, crushed
Pinch of ground cinnamon
Pinch of cayenne pepper

## THE MUSHROOMS

4 oz. (120 g) fresh white button mushrooms
Juice of a quarter lemon
2.5 fl. oz. (75 ml) olive oil
2.5 fl. oz. (75 ml) water

4 crushed peppercorns
8 coriander seeds
1 bayleaf
Sprig of thyme
Salt

## POACHING THE FISH

8 oz. (240 g) monkfish fillet
2 fl. oz. (60 ml) dry white wine

4 fl. oz. (120 ml) fish stock

## THE SALAD

Lettuce, sorrel and rocket, and some slightly bitter-tasting salad leaves like endive or chicory. A red lettuce or red chicory like radicchio would add to the visual impact of the dish (see p. 82)

## ORDER OF WORK

1. Pickle the cherries.
2. Cook the mushrooms.

3. Poach the fish.
4. Assemble the dish.

The pickled cherries should be made a few days before. The mushrooms and fish should be cooked some hours before serving.

Put all the pickling ingredients except the cherries into a pan, bring to the boil and simmer for 5 minutes. Add the cherries and cook till soft but still whole if fresh (just warm them through if they were tinned). Pour into a small bowl and chill till required.

Wash the mushrooms, place in a bowl and squeeze the lemon juice over them. Bring all the other ingredients for poaching the mushrooms to the boil and simmer for 2 minutes. Add the mushrooms and simmer for 5 minutes. Remove the mushrooms and reduce the sauce by half, then pour the liquor through a sieve over the mushrooms. Chill.

Season the fillet of monkfish and poach in the white wine and fish stock till white on the outside but still a little translucent at the centre. Remove the fillet, reduce the cooking liquor to a couple of tablespoons and pour it back over the fish. Chill.

Wash and dry the salad ingredients well. Mix some of the cherry pickling juice with the marinade from the mushrooms to make a delicious pink dressing. Put the salad in a bowl and toss with this dressing. Place the salad on four plates. Slice the monkfish into thin rounds and turn over in the bowl in which you dressed the salad to coat the monkfish with the last of the dressing. Lay this out on the four salads together with any remaining cooking liquor, which will have jellified and should be chopped up. Remove the stones from the cherries and distribute them and the mushrooms over the salad.

# SLICED RAW FISH WITH HORSERADISH AND A SOYA SAUCE

Raw fish may not appeal to you; all I can say is just try it. The idea comes from Japanese cookery: you dip the slices into the accompanying sauce and add a little horseradish. I need hardly add that the fish must be perfectly fresh for this dish.

You need to buy two or three fillets of different types of fish. We might use sliced salmon, brill and bass on one occasion, sliced shark, scallops and lemon sole on another day, or sliced monkfish, squid and red mullet, aiming always to get a contrast in colour and texture. The Japanese tend to slice the fish quite thickly, about ¼ inch (6 mm); we prefer slicing everything as thinly as possible. Aim to buy about three-quarters of a pound (360 g) of fillet altogether for a first course for four. To facilitate slicing, the fish should be very well chilled, even put in the freezer for a while, but taken out just before it actually starts to freeze.

Ideally you should try to get hold of some wasabi, which is green Japanese horseradish powder, extremely strong when mixed with water. Fresh horseradish is perfectly acceptable: mix 2 oz. (60 g) of finely grated horseradish with 1 fl. oz. (30 ml) double cream and the juice of half a lemon.

## SOYA SAUCE
### WITH GINGER AND SPRING ONIONS

3 fl. oz. (90 ml) soya sauce
3 fl. oz. (90 ml) water
The zest and juice of a lime

1 oz. (25 g) ginger, peeled and finely
   chopped
4 spring onions, chopped

# MARINATED SALMON TROUT
# WITH LIME AND GINGER

Thinly sliced salmon trout marinated in a dressing made with ginger, fresh lime juice and pink peppercorns. If you can't get hold of pink peppercorns leave them out, but they are available nowadays in good delicatessens. It is quite hard to slice raw salmon trout very thinly, but if you do the best you can, sandwich the slices between two plates, and apply a little gentle pressure, you will find the results quite passable.

8 oz. (240 g) salmon trout fillet,
free from bones

### THE DRESSING

4 fl. oz. (120 ml) groundnut oil
¼ oz. (7.5 g) fresh ginger, peeled and
   finely chopped

1 teaspoon (5 ml) of pink peppercorns
Juice and zest of one lime
½ teaspoon (2.5 ml) salt

Place the fillet, skin side down, on a chopping board, take a very sharp thin-bladed knife and cut thin slices, cutting on the slant towards the tail as you would slice smoked salmon. Cut enough to cover 4 dinner plates. Flatten the fish if necessary by pressing a clean plate down on to the slices, cover with clingfilm and refrigerate until just before you want to serve the fish. As slicing the fish is quite tricky it is a good idea to do it some time in advance.

Make the dressing by combining all the ingredients.

Five minutes before serving, put the dressing on the fish, spreading it over with the back of a teaspoon.

# SALMON MARINATED IN FRESH LIME JUICE WITH A CHIVE MAYONNAISE

The less you have to cook salmon and salmon trout, the better it tastes; so when the slices of salmon are 'cooked' for only five minutes in fresh lime juice one can't do much better than to eat it absolutely raw like the Japanese (see p. 150).

The idea of cooking fish in citrus juice is common in Caribbean cookery.

For this recipe, follow exactly the same instructions for the salmon trout (p. 151) but five minutes before serving squeeze the juice of a lime on each plate of salmon, rub it around with the back of a spoon and sprinkle it with a very little salt. Serve with mayonnaise, to which you should add a little double cream and some freshly chopped chives.

# A WARM SALMON SALAD

This is the sort of dish I love in the early summer: an uncomplicated way of presenting some fresh salmon. For a change I have included salad ingredients that you can readily buy. But naturally I would use a variety of different types of lettuce and probably some sorrel, cress grown outside, and some young rocket too.

A 1-lb. (450-g) piece of salmon on the bone
Salt and freshly ground black pepper
½ teaspoon (2.5 ml) fresh chopped tarragon

1 lettuce
1 bunch of watercress
1 bunch of spring onions
3 fl. oz. (90 ml) olive oil dressing (see p. 104)

Set your oven to 300°F (150°C; gas mark 2).

Take a piece of aluminium foil about 12 inches (30 cm) square and brush it with olive oil. Brush the piece of salmon with oil, season well, and sprinkle it with chopped tarragon. Parcel the salmon up loosely in the foil by folding one half over the other and turning over the edges. Place the parcel on a baking tray and bake gently in the slow oven for about 45 minutes until just cooked. It should be slightly undercooked in the middle (a darker shade of pink).

Meanwhile prepare the salad. Wash the lettuce and dry it. Remove the thickest watercress stalks and the outer skins of the spring onions. Cut the white of the spring onions from the green and slice the white part diagonally. Put in a bowl with the lettuce and cress and toss with half of the olive oil dressing.

Chop the green part of the spring onions into ⅛-inch (3-mm) pieces and put in a small saucepan with the rest of the dressing.

When the salmon is cooked, unwrap it and pour the cooking juices into the saucepan with the chopped spring onion and dressing. Remove the skin and bones from the salmon, break the fillet into pieces and arrange over the salad. Warm the dressing in the saucepan through and pour over the warm salmon; serve at once.

You can make a main course of this dish by using a 1½-lb. (700-g) piece of salmon and adding some new potatoes boiled with mint.

# A WILTED SALAD OF SCALLOPS, PRAWNS AND MUSSELS

A seafood salad which is slightly warmed up under the grill so that the leaves go limp. Salad leaves treated in this way taste totally different. By increasing the quantities, this will make a very pleasant main course.

4 scallops
20 mussels
1 courgette
Salad leaves for 4 people (as varied as possible, e.g. lettuce, spinach, rocket, sorrel, and a few dandelion leaves)

2 fl. oz. (60 ml) olive oil dressing (see p. 104)
2 good-sized tomatoes, peeled, deseeded and chopped
½ oz. (15 g) onion, finely chopped
5 leaves of basil
20 shelled prawns

Clean the scallops (see pp. 64–5) and slice each one into three. Brush a small grilling tray with a little oil and brush the scallops. 'Set' the scallops under the grill (i.e. cook them only enough to firm them up). Remove and cool down.

Clean the mussels (see p. 65), then open them in a pan with the lid on over a high heat. Strain through a colander; keep the cooking liquor for another dish. Shell and remove the beards from the mussels.

Cut the courgette into *julienne* strips, ⅛ by ⅛ by 1¾ inches (3 mm by 3 mm by 4.5 cm).

Toss the salad leaves in a bowl with half the olive oil dressing and the courgette strips.

Mix tomato, onion, the rest of the olive oil dressing and the basil (which should be roughly chopped) in a small saucepan. Add the scallops, mussels and prawns. Warm this through, but do not let it get hot.

Turn on your overhead grill.

Place salad leaves on 4 plates and arrange the scallops, mussels, prawns and the tomato and basil dressing on top.

Finally place the 4 salads under your grill for only enough time to wilt the salad leaves – about 20 seconds. Serve immediately.

# SKATE MAYONNAISE
# WITH A VEGETABLE SALAD

Skate is ideal for poaching and serving cold as a salad, having no bones and a firm texture.

1½ lb. (720 g) skate
*Court bouillon* (see p. 93)

---
### THE VEGETABLE SALAD
---

2 oz. (60 g) celery
2 oz. (60 g) carrot
2 oz. (60 g) leek
1 fl. oz. (30 ml) groundnut oil

1 fl. oz. (30 ml) white wine
Salt, black pepper
2 oz. (60 g) French beans
2 oz. (60 g) mange-tout peas

---
### THE MAYONNAISE
---

4 oz. (120 g) mayonnaise
  (see pp. 97–8)
3 oz. (90 g) tomato, peeled, deseeded
  and roughly chopped

1 avocado pear, peeled and chopped
4 oz. (120 g) potato, peeled and diced

Poach the skate in the *court bouillon* for 15 to 20 minutes. Leave to cool in the *bouillon*.

Cut the celery, carrot and leek into strips ⅛ by ⅛ by 2 inches (3 mm by 3 mm by 5 cm). Heat the oil in a sauteuse and gently cook the vegetables in the oil for a minute, add the white wine, salt and pepper, and cook till the wine has disappeared in steam. Turn out on to a plate and chill.

Top and tail the beans and mange-tout peas. Cut the beans into similar lengths to the rest of the vegetables; the peas can be left as they are. Bring a pan of salted water to the boil and blanch the beans and peas for half a minute, then plunge them into cold water, preferably iced. Drain through a colander and mix with the rest of the vegetables. Season with salt and black pepper.

Remove the skin and cartilage from the skate and mix with the mayonnaise, tomato, avocado, and potato. Test for seasoning. Serve with a couple of leaves from the heart of a lettuce and the vegetable salad.

# Ten

# FISH DISHES FOR A FIRST COURSE

# ANGUILLES AU VERT

I know of no better cookery book on the subject of fish and shellfish than Jane Grigson's *Fish Cookery*. I had it before I opened the restaurant twelve years ago and I still look at it every day. On the subject of eels, she makes one want to go out and buy some immediately:

I love eel. Sometimes I think it's my favourite fish. It's delicate, but rich; it falls neatly from the bone; grilled to golden brown and flecked with dark crustiness from a charcoal fire, it makes the best of all picnic food; stewed in red wine, cushioned with onions and mushrooms, bordered with triangles of fried bread, it's the meal for cold nights in autumn; smoked and cut into elegant fillets, it starts a wedding feast or Christmas eve dinner with style and confidence.

Like Jane Grigson, I think that once you've eaten eel it becomes something of a passion. It's the contrast between its fresh river-watery delicacy and its oily richness that makes it so satisfying.

This recipe for *anguilles au vert* shows off that contrast at its very best: fried fillets of eel with a white wine and egg sauce flavoured with spinach, sorrel and tarragon all on a *croûte* of fried French bread.

This is a traditional French recipe which we have slightly changed. In the original recipe, the eel is cooked and served on the bone, but we find at the restaurant that dishes which serve unfilleted fish completely covered in sauce are unpopular because people don't like having to search through the sauce for the bones.

Unlike the original recipe too we cook eel and sauce separately and combine them only when the dish is assembled to be sent out. In this way the flavours of fried eel, sauce, and fried bread are kept separate and, I think, combine more pleasingly when eaten.

The skinning and filleting of eels is quite a business (refer to p. 57 for the details). If you have to kill the eels first, I'm afraid it's a matter of whacking them over the back of the head with something heavy. They wriggle about for a long time after having been killed. An American cookery book I have suggests putting them alive in a deep freeze to kill them. I think dispatching them with a blow is more humane.

2 pieces of French bread about 5 inches (12.5 cm) long, cut in half lengthways
1½ fl. oz. (45 ml) oil
3 fl. oz. (90 ml) clarified unsalted butter
8 oz. (240 g) eel fillets
2 oz. (60 g) sorrel
3 oz. (90 g) spinach

½ oz. (15 g) parsley, roughly chopped
1 teaspoon (5 ml) fresh tarragon, chopped
6 fl. oz. (180 ml) dry white wine
Juice of a quarter lemon
¼ teaspoon (1.5 ml) salt
5 turns of the black peppermill
1 large egg yolk

### Order of work

1. Fry the croutons.
2. Fry the eel.

3. Make the sauce.
4. Assemble the dish.

Fry the four slices of bread very gently in the oil and 1 fl. oz. (30 ml) butter until golden brown. Drain on kitchen paper and keep warm.

Fry the fillets of eel in the same oil and butter, adding a little more butter if necessary until they are just cooked through. Remove and keep warm. Add the rest of the butter and all the rest of the ingredients except the egg yolk and bring to the boil, then simmer until the volume has reduced by a half.

Beat the egg yolk with a teaspoon of water. Take the pan off the heat and cool a little. Stir the egg yolk into the pan and heat until the sauce thickens. Don't overheat or the egg will scramble. Put the eel pieces on the four croutons, cover with the sauce and serve.

## FILLETS OF BASS WITH MUSSELS IN A SAFFRON SAUCE

20 mussels
A splash of white wine
2 fl. oz. (60 ml) Noilly Prat
4 fl. oz. (120 ml) fish stock (see p. 92)
A large pinch of saffron

4 fillets of bass, each weighing 3 oz. (120 g)
2 oz. (60 g) unsalted butter
Salt and white pepper from the peppermill

Open the mussels by putting them in a saucepan with the wine and cooking them over a high heat with the lid on. Remove from the heat as soon as they are open; strain them, reserving the liquor, and remove the shells and beards. Place the mussel cooking liquor in a sauteuse with the Noilly Prat, the fish stock and the saffron. Reduce the liquid by two-thirds by rapid boiling. Turn on the overhead grill, brush the fillets of bass with melted butter, season with salt and ground white pepper, and cook them. Finish off the sauce by whisking the butter, cut into 3 or 4 pieces, into the reduced liquid.

Put the mussels in the sauce to warm through and serve each fillet with 5 mussels and a quarter of the sauce.

# BREAM
# WITH AUBERGINES AND
# A RETSINA SAUCE

Retsina, the resinated Greek wine, makes a slightly aromatic but not assertive white wine sauce. With some thinly sliced aubergine crisply fried in olive oil, this dish combines some of the flavours of the Mediterranean in a northern European style.

½ pint (300 ml) fish stock (see p. 92)
1 fl. oz. (30 ml) retsina
2 fl. oz. (60 ml) double cream
Four 3-oz. (90-g) fillets of red or black bream (or you can use whole small fish)

12 very thin slices of aubergine
Seasoned flour
Olive oil

Reduce the fish stock and retsina by three-quarters. Add the double cream and reduce until the sauce coats the back of a spoon. Just before serving the sauce, sprinkle a little more retsina into it.

Very lightly dust the fish and aubergine with the seasoned flour. Heat some olive oil in a frying pan and quickly fry the fillets on both sides. Take them out and keep them warm, then quickly fry the aubergine until golden brown and crisp, adding more olive oil if necessary. Place one fillet and three slices of aubergine on each plate and pour a small pool of sauce beside them.

# GRILLED FILLETS OF BRILL IN BREADCRUMBS WITH A FRESH TOMATO AND COURGETTE SAUCE

We have some difficulty selling dishes made with brill at the Seafood Restaurant because it is not that well known. It is a marvellous flat fish, nearly as good as turbot but about 25 per cent cheaper. If you cannot find brill, you will get good results using either lemon sole or plaice in this recipe. Even the fussiest of people (like my children) enjoy this.

3 oz. (75 g) fresh white breadcrumbs
Flour for dipping the fillets
6 oz. (180 g) butter
4 skinned fillets of brill, each weighing about 2½ oz. (75 g) when skinned (they should not be more than ½ inch (15 mm) thick, so should be cut from a smallish brill)

2 oz. (30 g) courgettes
½ oz. (15 g) fresh parsley
3 oz. (90 g) tomato, peeled, deseeded and chopped
2 fl. oz. (60 ml) reduced fish stock
Salt and pepper from a mill

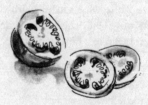

Make the breadcrumbs (using sliced white bread) in a liquidizer or food processor and put them into a shallow dish. Put the flour in another shallow dish. Melt 2 oz. (60 g) of the butter. Dip the fillets into the flour, brush them liberally with the melted butter, then press them into the breadcrumbs. Butter a baking tray, lay the fillets on it and dab the tops with more butter (any left-over butter can be added to the rest when finishing off the sauce). Put the fillets to one side while you make the sauce. Turn on your overhead grill.

Cut the courgettes into matchsticks as follows: first cut them into 1½-inch (4-cm) lengths; cut these into ⅛-inch (3-mm) slices and then into ⅛-inch (3-mm) sticks. Chop the parsley. Cut the butter into 6 pieces. Gently fry the courgettes in a little butter for one minute. Add the chopped tomato and cook for another minute. Put the stock in a small saucepan and bring to the boil. Whisk in the butter piece by piece, keeping the sauce on the boil. Add the parsley, tomato and courgettes and season to your taste. The sauce is ready.

Put the fillets under the grill. They will be cooked after 5 minutes, when the breadcrumbs will be a nice golden brown. They do not need to be turned. Serve the fish on four warm plates with the sauce beside the fillets.

# FILLETS OF BRILL
# WITH A PINK PEPPERCORN *SABAYON*

Dishes like this are a very popular first course at the Seafood Restaurant, light and delicate and with almost no fat.

| | |
|---|---|
| 1 pint (600 ml) fish stock (see p. 92) | A little melted butter |
| 2 fl. oz. (60 ml) Noilly Prat | Salt and ground white pepper |
| A pinch of salt | 3 egg yolks |
| 4 fillets of brill, each weighing 3 oz. (90 g) | 1 teaspoon pink peppercorns |

Put the fish stock, Noilly Prat and salt into a wide shallow pan (for quick reduction) and boil rapidly till you have reduced the volume of liquid down to about 5 fl. oz. (150 ml).

Turn on your overhead grill. Place the fillets of brill on a grilling tray, brush with melted butter and season with a little salt and a couple of twists from the white peppermill. Five minutes before serving the dish, place the fillets under the grill and cook. Place on four warm plates and keep warm while you finish the sauce. Whisk the Noilly Prat and fish stock reduction into the egg yolks in a tinned copper, stainless steel or enamelled saucepan (i.e. anything but aluminium, which discolours the sauce).

Return the pan to the heat and bring up the temperature of the sauce, whisking all the time. Keep checking the temperature of the sauce with your little finger. When the sauce begins to feel uncomfortably hot, remove from the heat because now the sauce will have thickened enough and any further heat would turn it into scrambled eggs. Mix in the pink peppercorns and pour the sauce over the four fillets of fish. Serve at once.

# SAUTÉED CHEEK OF COD
# WITH ARTICHOKES AND BASIL

This is the sort of recipe that may irritate you, because neither of the main ingredients is exactly easy to lay your hands on. You might well say that there are better things to do with artichokes; and as for cod's cheek, well! But I like to include some dishes with unusual ingredients on the restaurant menu, and I never serve anything there without having tried the recipe at home first. Quite often the ideas I come up with don't turn out well when we test them, but this dish was an instant success. I evolved it because I have so many artichokes growing in my garden, and some of them are left so long that only the base can be eaten. In the absence of cod's cheek, use cod fillet, but if you can get hold of cods' heads, you not only have excellent raw material for a fish stock, you will find that the two cheeks provide a nugget of sweet firm meat. It is well worth asking your fishmonger to keep the heads back for you; a large cod will yield two 3- or 4-oz. (90–120-g) cheeks.

| | |
|---|---|
| 4 artichokes | 1 teaspoon (5 ml) fresh chopped basil |
| 3 fl. oz. (90 ml) wine vinegar | 2 oz. (60 g) salted butter for *beurre* |
| 12 oz. (360 g) cod cheek | *noisette* |
| A little seasoned flour | Juice of a quarter lemon |
| Clarified butter for frying | |

Some time before cooking the dish, prepare the artichokes. Put on a pan of salted water big enough to cover them. Pour in the wine vinegar and bring to the boil. Cut the stems away from the base and boil the artichokes for 30 minutes. Test them by pushing the point of a small knife through the base; when they are cooked, the knife will slip through easily.

Pull off all the leaves when they have cooled a little and remove the white hairy choke; the artichoke bases are all you use in this dish. Keep the leaves; they make exquisite soup (sweat onions in butter with vermouth, add leaves and chicken stock, simmer, liquidize, pass, finish with cream).

Cut the cod into slices about the size of your little finger. Cut the artichoke bottoms into thin slices. Pass the fish fillets through the seasoned flour and pat them to remove excess flour. Heat the clarified butter in a frying pan. Fry the fish, turning once. They will only take a couple of minutes. Right at the end of the cooking, add the artichokes to warm through and finally the basil. Remove to a warm dish with a perforated spoon and empty out the butter you cooked the fish in. Return the pan to the heat and add the 2 oz. (60 g) of butter. Heat till it starts to foam and gives off a nice nutty smell, squeeze in the lemon juice and pour over the fish and artichokes.

# FISH TORTELLINI
# WITH BASIL AND SOURED CREAM

You can use any cooked fish for these, so it is a good recipe for using anything left over. I make them with cooked skate.

## THE PASTA

10 oz. (300 g) strong flour
½ teaspoon (2.5 ml) salt

3 eggs (size 2)
2 tablespoons (30 ml) olive oil

## THE FILLING

4 oz. (120 g) cooked fish, free from skin and bone
2 tablespoons (30 ml) soured cream

1 teaspoon (5 ml) chopped basil
1 clove of garlic
Salt and black pepper

## THE SOURED CREAM AND MUSHROOM SAUCE

2 oz. (60 g) sliced mushrooms
1 oz. (30 g) butter
½ pint (300 ml) fish stock (see p. 92)

4 fl. oz. (120 ml) soured cream
1 oz. (30 g) butter (to finish off the sauce)

## ORDER OF WORK

1. Make the pasta.
2. Prepare the filling.
3. Stuff the pasta.
4. Cook the pasta.
5. Make the sauce.

Put the flour and salt in a bowl and make a well in the centre. Add the eggs and olive oil and work into a stiff dough. Leave this covered in clingfilm for an hour before using (to relax the gluten and make rolling out easy). Mix all the filling ingredients together, breaking the fish fillet up as you do this.

When the pasta dough has rested, divide it into two balls and roll out on a floured surface as thinly as you can, continually turning the piece as you roll to ensure an even thickness. Take a 3-inch (7.5-cm) pastry cutter and cut 24 disks out of the paste. Put a teaspoon of the filling on the centre of each disk and brush the outside with water. Fold the disk over to form a crescent shape and pinch the edge with your finger and thumb. Turn up about ¼ inch (6 mm) of the edge, then bend the straight side of the crescent around your index finger until the two ends meet. Pinch the two ends together.

Cook the tortellini in boiling salted water for about 5 minutes. Drain and keep warm.

———————————————— THE SAUCE ————————————————

Lightly sauté the mushrooms in the first ounce (30 g) of butter. Remove the mushrooms, add the fish stock, bring to the boil and reduce the volume of liquid to just under half. Add the cream, bring to the boil and whisk in the second ounce (30 g) of butter; add the mushrooms and the tortellini, warm up a little and serve.


# STEAMED GREY MULLET WITH GARLIC, GINGER, SPRING ONIONS AND JAPANESE GREENS

During the time it has taken to write this book, chefs in good restaurants in Great Britain have begun to be far less lavish in their use of dairy produce, a change brought about by general worries about high intake of fat and ill health and obesity. Chefs who have virtually given up using cream and butter are very much in fashion. I take the view that cream and butter in fish cookery have their uses and that moderation is the answer; so you will find plenty of recipes in this book including dairy produce, and plenty that don't. This is one that doesn't, and it is proving extremely popular on our menu. It certainly brings out the best in a grey mullet, but it is also highly successful with sea bass for a special occasion. The Chinese would normally steam a whole fish for this dish; you could do that and turn it into a main course.

4 oz. (120 g) Japanese greens (see p. 85)

Four 3-oz. (90-g) fillets of grey mullet with the skin left on

2 teaspoons (10 ml) fresh ginger, finely chopped

1 tablespoon (15 ml) soya sauce

1 fl. oz. (30 ml) water or fish stock

3 spring onions, cut into ¼-inch (6-mm) lengths

1 fl. oz. (30 ml) sesame oil

2 cloves of garlic, finely chopped

See p. 70 for details on making a steamer. The Japanese greens can be cooked in the steamer, either during part of the cooking time of the fish or after you have cooked the fish, or alternatively they can be plunged briefly into boiling but not salted water. They should be little more than wilted in the water or steam, remaining crunchy so that they add a pleasing contrast of texture to the fish. Spinach or rocket would make a good alternative.

Place the fillets, flesh side up, on a plate which will fit into the steamer, leaving a gap of at least half an inch (1.25 cm) around the side. Sprinkle all the ginger on to the fish. Bring the water in the steamer up to a fast boil, put the plate in and a lid on top. Steam for 5 minutes for a fillet up to half an inch (1.25 cm) thick, increasing to 10 minutes for an inch-thick (2.5-cm) fillet. Transfer the fish to a warmed serving plate. Pour the juice from the steamer plate into a small sauteuse and add the soya sauce and water or fish stock. Heat up and pour over the fish and greens. Scatter the spring onions over the fish. Heat the sesame oil up in the small frying pan. When it is very hot, add the garlic and let it fry for only about 5 seconds; then pour oil and garlic over the fish.

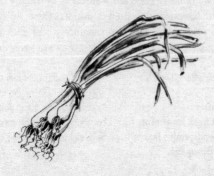

# JOHN DORY
# WITH BASIL AND MONBAZILLAC

Monbazillac is like Sauternes and goes exceptionally well with chopped basil in a cream-based sauce.

Four 2½–3-oz. (75–90-g) fillets of John Dory, or 4 small fish each weighing 6–8 oz. (180–240 g)
Butter for grilling
Salt and freshly ground pepper
½ pint (300 ml) fish stock (see p. 92)

1 fl. oz. (30 ml) Monbazillac (or Sauternes, or perhaps Muscat de Beaumes de Venise)
3 fl. oz. (90 ml) double cream
10 basil leaves

Turn on your overhead grill. Butter a shallow grilling tray and place the fillets on it, skin side down. Butter and lightly season them. Place the fish stock and wine in a small pan and reduce by three-quarters. Add the cream and reduce by rapid boiling until the sauce coats the back of a spoon. Add the basil and serve.

# FILLETS OF JOHN DORY
# WITH A BEAUJOLAIS SAUCE,
# ACCOMPANIED BY LEEKS AND MINT

I am not an enthusiast for fish in a red wine sauce when the fish has been poached or braised in the wine, though something like conger eel which is cheap and meaty makes a good red wine stew. Normally red wine gives the fish a metallic flavour which then dominates the dish. Nevertheless, if you cook fish and red wine sauce separately and choose, as in this recipe, a good-quality light red wine, the results are exceedingly good.

4 oz. (120 g) leeks, washed, tops removed
3½ oz. (105 g) butter
1 teaspoon (5 ml) fresh spearmint, chopped; plus 4 spearmint leaves
6 fl. oz. (180 ml) Beaujolais

½ pint (300 ml) of fish stock (see p. 92)
¼ teaspoon (1.5 ml) sugar
Four 3-oz. (90-g) fillets of John Dory
Salt and white milled pepper

Cut the leeks, lengthways, in half or into quarters if they are large. Cut these strips into ½-inch (1.25-cm) triangles by cutting across the leek diagonally in alternating directions.

Bring a small pan of salted water to the boil and simmer the leeks till they are cooked through but still *al dente*. Drain them and place them in a small pan with ½ oz. (12 g) of the butter. Sweat the leeks gently in the butter to drive off any excess moisture, then when they are dry and buttery add the mint. Keep warm.

Turn on the overhead grill.

Place the Beaujolais, fish stock and sugar in a sauteuse and reduce the volume by three-quarters over a high heat. Brush the John Dory fillets with a little melted butter, season with salt and milled white pepper, and cook under the grill. Cut the remaining butter into a few lumps. Bring the reduction back to the boil and whisk in the butter. Spoon the leeks on the 4 warm plates, placing them off centre. Put the fillets on the other side of the plate, with a pool of sauce next to each fillet. Place a single mint leaf next to each pile of leeks.

# TERRINE OF LEMON SOLE, PRAWNS AND FRESH HERBS WITH A PRAWN SAUCE

The amount of egg white that goes into a fish terrine is critical: too much and the terrine becomes rubbery, too little and it won't hold its shape. This one hovers on the edge of being difficult to handle, but it melts in the mouth.

Enough for 8–10 portions of terrine.

8 oz. (240 g) prawns in their shell
8 oz. (240 g) skinned lemon sole fillet
1 egg (size 2)
¼ oz. (7.5 g) onion
Juice of a quarter lemon

1½ teaspoons (7.5 ml) salt
8 fl. oz. (240 ml) double cream
1 teaspoon (5 ml) chopped fresh
   chives or parsley (or both)

The shells and heads from the prawns
1 teaspoon (5 ml) tomato purée
1 oz. (30 g) chopped onion
1 small stick of celery, chopped

5 fl. oz. (150 ml) double cream
Juice of a quarter lemon
Pinch of cayenne pepper

## The sauce

Peel the prawns and reserve them. Keep the heads and shells and put them in a saucepan with the tomato purée, onion and celery. Cover with water, bring to the boil and simmer for 25 minutes. Liquidize and pass through a sieve.

## The terrine

Make sure all the ingredients are cold before starting. When chilled, place fish, egg, onion, lemon juice and salt in a food processor. Reduce to a smooth, thick purée. Now pour the cream in over a period of 15 seconds and add the herbs at the same time. Chill this mousseline.

Set the oven at 350°F (180°C; gas mark 4).

Butter a 1½-pint (900-ml) terrine or mould. Fold the prawns into the mousseline and fill the mould; cover loosely with buttered foil. Place the dish in a baking tin, half fill the tin with hot water, bring to the boil then transfer to the oven and bake for about 40 minutes. Test that the terrine is cooked by pushing a thin knife or trussing needle into the centre and testing the temperature on your top lip; if it feels warm and the needle has come away cleanly from the centre of the terrine, it is done.

When cooked, remove the terrine from the oven and leave it to stand for about 10 minutes before turning out carefully. Add the cream to the sieved prawn stock and reduce the volume by rapid boiling till you have a sauce that will coat the back of a spoon. Season with lemon juice and cayenne pepper.

Serve the terrine in slices with what some restaurants rather coarsely describe as 'a puddle of sauce'.

# FILLETS OF PLAICE
# WITH HAMBURG PARSLEY

Plaice poached with white wine and served with Hamburg parsley cut into small dice and cooked gently with butter and a little white wine vinegar. The dish is finished with a simple sauce made from the fish cooking juices and cream.

Celeriac makes an admirable substitute for Hamburg parsley root.

3 oz. (90 g) Hamburg parsley root, peeled
3 oz. (90 g) onion
1 fl. oz. (30 ml) white wine vinegar
4 oz. (120 g) butter
Salt and freshly ground black pepper
4 fillets of plaice each weighing about
    3 oz. (90 g)

2 fl. oz. (60 ml) dry white wine
5 fl. oz. (150 g) double cream
1 teaspoon (5 ml) finely chopped
    celery leaf
Squeeze of lemon juice
Pinch of cayenne pepper

Set the oven at 400°F (200°C; gas mark 6).

Place the Hamburg parsley on a chopping board and cut a ⅛-inch (3-mm) slice off one side. Turn the parsley over on to the flat surface you have thus created (this steadies it), and cut it into ⅛-inch (3-mm) slices. Assemble these slices neatly into two piles and cut them into ⅛-inch (3-mm) strips. Now cut these strips across into ⅛-inch (3-mm) dice. Cut the first slice you removed into dice too.

Peel and finely chop the onion and put three-quarters of it into a small saucepan with the white wine vinegar, bring it to the boil and reduce till there is no more than a teaspoon (5 ml) of liquid left. Add the Hamburg parsley and 1 oz. (30 g) of the butter, season and cook gently without colouring, with a lid on, until the parsley is cooked through but still crunchy.

Butter an oven-proof dish and scatter in the remaining onion. Place the fish on top and sprinkle over the wine. Cover with buttered greaseproof paper and bake for 4–5 minutes. Pour the cooking juices into a saucepan by holding the fillets with the paper and tilting the dish. Add the cream to the juices, bring to the boil and reduce by half. Whisk the butter into the sauce in two halves. Sprinkle in the chopped celery leaf. Add the lemon juice and cayenne.

Place each fillet on a warm plate. Put a pile of Hamburg parsley next to it and cover the fillets with the sauce.

# RED MULLET
# STEAMED OVER SEAWEED

Bladderwrack, the seaweed that grows everywhere on the seashore with its distinctive air-filled 'bladders', not only gives fish steamed over it a fresh, ozone-filled aroma and flavour, but also provides body for a superb and utterly simple sauce.

| | |
|---|---|
| 1½ lb. (750 g) bladderwrack | 4 fillets of red mullet, each weighing |
| ½ pint (300 ml) fish stock | about 3 oz. (90 g) |
| | ½ oz. (15 g) butter |

Bring a large pan of water to the boil and blanch the seaweed in it for a minute. Pour it into a colander and run it under the cold tap, rinsing well. Place the seaweed in a pan big enough to take the fillets in one layer and pour in the fish stock. Bring the stock to the boil, then turn the heat down. Lay the fillets on top of the seaweed, put a lid on and steam over a low heat till the fillets are just cooked. Don't allow the stock to boil at all furiously or it will envelop the fillets and poach rather than steam them.

Put the fillets on a warm serving dish and keep warm. Strain the stock into a shallow pan and reduce the volume by two-thirds by rapid boiling. Whisk in the butter, pour over the fish and serve.

# RED MULLET
# WITH A TOMATO
# AND TARRAGON DRESSING

We often have this dish on the menu at the restaurant, but for some reason it doesn't sell very well. This is a great pity, because it is a treat too good to be missed.

It is usual to cook red mullet with the liver left in, because it adds immeasurably to the flavour of the fish (see p. 37). Even if I am cooking a dish of fillets of red mullet I try to put the liver in somewhere.

4 small red mullet, each weighing
about 6–7 oz. (180–210 g)

——————————— FOR THE DRESSING ———————————

3 good-sized tomatoes, peeled, deseeded and chopped
1 teaspoon (5 ml) chopped fresh tarragon
1 shallot or half a small onion, very finely chopped

3 fl. oz. (90 ml) olive oil
1 tablespoon (15 ml) fresh lemon juice
Salt and freshly ground black pepper

Scale and remove the fins from the mullet. Make a small incision in the belly and remove the gut, but not the liver. Turn on your overhead grill.

Brush the grilling tray with a little olive oil and place the fish on it. Season them with salt and ground black pepper and grill. Being a dense fish, they may take longer than you expect: about 4 minutes a side for fish this small. While they are grilling, mix together the dressing ingredients and warm through in a small saucepan; don't let it get too hot.

Lay the fish on warm plates, put the sauce beside, and decorate each plate with a tarragon leaf.

# GRILLED SARDINES
# WITH A SHALLOT DRESSING

Sardines need no more than simple grilling. This dressing is a change from the normal slices of lemon.

| | |
|---|---|
| 8 sardines | 2 fl. oz. (60 ml) olive oil |
| 1 oz. (30 g) finely chopped shallot | ½ fl. oz. (15 ml) white wine vinegar |
| ½ oz. (15 g) freshly chopped parsley | Salt and black pepper |

Cook the sardines on a barbecue grill (see pp. 75–6). Combine the other ingredients to make the dressing and serve with the fish.

# FILLETS OF SOLE FROM PADSTOW

One of the daunting parts of learning about classic French fish cookery is the vast number of recipes for fillets of Dover sole: page after page of unlikely-sounding names like Sole Ismailia, Sole Jules Janin, Sole Montgolfier; hundreds of recipes, most of them very similar but with slight variations, this one with mussels, prawns and mushrooms, this one with just mussels and prawns, this one with mushrooms and prawns but no mussels, this one with mussels but shrimps rather than prawns, and so on. At catering college (which I attended as an adult student) the implication was that I had to learn them all. Now I realize I could invent countless variations for fillets of sole which would be just as good as most of those listed in the chef's pocket reference book, *Le Répertoire de la Cuisine*.

These recipes are slavishly followed by many chefs up and down the country, using frozen mussels and prawns because they just can't get fresh, when really they'd be much better off forgetting the mussels and prawns and sticking to a simple sauce with perhaps some undercooked fresh mushrooms.

Take the original Sole Normande, which was an intelligent combination of some of the fresh and good things particular to Normandy. How many times does this excellent recipe appear on menus as a sad frozen copy of the real thing? If the correct ingredients can't be bought, far better to go for something different – Sole from Padstow, perhaps. This is fillets of sole with tiny mussels from the bays around Padstow, in a sauce made with local farmhouse cider, mussel juice, clotted cream from a farm at Trevone and maybe flavoured with some chopped chives from my garden.

40 small mussels
3 fl. oz. (90 ml) dry cider
Four 3-oz. (90-g) fillets of Dover sole
2 oz. (60 g) clotted cream

10 chives cut into ¼-inch (6-mm) lengths (cut them diagonally rather than straight: they look better)

Turn on your oven to 350°F (180°C; gas mark 4).

Clean and wash the mussels in several changes of water, place them in a saucepan with some of the cider and open them over a high heat with the lid on. As soon as they have opened, empty them into a colander with a bowl underneath to collect the cooking juice. Remove the beards from all the mussels and discard the shells of all but 16.

Put the sole fillets in a shallow buttered cooking dish and pour a little of the mussel cooking liquor over them; cover with a buttered paper and poach in the oven till just cooked through (about 5 minutes). Pour the poaching liquor into a small saucepan and add the mussel liquor, the rest of the cider and the clotted cream. Bring to the boil and reduce by rapid boiling till the sauce coats the back of a spoon. Put the 24 shelled mussels, the 16 unshelled mussels and the chives in with the sauce and warm through. Put the fillets of sole on four warmed plates and pour the sauce and mussels over them.

## GRILLED SPRATS
## WITH A COBNUT SAUCE

This must be made with fresh Kent cobnuts, which are available only for a few weeks in early autumn, the same time (for us in Padstow anyway) as sprats are abundant.

I very much like putting on dishes in season, then leaving them alone for the rest of the year. But as my now famous friend Keith Floyd said to me after a long visit to Provence, where the French treat seasonal foods very seriously, 'You can get damn bored with flageolets after two weeks of nothing else.'

20 cobnuts
5 fl. oz. (150 ml) groundnut oil
1 sprig of fresh marjoram
½ oz. (15 g) parsley
½ oz. (15 g) Parmesan cheese

Half a clove of garlic
A few drops of lemon juice
A pinch of salt
16 sprats

Turn on the overhead grill.

Crack the cobnuts and put them in a liquidizer with all the other ingredients (except, of course, the sprats) and blend till smooth.

Brush the sprats with oil and grill for about two minutes. Turn them over and grill for a further one or two minutes.

# FRIED SQUID
# WITH AN INK SAUCE

The ink with which the squid screens itself from its enemies is very concentrated. One ink sac produces only a few drops, but the amount of squid in this recipe will give you enough ink to colour and flavour the sauce.

1 lb. (450 g) squid
3 tablespoons (45 ml) groundnut oil
Seasoned flour
1 medium onion, finely chopped
2 cloves of garlic

3 oz (90 g) tomato, peeled, deseeded
  and chopped
1 tablespoon (15 ml) brandy
1 tablespoon (15 ml) chopped parsley
1 tablespoon (15 ml) breadcrumbs
Salt, black pepper

See pp. 62–3 for details on preparing squid, including the removal of the ink sac. Mix the sacs with two tablespoons of water in a bowl. Slice the body of the squid into thin rounds and the tentacles and triangular fins into pieces.

Heat the oil in a frying pan. Pass the squid pieces through the seasoned flour and fry in the oil in batches (this ensures that the oil remains hot, so that the squid fries crisply).

Remove each batch with a perforated spoon to a warm serving dish, adding more oil to the frying pan if necessary. When the squid has been fried, lower the heat, put the onions and garlic in the pan and sweat them without colour; then add the tomato, brandy and strained black ink, and reduce the liquid a little. Finally add the chopped parsley and bread-crumbs. Season and serve on four plates with the sauce next to the squid.

# Eleven

# SHELLFISH DISHES
# FOR A FIRST COURSE

# COCKLES AND MUSSELS IN
# A HORN OF PLENTY

❧❦❧❦❧❦

ockles and mussels look much less appetizing out of their shells than in them. I thought, therefore, that an intricate-looking pastry case and an interesting sauce would help to present these delicious molluscs in the most favourable light. On a plate, spilling out of a pastry horn and glistening with a parsley and garlic sauce, they look worth eating with serious attention. Cockles and mussels should be cooked only long enough to open their shells. You will need four horn moulds.

| | |
|---|---|
| 1 lb. (450 g) butter puff pastry (see pp. 107–9) | ½ oz. (15 g) finely chopped onion |
| 24 cockles | 1 clove of garlic |
| 24 mussels | ½ oz. (15 g) freshly chopped parsley |
| 2 fl. oz. (60 ml) dry white wine | 1 tablespoon (15 ml) lemon juice |
| | 3 oz. (90 g) unsalted butter |

───────────── ORDER OF WORK ─────────────

1. Make pastry horns.
2. Open cockles and mussels.
3. Make sauce and assemble.

Set your oven to 450°F (230°C; gas mark 8).

Lightly grease four horn moulds. Roll out the pastry ¹⁄₁₆ inch (1 mm) thick and about 16 inches (41 cm) long. Cut into ¾-inch (20-mm) strips. Brush one side of the strip with a little water and wind the strips on to the moulds, starting from the point and overlapping each wind by about one-third. Place on a baking sheet and brush the top side with egg wash. Bake at the top of the oven for about 12 minutes.

Take out, leave to cool a little, then remove the horn moulds. Cool on a wire rack. You can make the pastry horns some time before serving; indeed you can do it the day before, providing you keep them in an airtight container. They won't taste quite as good as if they were made just before serving, but it's often as well to sacrifice perfection to avoid getting in a panic when you find you've given yourself too many things to do at the last minute. If you make the horns beforehand, warm them through in the oven before serving.

## PREPARING THE COCKLES AND MUSSELS

See the notes on cleaning molluscs on pp. 65–6. Place the cockles in a pan with the wine and chopped onion. Put them on a high heat with a lid on and shake the pan occasionally as you heat the shells up. As soon as the shells open, drain the cockles through a colander with a bowl underneath to catch the cooking liquor. Return some of the cooking liquor to the pan and cook the mussels in the same way draining through the colander and saving the cooking liquor, as with the cockles. Pour all but the last tablespoon of the juice (where there might be some grit) through a sieve into a saucepan and reduce this down by rapid boiling to a couple of tablespoons (about 30 ml).

Take the meats out of the shells and remove the beards from the mussels.

Crush the garlic and chop. Add to the parsley. Bring the reduced cooking liquor back to the boil, add the garlic, parsley and lemon juice. Whisk in the butter, chopped into a few lumps, then when the sauce is smooth add the cockles and mussels and warm them through. Place the horns on four warm plates, fill them with the molluscs and sauce and place the remainder of the filling at the mouth of each horn as if it were spilling out in abundance.

# STUFFED COCKLES

| | |
|---|---|
| 80 cockles | The *beurre blanc* on p. 187 |
| 3 oz. (90 g) spinach | 2 oz. (60 g) grated Emmenthal cheese |

Prepare the cockles as described on pp. 65–6. Open them by steaming them with a splash of dry white wine or water in a saucepan with the lid on over a fierce heat. Remove from the heat as soon as they have opened. (Keep the cooking liquor for another dish.)

Blanch the spinach, plunge into cold water, drain, dry out and finely chop and add to the *beurre blanc*. Leave to go cold. Stuff the cockles with this, sprinkle the tops with the cheese and heat up in a moderate oven or under the grill.

# A *FEUILLETÉE* OF CRAB
# WITH HOLLANDAISE SAUCE

The light hollandaise sauce on p. 95     8 oz. (240 g) white crab meat
8 oz. (240 g) butter puff pastry (recipe
    pp. 107–9; or use frozen)

Make the hollandaise sauce. Set your oven to 450°F (230°C; gas mark 8).

Roll out the pastry to about ¼ inch (6 mm) thick. Cut out four parallelogram shapes with sides 5 by 3 inches (13 by 8 cm). Brush them with beaten egg and bake for about 10 minutes. Cut in half horizontally and remove any soft pastry inside.

Warm the crab up with a little melted butter in a small pan. Put the bottom half of the *feuilletées* on four warm plates and spoon the crab meat over them. Pour the hollandaise over the top of the crab meat, spilling on to the plate, and put the lids of the *feuilletées* on top.

# SOLE AND LOBSTER FLAN
# WITH CHERVIL

Individual flans of Dover sole and lobster baked with cream and eggs and flavoured with shellfish *fumet* and chervil.

The cases can be baked in the morning and the filling prepared at the same time and chilled. The assembly and final baking can be left till the last minute. If there is any lobster coral or berries (under the tail), add to the filling. Small quantities of lobster meat are of course hard to come by. You could use prawns instead, but you would get 3 oz. (90 g) meat from half of a lobster weighing 1¼ lb. (600 g); so why not buy one of this size? You could use the rest for a simple salad of sliced lobster with some peeled, deseeded and chopped tomato and some olive oil dressing with freshly chopped tarragon. Serve the salad first and then the flans. In this way, you will derive maximum enjoyment from a very expensive raw material.

| | |
|---|---|
| 8 oz. (240 g) shortcrust pastry (see p. 109) | Salt and freshly ground white pepper |
| 1 fl. oz. (30 ml) shellfish reduction (see pp. 92–3) | 1 teaspoon (5 ml) chopped chervil, plus extra fronds for decoration |
| 5 fl. oz. (150 ml) double cream | 3 oz. (90 g) lobster meat |
| 1 egg and 1 egg yolk | 3 oz. (90 g) Dover sole fillet |

Set your oven to 350°F (180°C; gas mark 4).

You will need four individual 4-inch (10-cm) flan cases. Line these with the shortcrust pastry, rolled as thin as you can handle. Prick the pastry base with a fork, line it with greaseproof paper and fill with dried beans (or peas or rice). Bake for about 9 minutes; remove the beans and greaseproof paper. Beat the shellfish reduction, double cream and eggs together, season to your taste and add the chervil. Fill the tarts with the egg/cream mix and the lobster and sole. Bake in the oven for 15 to 20 minutes. Take out while the centre of the tart is still moist and soft. Serve with a single frond of chervil on top of each tart, slightly off centre.

## MOULES MARINIÈRE

I feel that *moules marinière* usually come unnecessarily complicated with extras. I have even had them once in Brittany flavoured with sage, which was not nice. I believe this should be a dish of great simplicity, not thickened with flour, and with no garlic and no cream.

| | |
|---|---|
| 60 good-sized mussels (or 80 small ones) | 2 fl. oz. (60 ml) dry white wine (or dry cider) |
| 1 medium onion, finely chopped | 2 oz. (60 g) unsalted butter |
| 1 oz. (30 g) parsley, roughly chopped, with some stalks too | Freshly ground black pepper |

Clean the mussels (see p. 65) and put them in a large saucepan with the onion and three-quarters of the parsley. Pour in the white wine and put on a high heat to steam open. As soon as the shells have opened, pour into a colander with a bowl underneath to collect the juice. Leave the juice to settle, then pour back into the saucepan all but the last tablespoon or so of juice (which may contain grit). Check the mussels in the colander for any beards and remove them. Put the mussels in a big bowl. Return the juice to the heat, bring to the boil, whisk in the butter, pour over the mussels, and add the remainder of the parsley and 3 or 4 turns of the peppermill. Serve with plenty of fresh bread, soup bowls for each person and a large bowl for the empty shells.

# MUSSEL TART
# WITH A SAFFRON SAUCE

A popular dish at the restaurant. The parsley should ideally be the broad-leaved variety and is added to the filling chopped up with the garlic. The parsley and garlic are only briefly simmered so that the tart is noticeably imbued with the fresh flavours of both.

| | |
|---|---|
| 8 oz (240 g) shortcrust pastry (see p. 109) | 2 oz. (60 g) unsalted butter |
| 24 mussels | 1 fl. oz. (30 ml) dry white wine |
| A splash of dry white wine | Juice of a quarter lemon |
| 6 oz. (180 g) fennel, finely sliced | 1 oz. (30 g) parsley, and a few sprigs for decoration |
| 2 oz. (60 g) onion, finely chopped | ½ oz. (15 g) garlic |

## FOR THE SAUCE

| | |
|---|---|
| 6 fl. oz. (180 ml) fish stock (see p. 92) | Juice of a quarter lemon |
| 1 pinch saffron | ½ oz. (15 g) butter |

## ORDER OF WORK

1. Make the pastry cases.
2. Open the mussels.
3. Make filling and sauce.
4. Assemble the dish.

Set your oven to 350°F (180°C; gas mark 4).

Roll out the pastry as thinly as possible and line four 4-inch (10-cm) tart tins with it. Line with greaseproof paper and fill with cooking beans, peas or rice. (A quick way of baking blind if you've got plenty of tart tins is to put a spare tin on top of the pastry rather than paper and beans.) Bake in the oven for about 12 minutes, removing the filling for the last two minutes to colour the pastry.

Clean the mussels (see p. 65), put them in a large pan with the splash of white wine, and cook them over a high heat with the lid on till they open. Drain through a colander, reserving the cooking liquor in a bowl below.

Soften the fennel and onion in the butter, add 2 fl. oz. (60 ml) of the mussel cooking liquor, the white wine and lemon juice. Reduce this by rapid boiling to 1 tablespoon (15 ml) of liquid. Add the garlic and parsley and simmer for no more than half a minute.

To make the sauce, put the fish stock, saffron, lemon and butter in a pan and reduce the volume of liquid by two-thirds by rapid boiling.

Heat up the pastry cases in the oven if you baked them some time beforehand. Gently heat the mussels in the filling. Spoon into the pastry cases and serve on four warmed plates with the sauce spooned around. Garnish with sprigs of parsley.

# MUSSELS WITH MANGE-TOUT AND SPAGHETTI

A dish which highlights the sweetness of fresh mussels.

| | |
|---|---|
| 40 mussels | 10 oz. (300 g) spaghetti |
| A splash of dry white wine | 2 fl. oz. (60 ml) olive oil |
| 4 oz. (120 g) courgettes | 2 cloves of garlic, chopped |
| 4 oz. (120 g) mange-tout peas | 1 tablespoon (15 ml) chopped parsley |

Clean the mussels (see p. 65), put them in a saucepan, splash in some wine and put them on a high heat with a lid on till they open. Remove them and strain through a colander, collecting the juice. Remove the beards and shells.

Cut the courgettes into 1-inch (2.5-cm) lengths. Cut these into ⅛-inch (3-mm) slices and then into ⅛-inch (3-mm) matchsticks. Cut the mange-tout into similar strips.

If the spaghetti is the long, 20-inch (50-cm) type, break it in half. Boil

3½ pints (2 litres) of salted water and cook the spaghetti till it is *al dente* (cooked through but still firm).

Heat the olive oil and add the mange-tout. Cook for 2 minutes, then add the courgettes. Cook for another minute (the vegetables must remain *al dente*), then add the mussels, 3 tablespoons (45 ml) of the mussel cooking liquor, and the garlic.

Warm the mussels through, then stir in the pasta and parsley and serve, perhaps with a bottle of *sur lie* Muscadet.

# MUSSELS WITH TOMATO AND BASIL

50 to 60 good-sized mussels (more if you can only get small ones)
A splash of white wine
1 oz. (30 g) finely chopped shallot or onion
1 fl. oz. (30 ml) olive oil

6 oz. (150 g) tomato, peeled, deseeded and chopped
3 cloves of garlic, finely chopped
8 basil leaves
1 teaspoon (5 ml) chopped parsley

Clean the mussels (see p. 65) and put them in a large saucepan on a fierce heat. Sprinkle in some white wine, put a lid on and cook till the mussels open. Remove from the heat as soon they have opened, strain off the liquor and keep it. Remove the beards from the mussels, and discard one half of each shell. Set the mussels in the half shells on a dish.

Soften the shallots in the olive oil over a moderate heat and add about 3 fl. oz. (90 ml) of the mussel cooking liquor (keep the rest for other dishes: for example, add some to fish stock to improve its flavour). Reduce the mussel liquor down till it has almost disappeared, then add the tomatoes, heat through and add the garlic. Warm through again to drive off some but not all of the volatility of the garlic, then add the basil freshly snipped up with a pair of scissors in a glass (this passes as much as possible of the ephemeral basil flavour into the dish). Add the parsley and season the sauce with salt and ground black pepper.

Heat the mussels through in the oven; don't overdo it or they will toughen up. Spoon the sauce into the mussel shells and serve.

# STUFFED GRILLED MUSSELS

You can make this dish with either the garlic butter, the garlic and roasted hazelnut butter, or the coriander and parsley butter described in Chapter 6.

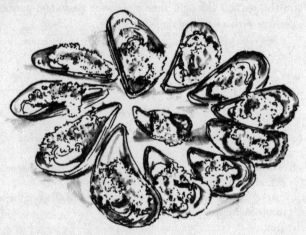

| | |
|---|---|
| 48 good-sized mussels | 2 oz. (60 g) grated Emmenthal cheese |
| Splash of dry white wine or water | 1 oz. (30 g) dried breadcrumbs |
| The garlic butter on p. 102 (or garlic | |
| and roasted hazelnut butter, p. 102, | |
| or coriander and parsley butter, | |
| p. 102) | |

Clean the mussels (see p. 65) and open them by steaming them with a splash of dry white wine or water in a saucepan with the lid on over a fierce heat. Remove from the heat as soon as they have opened. Keep the cooking liquor for another dish. Remove the beards from the mussels and discard one half of each shell. When the mussels have cooled, put a piece of the flavoured butter in each. Mix together the grated cheese and the breadcrumbs and sprinkle over each shell.

When ready to serve the mussels, heat up in a moderate oven or under the grill.

# OYSTERS WITH
## *BEURRE BLANC AND SPINACH*

The oysters in this dish are hardly cooked at all and the combination is fresh and pleasing.

16 oysters
16 spinach leaves (washed, stalks removed)
1 oz. (30 g) finely chopped shallot or onion

½ fl. oz. (15 ml) white wine vinegar
½ fl. oz. (15 ml) white wine
2 fl. oz. (60 ml) water
5 oz. (150 g) unsalted butter

Prepare a steamer to cook the oysters, using the perforated steamer described on p. 70. Thoroughly wash the oysters and steam for about 4 minutes. Remove and open, keeping the liquor that comes out of them.

Put the spinach leaves in the steamer and steam for 2 minutes. While you are steaming the oysters, put the shallots, vinegar, wine and water in a small pan; add the juice from the oysters and simmer till only about 2 tablespoons (30 ml) of liquid are left. Cut the butter into small squares and whisk it in a little at a time off the heat, building up a light emulsion.

Remove the oysters from their shells and lay a folded leaf of spinach in the bottom of each. Place these shells on a suitable serving dish and push briefly under the grill to warm up the spinach. Put the oysters on top and pour the *beurre blanc* over each. Place under the grill again just to warm through and serve, perhaps with a chilled bottle of Bourgogne Aligoté.

# DEEP-FRIED SCALLOPS WRAPPED
## IN PARMA HAM

Most frozen scallops have been soaked in water before freezing, so that they swell up to about twice their natural size, which rather spoils their flavour. But you can sometimes get them quite cheap, and this recipe, though it would not be the right treatment for perfectly fresh scallops, turns the frozen variety into something extremely pleasant to eat.

You could also use this recipe for scallop-shaped pieces of cod or monkfish.

8 scallops
4 oz. (120 g) Parma ham (or any other very thin-sliced ham)
2 oz. (60 g) flour
2 eggs
2 oz. (60 g) fresh breadcrumbs
Tartare sauce (see p. 100)

Cut each scallop in half, and roll each half in a piece of Parma ham. Put the flour in one small tray; whisk the eggs and put them in a second tray; put the breadcrumbs in a third, and pass the scallops through the flour, then the egg, then the breadcrumbs. A small tip on how to do this – probably obvious to you, but it took me some time to think of it – put all the scallops in the flour, then all in the egg, then all in the breadcrumbs. (I used to do them one at a time and got in an awful mess, with the egg everywhere.) Deep-fry until golden brown (about 2 minutes). Serve with home-made tartare sauce.

# SAUTÉED SCALLOPS
# WITH CHICORY AND NOILLY PRAT

Noilly Prat is a vermouth much favoured by fish cooks, so much so that in some circles it is considered rather hackneyed. But I think it gives a combination of faint sweetness and bitterness hard to better. In this dish the bitterness is underpinned by the chicory.

8 good-sized scallops
3 oz. (90 g) chicory
2 fl. oz. (60 ml) Noilly Prat
15 fl. oz. (450 ml) fish stock (see p. 92)
5 fl. oz. (150 ml) double cream
2 oz. (60 g) butter

Slice each scallop into three rounds and separate the corals.

Cut the chicory into thin strips about 1 inch (2.5 cm) long. Reduce the vermouth and fish stock by about two-thirds by rapid boiling. Add the chicory and cream and reduce still further till the sauce coats the back of a spoon. Brush a frying pan with oil and put on the stove to heat. Whisk the butter into the sauce and spoon it out on to four hot plates. When the frying pan is smoking hot, put in the scallops, and turn them over almost immediately. They should be removed very soon afterwards on to the chicory sauce on the plates, the idea being to slightly caramelize the outside of the scallops but keep the inside almost raw, just warmed through.

## SAUTÉED SCALLOPS WITH MANGE-TOUT PEAS

Very much a dish for perfectly fresh scallops. They are just seared in a very hot pan, so that you get the best of both worlds, the sweet caramelized taste of fried scallops on the outside and with the delicacy of undercooked scallops as well.

4 oz. (120 g) mange-tout peas
8 scallops
1 oz. (30 g) unsalted butter

1 teaspoon (5 ml) chopped parsley
Salt and ground black pepper

Wash, top and tail the mange-tout peas and blanch them in boiling salted water for 2 minutes. Drain and refresh in cold water.

Cut the scallops into 3 slices. Take a thick-bottomed frying pan and heat until extremely hot. Put in a small knob of the butter, quickly brush it around the bottom of the pan with a pastry brush, and immediately throw in the scallops. Cook for about 10 seconds and turn over with a palette knife or toss. Cook for a further 20 seconds, take off the heat and lift the scallops out with a fish slice into a warm dish.

Put in the rest of the butter and then the mange-tout peas and the parsley. Return to the heat and let the peas warm through in the butter. Season with salt and black pepper. Add the peas, parsley and cooking butter to the warm scallops and serve.

## SCALLOPS BAKED IN THEIR OWN SHELLS

The scallops are removed from their shells, sliced and put back with carrot, celeriac and white of leek, which have been cooked in a little butter and Vouvray. The two shells are sealed with puff pastry and baked. You can make this dish as much as a day in advance.

12 scallops

2½ oz. (75 g) carrot, peeled

2½ oz. (75 g) celeriac, peeled

2½ oz. (75 g) white of leek, well washed

1 fl. oz. (30 ml) Vouvray or other white wine (preferably a chenin blanc)

2 oz. (60 g) unsalted butter (for cooking the vegetables)

Salt and black pepper

1 oz. (30 g) shallot or onion, finely chopped

1 tablespoon (15 ml) white wine vinegar

1 tablespoon (15 ml) water

½ oz. (15 g) parsley

4 oz. (120 g) unsalted butter

8 oz. (240 g) puff pastry (pp. 107–9)

1 egg for glazing the pastry

———————— ORDER OF WORK ————————

1. Cut out scallops, clean shells.
2. Cut and cook vegetables.
3. Fill scallops.
4. Roll out pastry and seal scallops.
5. Bake.

If possible, buy scallops in the shell for this dish and cut them out according to the instructions on pp. 64–5. If you can get hold of some empty shells, then by all means buy fresh scallops cut out of the shell, but frozen scallops are not suitable.

Cut the carrot, celeriac and leek into slices 1½ by ⅛ inches (4 cm by 3 mm). Cut these slices into julienne strips 1½ by ⅛ by ⅛ inches (4 cm by 3 mm by 3 mm).

Place the carrots in a small pan with the Vouvray and butter, and cook gently with a lid on for 2 minutes; add the celeriac and cook for a further 2 minutes; add the leek and cook for another minute. Season with salt and freshly ground black pepper.

While these vegetables are cooking, put the chopped shallots in another small pan and add the white wine vinegar and water. Simmer until all the liquid has evaporated away, then add these slightly crunchy, sharp shallots to the vegetables.

Put the vegetables in the deep half of 8 scallop shells.

Now take the 12 scallops and check that there is no sand on them (wash in a colander if there is). Cut away any white sinew that attaches the scallop meat to its shell. Slice each scallop into three (or four if they are particularly big). Divide these scallop slices among the eight shells, putting them on top of the vegetables. Sprinkle the chopped parsley over each.

Take 4 oz. (125 g) – half a 250-g block – of unsalted butter, cut it into 8 pieces and put a piece on top of everything else in the shell. Put a flat lid shell on each deep base.

Set the oven at 450°F (230°C; gas mark 8) half an hour before you intend to bake the scallops.

Roll out the puff pastry into a rectangle about 7 by 16 inches (18 by 40 cm). Cut this into eight 16-inch (40-cm) strips. Chill the strips to make them easy to handle. When the pastry is stiff, take each strip and push it on to the join between top and bottom shell, working all the way around the shell. Smooth the pastry against the shells to make a good seal. Paint the pastry with beaten egg and bake in the oven for 9 minutes.

Bring to the table unopened and let each person open their own by pushing a knife through the pastry between the top and bottom shells and twisting it. The aroma will please, I'm sure.

## SCALLOPS WITH BACON

This simple dish is improved immeasurably by leaving a trace of garlic on each skewer.

12 scallops
4 rashers of best back bacon
  (unsmoked)

1 clove garlic
Melted butter
Salt
4 lemon quarters

Remove corals from scallops and slice each scallop meat into three. Cut each rasher of bacon into eight pieces. Take four barbecue skewers, impale each one with the clove of garlic and push the garlic up to the handle and back.

Now thread the skewers with first a piece of scallop, then a piece of bacon, then a piece of scallop and so on, including the corals. Brush with melted butter and cook under the grill until the scallops have turned from opaque to white. Season with salt and serve on the skewer with lemon wedges.

# SEAFOOD PANCAKES

This was one of the most popular dishes at the restaurant until every frozen food company in the land started producing them and so debased the idea that we gave them up. It doesn't alter the fact that they are very nice.

The filling is enough for about eight pancakes.

---
### PANCAKES
---

½ oz. (15 g) butter
4 oz. (120 g) flour
1 egg

½ pint (300 ml) milk
½ teaspoon (2.5 ml) of salt
Oil for frying

---
### FILLING
---

4 oz. (120 g) skinned fillet of lemon sole, plaice, whiting or any other white fish
1 small onion, finely chopped
4 tablespoons (60 ml) dry white wine
Salt and ground white pepper
½ pint (300 ml) *velouté* (see p. 94)

Juice of a quarter lemon
3 fl. oz. (90 ml) double cream
1 egg yolk
Pinch cayenne pepper
4 oz. (120 g) shelled prawns
2 oz. (60 g) white crab meat

---
### ORDER OF WORK
---

1. Make the batter.
2. Make the pancakes.
3. Prepare the filling.
4. Assemble the pancakes.

Melt the butter in a small saucepan. Sift the flour into a medium bowl, make a well in the centre and add the egg. Gradually add the milk and whisk well to make a smooth batter. Add salt and melted butter. Leave to stand for half an hour or so.

Place a tablespoonful (15 ml) of oil in a small frying or crêpe pan and allow it to heat for a few minutes. When the oil is shimmering hot, tip it out into a small dish and pour about 1 fl. oz. (30 ml) of batter into the pan, tilting it quickly so that the batter covers the base. Cook over a medium heat until golden. Turn, using a palette knife, and cook the second side. Repeat for the remaining batter, adding a little oil and pouring it out of the pan again before cooking each pancake.

Cut the sole into 1-inch (2.5-cm) strips. Place the onion in a shallow buttered pan and lay the sole on top, pour on the white wine and season lightly with salt and freshly ground white pepper, cover with a butter paper and poach very gently on top of the stove till the sole has 'set', i.e. has just firmed up.

Heat the *velouté* up in a pan and add the cooking juices from the fish, the lemon juice, the cream and the egg yolk. Season with cayenne pepper. Turn on your overhead grill.

Add the prawns and crab meat to the poached sole and pour on enough sauce to bind all the fish and shellfish. Spoon this into the centre of the pancakes. Roll them up and place in shallow oven-proof dish. Pour the rest of the sauce right over the rolled pancakes and gratinate under the grill till brown and bubbling.

# Twelve

# EVERYDAY MAIN COURSES

This chapter is devoted to recipes for fish served as the main part of a meal, the common link between the dishes being that they are all based on the cheaper varieties of fish, and although some of the recipes are quite elaborate, none of them will cost you a great deal. These are the sort of main courses we use on our fixed price menu, which we run alongside our *à la carte* dishes to give customers a three-course dinner for a lot less than the *à la carte* prices. I hope you will try them out at home.

# CONCHIGLIETTE
# WITH SEAFOOD AND SAFFRON

Shell pasta with mussels, prawns and lemon sole in a saffron-flavoured sauce. The small shells called *conchigliette* look best, but the bigger *conchiglie* will do. In fact you can use any pasta, but if it's long strands like spaghetti, it is best to cut it up after cooking and before mixing it with the seafood. This dish is really quite easy to make and always appreciated; my children love it.

14 oz. (420 g) shell pasta
20 to 35 mussels (depending on size)
1 fl. oz. (30 ml) white wine
1 oz. (30 g) finely chopped onion
12 oz. (360 g) skinned lemon sole fillet
8 fl. oz. (240 ml) fish stock (see p. 92)

Salt and pepper
2 fl. oz. (60 ml) mussel liquor (from cooking the mussels)
A good pinch of saffron
5 fl. oz. (150 ml) double cream
4 oz. (120 g) shelled prawns

Cook the pasta in 4 pints (2.3 litres) of well-salted water till it is *al dente* (not totally soft).

Put the mussels in a saucepan, sprinkle with half of the wine and some of the chopped onion, and cook over a high heat with the lid on until the mussels open. Strain through a colander into a bowl, reserving the liquid. Remove the beards and shells from the mussels.

Cut the sole fillet into *goujons* about the size of your little finger. Put them in a shallow pan with the rest of the wine, the rest of the chopped onion and a couple of tablespoons of the fish stock. Season with salt and white pepper, cover with a butter paper and cook gently on the stove until the fish has just turned white.

Strain carefully through a colander and put the strained cooking juice, the rest of the fish stock, the mussel liquor and the saffron into a pan large enough to take the pasta (this pan will also be the serving dish). Bring to the boil and simmer for a couple of minutes, then add the cream. Bring back to the boil and reduce till the sauce is the consistency of single cream.

Add the prawns, pasta and mussels and warm through. Finally, add the lemon sole – with care, as it breaks up easily.

I suggest a simple green salad to go with this and a bottle of Verdicchio, the clean, dry, white wine from the Adriatic coast of Italy.

# CHAR-GRILLED CONGER EEL WITH A RICH RED WINE SAUCE

The red wine sauce in this recipe could just as easily be served with steak, but it works well with these slightly charred fish steaks. They should ideally be cooked on a charcoal grill, but you can also achieve good results under a domestic grill.

Four 8-oz (240-g) steaks of conger eel
1 teaspoon (5 ml) chopped fennel
2 bayleaves, sliced up

Salt and black pepper
Juice of a quarter lemon

--- FOR THE SAUCE ---

8 oz. (240 g) onions, finely chopped
5 fl. oz. (150 ml) red wine
1 fl. oz. (30 ml) red wine vinegar

4 fl. oz. (120 ml) strong meat stock
½ teaspoon (2.5 ml) sugar
3 oz. (90 g) unsalted butter

Put the conger steaks in a shallow dish with the fennel, bayleaves, salt, pepper and lemon juice. Leave to marinate for 30 minutes, turning occasionally.

Turn on your grill well in advance of cooking the steaks. If cooking over a charcoal fire, wait till the coals have just started to turn to ash before grilling the steaks.

Put the onions, red wine, red wine vinegar, stock and sugar in a sauteuse, bring to the boil and simmer gently till you have reduced the liquid right down to a thick juice with the onions.

Grill your steaks for about 5 minutes on each side; baste them by brushing a little of the marinade over them with a pastry brush. Test whether they are done by pushing the point of a small knife into the centre; the flesh should be white rather than translucent and should come away from the bones.

To finish off the sauce, cut the butter into a few lumps. Put the onion reduction back on to boil and whisk in the butter on the boil to form a shiny, viscous sauce. A simple green salad would go very well with this dish.

# GRILLED MARINATED DOGFISH
# WITH A GARLIC SAUCE

Dogfish has a rather insistent flavour which can become overpowering, but it is extremely cheap, and having no bones it is easy to prepare. This presents the occasion for a liberal use of strong tastes, and in conjunction with these, dogfish can be very pleasant.

| | |
|---|---|
| 1¼ lb. (600 g) dogfish fillet in four pieces | ½ teaspoon (2.5 ml) oregano |
| | Juice of a quarter lemon |
| 1 clove of garlic, finely chopped | ½ oz. (15 g) fresh bread |
| ½ fl. oz. (15 ml) olive oil | ½ oz. (15 g) grated Parmesan |
| ¼ teaspoon (1.5 ml) salt | |

#### FOR THE GARLIC SAUCE

| | |
|---|---|
| 1 clove of garlic, finely chopped | 1 small tomato, peeled, deseeded and chopped |
| 1 oz. (30 ml) mayonnaise | |
| 3 fl. oz. (90 ml) fish stock (see p. 92) | |

Place the fillets in a shallow dish. Add the chopped clove of garlic, the olive oil, salt, oregano and lemon juice, and leave to marinate for at least 30 minutes, stirring occasionally.

Liquidize the bread to make fresh breadcrumbs and mix with the Parmesan.

Mix the second chopped clove of garlic into the mayonnaise.

Turn on your grill.

Remove the fillets from the marinade. Mix the breadcrumbs and

Parmesan into the marinade and thoroughly coat the dogfish with the mixture.

To make the sauce, place the fish stock in a small pan, bring to the boil and reduce by half. Remove from the heat. Put the mayonnaise in a mixing bowl and pour on the hot stock, whisking all the time as you pour. Keep the sauce warm while you cook the fish, but don't stir the chopped tomato into the sauce till just before serving the fish: in this way it will taste tart and fresh.

Place the dogfish fillets on a grilling tray. Cook them under the grill, keeping the tray near the bottom so that the breadcrumbs do not burn. When the coating is a golden brown, the fillets will be cooked. Serve the fillets on warm plates with the sauce poured to one side of them.


# LEMON SOLE IN PUFF PASTRY
# WITH CIDER, MUSHROOMS AND CREAM

The filling for this puff pastry *tourte* is not baked with the pastry; the two are combined just before serving so that the crust stays crisp and light.

| | |
|---|---|
| 1 large lemon sole, about 1½ lb. (720 g) | 3 fl. oz. (90 ml) dry cider |
| 1 lb. (450 g) puff pastry, butter (see pp. 107–9) or frozen | 4 oz. (120 g) fresh white button mushrooms, thinly sliced |
| 1 egg (for egg wash) | 4 fl. oz. (120 g) double cream |
| 2 oz. (60 g) onion, finely chopped | 10 fl. oz. (300 ml) fish *velouté* (see p. 94) |
| ½ teaspoon (2.5 ml) salt | Cayenne pepper and lemon juice |

Turn on the oven at 450°F (230°C; gas mark 8).

Remove the four fillets from the lemon sole (see p. 56). Skin them and cut each in two. Make a fish stock with the bones, using a pint (600 ml) of water and about 10 oz. (300 g) vegetables (see p. 92).

Roll out the puff pastry on a lightly floured surface till it is a quarter inch (6 mm) thick. Cut out a circle 12 inches (30 cm) in diameter, then place a 10-inch (25.5-cm) dinner plate on the pastry and gently cut a circle round it, halfway through the pastry. Put the pastry on a suitable baking sheet and rest it in the refrigerator for 10 minutes. Break the egg, whisk it up with a fork and brush the top of the pastry with it, using a pastry brush. Bake for about 12 minutes until golden brown and nicely risen.

Butter a shallow pan and place the onion then the fish fillets in it. Season with salt and pour on the cider. Cover with a butter paper and cook gently on the top of the stove until the fish has just turned white.

Cook the sliced mushrooms gently in a little butter.

Cut the top from the baked puff pastry (this will be easy to do because of the circle you marked on it). Scoop out any moist pastry underneath. Place the cooked fish fillets and the mushrooms inside, replace the lid and keep warm.

Add the fish cooking liquor and the double cream to the *velouté* and reduce the sauce till it is thick enough to coat the back of a spoon. Add a little lemon juice and a pinch of cayenne pepper.

Take the lid off the pastry case, pour the sauce over the fish and mushrooms, replace the lid and serve at once. The rest of the bottle of dry cider you used for the sauce would be nice chilled and served with this.

# SEAFOOD THERMIDOR

It would not be exaggerating to say that the success of our restaurant in our first ten years was due to this dish, which seemed to appeal to almost everyone. It had lots of different seafood in it, it was robustly flavoured, and it was the cheapest main course we sold. I still think it is a thoroughly delightful dish, even though I have given up serving it in the restaurant – mainly through boredom, but also because it is not at all fashionable at present. I shall revive it one day, if the taste for flour-based sauces returns (as it probably will). Until then here is the recipe for you to try.

4 oz. (120 g) onion, finely chopped
2 oz. (60 g) unsalted butter
3 fl. oz. (90 ml) dry white wine
10 fl. oz. (300 ml) fish stock (see p. 92)
3 oz. (90 g) fresh button mushrooms
20 fl. oz. (600 ml) *velouté* (see p. 94)
4 fl. oz. (120 ml) double cream
6 oz. (180 g) skinned lemon sole fillet
6 oz. (180 g) skinned monkfish fillet

4 large scallops
4 oz. (120 g) shelled North Atlantic prawns
1 tablespoon (15 ml) Colman's English mustard powder, made up with a little water
Juice of a quarter lemon
3 oz. (90 g) grated cheese
1 oz. (30 g) breadcrumbs
Pinch of cayenne pepper

Turn on your overhead grill. Soften the onion in the butter and pour on the white wine. Reduce a little, then add the fish stock and 1 oz. (30 g) of the mushrooms. Simmer for 10 minutes, then reduce the volume by two-thirds by rapid boiling. Heat the *velouté* carefully and add the reduction to it (there is no need to strain this). Stir in the cream and leave simmering on a very low heat while you prepare the fish.

Cut the lemon sole and monkfish into ½-inch (1.2-cm) pieces. Slice each scallop into three. Put all the fish into a large shallow gratin dish. Sprinkle the rest of the mushrooms on top and brush with melted butter. Season with salt and place under the grill. Remove when the fish has turned white but is still a little underdone (it will cook more when you finish the dish by gratinating it under the grill). Now add the prawns to the rest of the fish. Add the mustard and lemon juice to the sauce and taste it; it should be slightly hot with mustard but not overpoweringly so. Pour the sauce over the fish and mushrooms. Mix the grated cheese with the breadcrumbs, the cayenne pepper and a couple of twists of the black peppermill and sprinkle over. Gratinate under the grill to a nice golden brown.

# COD *EN PAPILLOTE* WITH *BEURRE BLANC*

It was my misfortune to attempt to demonstrate this dish to a Women's Institute in Perranporth. Never having demonstrated outside my own kitchen before, I should have thought twice beforehand. I realize now why cookery demonstrators on television say 'We'll just leave that one cooking, and meanwhile I've got another one already in the oven.' If you haven't made such arrangements, you find you have to fill in the time when dishes are cooking and sauces are reducing with a great deal of general chat, and not knowing immediately what would interest eighty-four rather formidable-looking women, I found the whole experience utterly harrowing.

Cod is usually considered to be cheap, plentiful but rather dull. However, the best fish and chips I have eaten were made with cod, in the Yorkshire fishing port of Whitby. The fish was so fresh, it was sweet and milky. That taught me two things: first, that fish and chips can be a wonderful dish; second, that cod is far from dull if it is perfectly fresh.

4 pieces of aluminium foil, each
  12 × 15 inches (30 × 38 cm)
4 pieces of greaseproof paper, each
  12 × 15 inches (30 × 38 cm)
A little melted butter
2 oz. (60 g) butter
3 oz. (90 g) carrot, thinly sliced
3 oz. (90 g) celery, thinly sliced
3 oz. (90 g) leek, thinly sliced

3 oz. (90 g) button mushrooms
4 cod fillets, each weighing 6–8 oz.
  (180–240 g)
Salt and freshly ground black pepper
A little lemon juice
½ fl. oz. (15 ml) dry white wine
½ pint (300 ml) *beurre blanc* (see
  p. 187)

Lay a piece of aluminium foil on top of each piece of greaseproof paper, and brush the top side of the foil with melted butter. (The use of both foil and paper ensures an absolutely airtight seal, with the result that the *papillotes* always puff right out and look much more attractive when served.)

Turn on the oven at 400°F (200°C; gas mark 6).

Melt the 2 oz. (60 g) butter and cook the carrot, celery and leek without colouring for 7 minutes. Wash the mushrooms, add them to the vegetables and cook gently for a further 2 minutes. Divide the vegetables into eight. Place one eighth on one half of each piece of foil; place a fillet of fish on top, and then another eighth of the vegetables on top of the fish. Season with salt and pepper, and add a few drops of lemon juice and a splash of white wine.

Fold the other half of the foil and greaseproof paper over the fish and vegetables, and seal the edges by folding over a couple of inches (5 cm) at a time, working round the *papillote* to form a semicircular parcel.

Cook in a roasting tray for 10 minutes, or 15 minutes if the fillets are more than an inch thick. Let each person open their own parcel to enjoy the pleasant aroma of fish, wine and vegetables. Serve the *beurre blanc* separately, perhaps with a Savennières such as Clos du Papillon.

# A *POÊLE*
# OF CONGER EEL

In this recipe, the conger eel is studded with slivers of garlic and wrapped in caul fat, which gives the fish a wonderful smooth moistness. The problem, of course, is getting caul fat: you need a good butcher. Caul is a membrane laced with fat from a pig's abdominal cavity. If you can get hold of it, buy plenty; it freezes well, and you can use it for lining pâtés and as a casing for *crépinettes*.

To make the caul manageable, put it in a bowl of warm water to which you have added a little vinegar.

If you can't get hold of any caul, wrap slices of streaky bacon around the piece of conger eel and secure them with string.

6 cloves garlic, peeled

A 2½-lb (1.2-kg) section of skinned conger eel, cut from just behind the gut cavity

Caul fat (or 4 slices of streaky bacon)

2 oz. (60 g) butter

4 oz. (120 g) carrot, peeled and cut into pieces 1½ by ½ inch (3.8 by 1.2 cm)

4 oz. (120 g) button onions, peeled

4 oz. (120 g) celery, cut into pieces 1½ by ½ inch (3.8 by 1.2 cm)

Salt and freshly ground black pepper

Set your oven to 450°F (230°C; gas mark 8).

Slice two of the cloves of garlic thinly, make incisions all over the fish and insert the garlic. Wrap in the caul fat, or tie with streaky bacon. Melt the butter in a solid casserole (such as a Le Creuset), add the carrot, onions, celery and the rest of the garlic, and stew the vegetables gently in the butter for 5 minutes with the lid on. Now add the conger; roll it around in the butter, season with salt and black pepper, and place it in the oven with the lid on for 20 minutes. Baste the fish with the butter twice during that time.

After 20 minutes, baste once more and remove the lid. Cook for a further 10 minutes with the lid off. Serve up like a joint of meat on a large oval dish with the vegetables and juice poured all around. Carve it lengthways in long slices.

With each serving, spoon out vegetables and the buttery sauce and drink a nice chilled Beaujolais like a crisp Moulin à Vent with it.

# FISH CAKES
## WITH TURMERIC, CORIANDER AND CARDAMOM

The amount of spice in these fish cakes gives them a subtle flavour and an interesting colour but doesn't overpower.

| | |
|---|---|
| 1 pint cider *court bouillon* (recipe on p. 93) | 1 oz. (30 g) chopped parsley |
| | ½ teaspoon (2.5 ml) ground turmeric |
| 1½ lb. (720 g) mackerel, herring or white fish | ½ teaspoon (2.5 ml) coriander seeds |
| | 2 cardamoms |
| 1 lb. (450 g) floury potatoes, peeled and sliced | Flour for coating hands |
| | 2 fl. oz. (60 ml) milk |
| 2 eggs | 2 oz. (60 g) breadcrumbs |
| 1 oz. (30 g) butter | Oil for shallow frying |

Bring the *court bouillon* to the boil, add the fish and poach gently until just cooked. Remove the fish and cook the sliced potatoes in the *bouillon* till they are falling apart. Drain and mash the potato. Take the fillets off the fish, removing the skin. Beat one of the eggs into the potato with the butter and parsley.

Grind the turmeric, coriander and cardamom together in a grinder. Add the spices and the fish to the potato mixture and season.

Divide the mixture into eight and mould into flat cakes using floured hands. If the cakes are a bit soft, chill them for 30 minutes. Beat the remaining egg and add the milk. Coat the cakes in the egg mixture, then the breadcrumbs. Heat the oil in a frying pan and fry the fish cakes for 3 minutes on each side or until golden brown. Drain on kitchen paper.

Serve the fish cakes with a green salad dressed with walnut dressing (p. 105) and sprinkled with chopped coriander leaf.

# FISH CASSOULET

In an idle moment at the restaurant, we were wondering how the traditional *cassoulet* from Languedoc would taste made with fish, using some robust, cheap varieties such as conger eel, dogfish, skate, shark and monkfish (not, alas, particularly cheap any more), with a good lashing of salt cod.

The fish in the *cassoulet* would first be part-cooked in a fish *ragoût* using the ingredients that go into a *bouillabaisse*, garlic, saffron, tomatoes, olive oil, and such herbs as fennel, bay, perhaps some savory and a little thyme.

We decided to use freshly dried green haricots, flageolets, and include some salt pork too. It all turned out very well. It is a lot of work and so is not worth making except for a fair number of people. It reheats as well as the normal *cassoulet* does, and it really is very pleasant to consume with gusto by the large plateful.

The quantities are for 8 people.

---

### THE FISH

2 lb. (900 g) fillets of any firm fish (I suggest conger eel, dogfish, monkfish)

8 oz. (250 g) salt cod fillet

---

### FOR COOKING THE BEANS

1 lb. (500 g) flageolets (or haricots)
2 bayleaves
1 onion, studded with 4 cloves
4 cloves of garlic

4 oz. (120 g) salt pork (a boned pork chop covered in salt for 12 hours and washed under the cold tap before use)

---

### THE FISH RAGOÛT

6 fl. oz. (180 g) olive oil
4 oz. (120 g) roughly chopped onion
4 cloves of garlic
4 oz. (120 g) celery
4 oz. (120 g) leek
6 oz. (180 g) tomato, peeled, deseeded and roughly chopped
1 teaspoon (5 ml) tomato purée

A large pinch of saffron
4 fl. oz. (120 ml) white wine
4 fl. oz. (120 ml) fish stock (see p. 92)
1 bayleaf
A sprig of thyme
1 tablespoon (15 ml) chopped fennel
Pinch of savory

---

### TO FINISH THE CASSOULET

½ pint (300 ml) bean cooking liquid
2 oz. (60 g) fresh breadcrumbs

3 tablespoons (45 ml) olive oil

---

### ORDER OF WORK

1. Soak the salt cod.
2. Soak the flageolets.
3. Cook the flageolets.

4. Make the *ragoût*.
5. Poach the salt cod.
6. Cook the *cassoulet*.

Soak the salt cod for at least 36 hours in a bowl of cold water (to make your own salt cod, see p. 110).

Soak the flageolets for 12 hours.

Keep both in the refrigerator.

---

## COOKING THE FLAGEOLETS

Having soaked the flageolets, drain them in a colander and run them under the cold tap. Put them in a saucepan with the bayleaves, studded onion, garlic and salt pork. Cover with water, bring to the boil and simmer till cooked (about one hour). Drain the beans, reserving the cooking liquor. Cut the pork up and add it to the beans; discard the onion, bayleaves and garlic.

## THE RAGOÛT

Heat the olive oil in a pan and add the onion, garlic, celery and leek. Sweat the vegetables in the oil, then add the tomato, tomato purée, saffron, wine, fish stock, bayleaf and thyme. Simmer for 5 minutes, then add the 2 lb. (900 g) of fish, cut into 1-inch (3-cm) chunks, together with the fennel and the savory. Bring to the boil, then simmer gently for a couple of minutes, turning the fish over in the *ragoût*. Season with salt and plenty of ground pepper. (The cooking of the fish will be completed in the oven.) Remove from the heat. Set your oven to 350°F (180°C; gas mark 4).

Poach the salt cod in the bean cooking liquor.

## ASSEMBLING THE CASSOULET

Select a deep casserole. Place a layer of beans and pork on the bottom, followed by some of the fish *ragoût* and salt cod, followed by more of the pork and beans, and so on till all are used up. Pour in the half pint (300 ml) of the bean cooking liquid. Put the breadcrumbs on top and pour the olive oil over. Put the lid on and bake in the oven for 45 minutes.

Halfway through the cooking, push the crust down into the beans with the back of a spoon so that it amalgamates with some of the cooking juices and reforms into a very pleasant-tasting new crust. Cook for the last 10 minutes with the lid off.

You need accompany this with no more than a simple green salad and a bottle of very chilled white Rioja, one of the old-style Riojas with plenty of oak, yellow and aromatic, such as Vina Tondonia, made by R. Lopez de Heredia. In fact, I think six bottles of Vina Tondonia over a very long lunch would be an excellent idea.

# FISH KEBABS
## WITH A PASTIS MAYONNAISE

One of the disadvantages of running a restaurant is that one misses out in summer, when friends seem to spend all their evenings having leisurely barbecues. This hurts me, because I love barbecued food. For these kebabs you need a firm-fleshed fish to stay on the skewer; I have specified monkfish, but suitable alternatives would be conger eel, eel, or members of the shark family such as dogfish, porbeagle and angel fish.

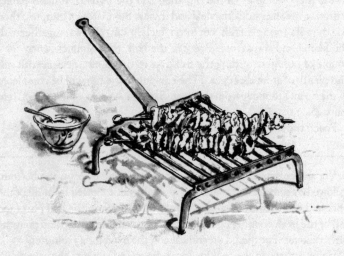

1 lb. (450 g) monkfish fillet
Sprig of thyme
Sprig of fennel
6 bayleaves
2 fl. oz. (50 ml) olive oil

Juice of a quarter lemon
4 tomatoes
1 large onion
4 oz. (120 g) bacon
Salt and black pepper from the mill

--- THE PASTIS MAYONNAISE ---

10 fl. oz. (250 ml) olive oil
   mayonnaise (see pp. 97–8)

1 fl. oz. (25 ml) pastis (Ricard or
   Pernod)
1 teaspoon (5 ml) chopped fennel

Cut the monkfish into ¾-inch (2-cm) slices. Pull the thyme leaves off the sprig and chop up the fennel. Cut each bayleaf into three pieces.

Place the herbs in a bowl with the fish and add the oil and lemon juice. Stir around and leave to marinate for at least an hour before cooking.

Cut the tomatoes and onion into wedges. Remove the rind from the bacon and cut it into 1-inch (2.5-cm) pieces. Thread four skewers with monkfish, pieces of bayleaf, bacon, tomato and onion. Chill until needed. Mix the pastis mayonnaise ingredients.

To cook the kebabs, make sure that the flames have died down on the barbecue. Brush the kebabs with some of the marinade and grill them for about 7 minutes, turning occasionally. Throw some dried fennel on to the fire for extra flavour. Season with salt and pepper. Serve with the mayonnaise, a green salad and, perhaps, some pitta bread.

# HAKE AND POTATO PIE
# WITH A GARLIC, PARSLEY AND
# BREADCRUMB CRUST

1 lb. (450 g) peeled potatoes
4 oz. (120 g) butter
1 lb. (450 g) skinned hake fillet
Salt and freshly ground black pepper

2 slices of white bread
2 cloves of garlic
½ oz. (15 g) parsley

Set your oven to 400°F (200°C; gas mark 6).

Cut the potato into ¼-inch (6-mm) slices. Parboil them in boiling salted water for 2 minutes. Smear half the butter round an oven dish; put the drained potato and the hake, cut into 1-inch (2.5-cm) slices, in it; season with salt and pepper and put the rest of the butter on top. Cover the dish and bake in the oven for 15 minutes, basting the fish and potatoes with the butter twice during that time.

Reduce the bread to crumbs in a food processor or liquidizer with the garlic and the parsley. Season the crumbs with a little salt and pepper.

Take the lid off the baking fish and potatoes and sprinkle with the breadcrumb mixture. Bake uncovered for a further 5 minutes or so till the top is crisp.

# A RATHER SPECIAL
# FISH PIE

The more familiar fish pie is made with mashed potato, flaked fish, eggs, parsley, and cheese, but this haddock pie is based on a medieval recipe and is topped with pastry. The original recipe contained a great deal of sugar and has too long a cooking time for modern tastes. I have left a pinch of sugar in – to good effect – and I have used puff pastry instead of shortcrust for a lighter result. The vegetables are sautéed in butter first, so the fish doesn't overcook.

1 lb. (450 g) haddock fillet
10 oz. (300 g) potatoes, peeled
2 oz. (60 g) butter
3 oz. (90 g) carrots, peeled and cut into thin rounds
3 oz. (90 g) onion, peeled and chopped
4 oz. (120 g) white of leek, sliced into thin rounds

Pinch of sugar
4 oz. (120 g) button mushrooms, thinly sliced
Salt and freshly ground black pepper
A little lemon juice
1 oz. (30 g) fresh chopped parsley
4 tablespoons (60 ml) double cream
8 oz. (240 g) puff pastry
1 egg

Cut the fish into ½-inch (1.25-cm) strips. Cut the potatoes into ¼-inch (6-mm) slices, place them in salted water, bring to the boil and boil for 3 minutes; drain.

Melt the butter in a heavy-based saucepan and cook the carrots, onion and leek gently for 5 minutes, stirring three or four times. Add the pinch of sugar and the mushrooms and cook for a further 3 minutes. Season with the salt and black pepper. Put into a pie dish. Add the drained potatoes, fish, lemon juice, parsley and cream; season again.

Set your oven at 425°F (220°C; gas mark 7).

Roll out the pastry on a lightly floured surface until it is 1 inch (2.5 cm) larger than the pie dish.

Beat the egg and brush the rim of the dish. Cut strips from the outside of the puff pastry and use it to line the rim. Brush with beaten egg. Cover with the main sheet of pastry, trim off the edges and crimp the pastry. Cut a small hole in the centre of the pie to allow steam to escape. Brush with beaten egg and bake in the top of the oven for 20 minutes.

A simple green salad goes excellently with this pie.

# BAKED GREY MULLET WITH TOMATO, OLIVES AND ANCHOVIES

1 oz. (30 g) chopped shallots
2 cloves of garlic, peeled and chopped
2 fl. oz. (60 ml) olive oil
1 grey mullet weighing about 3 lb. (1.4 kg)

Salt and black pepper
2 large tomatoes, skinned
4 large black olives
6 fillets of anchovy
1 spray of fennel

Turn on the oven to 450°F (230°C; gas mark 8).

Sweat the garlic and shallots in the olive oil. Turn out on to a plate to cool. Season the fish inside and out with salt and black pepper. Put half of the onion/garlic mixture inside the fish; spread half of the rest under the fish on a piece of foil about 18 inches (45 cm) square. Put the remainder on top of the fish. Cut each tomato into three and lay the slices along the fish. Stone the olives and cut into about 12 slices. Lay these over the tomatoes. Cut the anchovy fillets into 12 thin strips and lay these criss-cross over the tomatoes and olives. Finally, lay the fennel spray over the top. Carefully parcel up the fish with the foil and bake in the oven for 25 minutes. Serve the parcel at the table; it will smell wonderful.

# LEEK AND HAKE QUICHE

Fillets of hake with leeks cooked in butter in a light savoury custard flavoured with Noilly Prat and fish *fumet*.

8 oz. (240 g) shortcrust pastry (see p. 109)
3 oz. (90 g) leek (outer leaves and top removed, well washed)
½ oz. (15 g) butter
½ pint (300 ml) fish stock (see p. 92)

1 fl. oz. (30 ml) Noilly Prat (or other dry vermouth)
A little lemon juice and salt
Pinch of cayenne pepper
3 eggs
4 oz. (120 ml) double cream
6 oz. (180 g) hake fillet with skin removed

Preheat the oven to 375°F (190°C; gas mark 5).

You will need a deep 8-inch (20-cm) flan ring or flan case for this dish.

Roll out the pastry and line the flan case with it. Prick the pastry and cover it with greaseproof paper. Fill with baking beans. Bake for 10 minutes. Take out and remove beans and paper. Slice the leeks and soften them in the butter with a lid on the saucepan. Reduce the fish stock and Noilly Prat down to about 1 fl. oz. (30 ml) by rapid boiling. Add the lemon juice, salt and cayenne pepper. Add this to the eggs and cream and beat together. Line the pastry case with the leeks. Cut the hake fillet into slices about the size of your little finger and lay these on top of the leeks. Pour the custard over and bake in the oven for 25 minutes.

# TANDOORIED STEAKS OF HAKE

When this recipe appeared in my fish cookery column in *Woman's Realm*, I received a letter from a man who found it extraordinary that I should specify that the steaks of fish should be cut from the central section of the fish. He suggested that if he asked his fishmonger such a thing he would more or less be told to get lost on the grounds of 'What do you expect me to do with the rest of the fish?' It was a most revealing letter, showing how little we demand from those to whom we are paying good money.

| | |
|---|---|
| 2 oz. (60 g) onion | Good pinch of cayenne pepper |
| 4 cloves of garlic | ½ oz. (15 g) chopped mint |
| 1 green chilli | 1½ fl. oz. (45 ml) oil |
| 2 teaspoons (10 ml) black peppercorns | 4 fl. oz. (120 ml) natural yoghurt |
| 2 teaspoons (10 ml) coriander seeds | 8 steaks of hake, cut from the middle of the fish behind the gut cavity, and each weighing about 4 oz. (120 g) |
| 1 tablespoon (15 ml) turmeric | |
| 1½ fl. oz. (45 ml) lemon juice | |
| 2 teaspoons (10 ml) paprika | Salt |

Peel the onion, skin the garlic, and chop both very finely. Deseed the chilli and chop it finely. Grind the black pepper and coriander in the coffee grinder attachment of your liquidizer (if you haven't got one, use a pepper grinder or a pestle and mortar; or use ground pepper and coriander). Place them in a bowl with all the other ingredients except the fish, and mix really thoroughly. Lay the fish steaks in a shallow dish and pour the mixture over. Turn the fish over in the mixture to coat. Refrigerate for a minimum of 4 hours, turning the fish occasionally.

Turn on the grill. Oil the grill wire. Place the steaks on it and grill for 7 to 8 minutes each side. Season with salt after they are cooked.

Baste each side with the marinade once during grilling. Heat up the remainder of the marinade and serve it with the steaks. Accompany the fish with plain boiled rice and a simple green salad.

# HERRINGS IN OATMEAL

I was once advised by a fisherman in Padstow on the cooking of salmon. 'Take a piece of fat, put it in the pan, heat it up and chuck in the salmon,' he said. He suggested the same method for the cooking of young rabbit, and indeed almost any other piece of fish, meat, or fowl he hooked, netted, shot or trapped. The cooking of salmon in lard seemed a bit barbaric, considering the price; but to many fishermen in Padstow salmon is no more a luxury than the odd crawfish or lobster they take home for tea. If one can ignore the price, salmon cooked in lard is pretty similar to herrings cooked in bacon fat – which is quite the most satisfactory way of dealing with herrings, and I should think an eminently satisfactory way of serving up salmon too.

| | |
|---|---|
| Four 8-oz. (240-g) herrings | 3 oz. (90 g) lard |
| Salt and freshly ground black pepper | 4 rashers streaky bacon |
| 8 oz. (240 g) oatmeal | Lemon wedges |

Flatten out and bone the herrings (see p. 55). Season and press them with oatmeal until well covered.

Place the lard in a frying pan and fry the streaky bacon until crisp. Remove and keep warm. Fry the herrings in the fat, flesh side first, then skin side until golden brown. Serve with the bacon and lemon wedges.

# STIR-FRIED SLICES OF LEMON SOLE WITH GARLIC AND GINGER

This is slightly different from many similar Chinese dishes in that I have used quite a lot less soya sauce than would be called for in a Chinese recipe. Soya is a bit like chilli in Indian cookery: the more you use it, the less you yourself notice it. I find soya is best used with moderation for English tastes.

You could add a pinch of five spice powder to give this dish a more oriental lift. I haven't listed it because I wanted this recipe to be made up of ingredients you could easily get hold of, and there is already plenty of oriental flavour in the garlic and ginger. But all Chinese food shops sell five spice powder, which is a mixture of equal quantities of star anise, cinnamon, cloves, Chinese pepper and fennel seed. If you do use it – just a pinch!

12 oz. (360 g) lemon sole fillets with the skins removed
6 oz. (180 g) onion
¼ oz. (7.5 g) fresh ginger
3 cloves of garlic
2 mild green chillies (these are the long chillies which are usually available; if you can only get the hotter red chillies, use one instead)

2 oz. (60 g) white cabbage
½ oz. (15 g) cornflour
2 fl. oz. (60 ml) chicken stock
2 tablespoons (30 ml) dry sherry
2 tablespoons (30 ml) soya sauce
1 teaspoon (5 ml) sugar
4 fl. oz. (120 g) oil
1 oz. (30 g) cashew nuts

Cut the lemon sole into slices about the size of your little finger. Peel the onion, cut it in half and slice it as thinly as you can. Peel the ginger and chop it into a fine dice. Deal with the garlic in the same way. Remove and discard the seeds from the chillies and chop up the flesh.

Slice the cabbage thinly. Mix half the cornflour with the stock in a small bowl and add the dry sherry, soya sauce and sugar.

Shake the rest of the cornflour over the sole and stir around a little. Place the oil in a wok or frying pan and heat till shimmering hot. Throw in the pieces of fish, making sure that all are in contact with the pan. Turn the fish over once and cook for one minute only. Remove quickly with a perforated spoon.

Reheat the oil and add onions, ginger, chillies, cashew nuts and cabbage. Stir-fry them vigorously for one minute, add the garlic and then the liquid, bring to the boil, reduce a little, then gently mix in the fish. Turn out into a serving dish. Eat with some nicely undercooked green vegetables such as spinach or green beans.

# A TOURTE
# OF LING AND PRAWNS

A round, covered tart made with puff pastry filled with fillets of ling and prawns in a shellfish mousseline with a prawn-flavoured sauce. The *tourte* is glazed with egg to give it a beautiful brown finish and cut in radiating curves like a gâteau pithivier. This is a popular dish on our fixed-price menu.

1 lb. (450 g) prawns in the shell

8 oz. (240 g) ling fillet, skinned and free from bones

--- THE MOUSSELINE ---

1 fl. oz. (30 ml) shellfish reduction
1 oz. (30 g) butter
1 egg
½ teaspoon (2.5 ml) chopped shallot
½ teaspoon (2.5 ml) salt
3 fl. oz. (90 ml) cream

12 oz. (360 g) puff pastry (see pp. 107–9; or use frozen pastry)
½ oz. (15 g) tomato, peeled, deseeded and chopped
1 egg (for egg wash)

--- THE SAUCE ---

The rest of the shellfish reduction
5 fl. oz. (150 ml) double cream

3 oz. (90 g) butter
Juice of a quarter lemon

--- ORDER OF WORK ---

1. Make the shellfish reduction.
2. Make the mousseline.
3. Roll out the pastry.
4. Make the *tourte* and bake.
5. Make the sauce.

Peel the prawns and use the shells to make the shellfish reduction (see pp. 92–3). Chill.

Put half of the ling fillet in a food processor with 1 fl. oz. (30 ml) of the shellfish reduction, the butter, egg, chopped shallot and salt. Turn on and whiz till smooth. Add the cream right at the end, allowing only about 10 seconds to pour it in with the motor on. Turn out into a bowl, cover and chill for an hour (this stiffens it up).

Turn on the oven to 425°F (220°C; gas mark 7).

Roll the puff pastry out thinly to about 3⁄16 inch (4 mm). Cut two circles out of it with 9-inch (23-cm) dinner plate. Chill one of the circles. Put the other on a baking sheet and spread half the mousseline over it, leaving a margin of 2 inches (5 cm) at the edge.

Cut the remaining ling fillet into slices about the size of your little finger and lay them on top of the mousseline with the prawns. Scatter the chopped tomato over the fish; season with salt and freshly ground white pepper. Spread the rest of the mousseline over the fish and prawns.

Brush the edge of the pastry with water. Take the second piece of pastry out of the refrigerator and slightly increase its diameter by rolling it out gently, turning it as you go. Lift it off the board on a rolling pin and lay it over the first circle of pastry and the filling. Press the two edges together and crimp them by pushing the point of a knife right through both pieces all around the edge. Brush the top with beaten egg. Cut quite deep curved lines from the centre to the edge all the way round the *tourte*. Make a small hole in the centre. Bake in the preheated oven for about 30 minutes.

Put the rest of the shellfish reduction and the cream into a saucepan and bring to the boil. Simmer for 5 minutes. Just before serving the *tourte*, bring the sauce back to the boil and whisk in the butter, which should be cut into two or three pieces, and the lemon juice.

# SCROWLED PILCHARDS

I have a number of old Cornish recipe books, but they contain few recipes for fish cookery, and not many of those that are included are worth cooking. But scrowled pilchards – slightly cured split pilchards grilled in pairs pushed together on a gridiron – are very nice. You may not manage to get hold of pilchards; but herrings or fresh sardines make an ideal substitute.

8 pilchards, each weighing about 5–6
   oz. (150–180 g), or 8 similar-sized
   herrings, or 12 sardines.
1 tablespoon (15 ml) salt

1 teaspoon (5 ml) sugar
10 turns of a black peppermill
1 lemon

The pilchards need to be split and flattened. To do this, cut from the belly along to the tail and push out firmly with the flat of your hand on a chopping board. Turn over and pull out the backbone. Mix the salt, sugar and black pepper together, and sprinkle the insides of the fish with the mixture. Leave for 45 minutes, skin side up, on a wire rack in the refrigerator.

Turn on your grill, or light a barbecue.

Sandwich pairs of pilchards together, inside to inside. Grill on both sides; serve with wedges of lemon.

# BAKED PLAICE
# WITH CHEESE AND CIDER

This is a good dish to choose when you haven't much time, as it is quick to prepare and cook, and it tastes nice too.

2 oz. (60 g) cheddar cheese
½ oz. (15 g) butter
8 oz. (240 g) onion

4 large fillets of plaice
Salt and freshly ground black pepper
5 fl. oz. (150 ml) dry cider

Set the oven at 350°F (180°C; gas mark 4).

Grate the cheese. Melt the butter in a frying pan and fry the onions until soft. Transfer to a shallow baking dish. Place the fillets on top of the onions and season. Sprinkle with cheese, pour on the cider and bake in the centre of the oven for 20 minutes. I would serve this with mashed potatoes with a trace of garlic mashed up with a little salt and mixed in. Some chilled dry cider would go well with it; I like the Breton or Normandy ciders which you can buy in England quite easily now. I also like the dry unfiltered cider of the Cornish Cider Company (tel. Truro 77177).

# PLAICE AND ARTICHOKE PIE

The Jerusalem artichoke, when mashed half and half with potatoes, produces a purée with a sweet delicate flavour which goes very well with the plaice and the other vegetables in this pie. Serve it with cauliflower cooked *al dente* and then tossed in butter with some finely chopped onion.

| | |
|---|---|
| 1 lb. (450 g) Jerusalem artichokes | A splash of dry cider |
| 1 lb. (450 g) floury potatoes | Salt and ground black pepper |
| 3 oz. (90 g) onion | 2 oz. (60 g) butter |
| 4 oz. (120 g) button mushrooms | 2 fl. oz. (60 ml) double cream |
| 1 lb. (450 g) plaice fillet | |

Set your oven to 400°F (200°C; gas mark 6).

Peel the artichokes and potatoes and cut them into pieces. Bring to the boil in salted water and cook until soft. Peel and chop up the onion finely and slice the mushrooms. Butter a shallow oven-proof dish and sprinkle the onions over the bottom. Lay the mushrooms on the onions and put the plaice on top. Sprinkle with dry cider, lightly season with salt and ground black pepper and dot with a third of the butter.

Drain the artichokes and potatoes and mash them well. You may need to pass them through a sieve to get rid of the lumps in the artichoke; push it all through with the back of a large spoon.

Return the purée to the saucepan and heat gently while adding the cream and the remaining butter. Season to your taste and stir until it has stiffened up, then spread it over the fish and vegetables. Bake in the oven for 15–20 minutes until the top has browned nicely.

# BATTERED, SPICED AND MARINATED POLLACK
# WITH RAITA AND KACHUMBER

In a book essential to all enthusiastic fish cooks, *North Atlantic Seafood*, Alan Davidson refers to pollack as 'a fish of satisfactory quality'. Since he is an ex-diplomat, I take this to mean that it isn't particularly interesting – and indeed it isn't. Nevertheless, in south-west England it is cheap and plentiful, a fish that is often caught by people on holiday out for a day's mackerel fishing with feathers or a spinner. It is perfectly at home with other fish in a fish stew or soup, but shouldn't, I think, be cooked in any simple manner like grilling or frying, because it doesn't have enough flavour. This recipe works well because the pollack is a foil to some of the hotter, spicier flavours of the other ingredients.

## THE RAITA

2 cloves of garlic
2 oz. (60 g) onion
Half an inch (12.5 mm) fresh ginger, peeled
1 tablespoon (15 ml) oil
¼ teaspoon (1.5 ml) turmeric
1 teaspoon (5 ml) cummin powder

½ teaspoon (2.5 ml) cayenne pepper
1 red chilli, deseeded and finely sliced
Two 5-fl.-oz. (150-ml) cartons of natural yoghurt
Salt
1 teaspoon (5 ml) fresh coriander leaf (f you can get it), chopped

## THE MARINADE

2 red chillies, deseeded
4 cloves of garlic
½ teaspoon (2.5 ml) turmeric

½ teaspoon (2.5 ml) salt
2 tablespoons (30 ml) oil

4 pieces of skinned pollack fillet, each
weighing 5–6 oz. (150–180 g)

## KACHUMBER

6 oz. (180 g) onion, peeled and finely chopped
3 tomatoes, peeled, deseeded and chopped
A quarter cucumber, peeled and cut into small dice

¼ teaspoon (2 ml) salt
1 teaspoon (5 ml) chopped mint
3 tablespoons (45 ml) white wine vinegar

## THE BATTER

A plate spread with flour for dipping the fish

The baking powder batter recipe on p. 107

1. Make the raita.
2. Make the marinade and marinate the fish.
3. Make the kachumber.
4. Make the batter.
5. Fry the fish.

## THE RAITA

Purée the garlic using a garlic press. Grate the onion and the ginger.

Heat the oil in a frying pan and fry the garlic, onion and ginger for 3 minutes. Add the turmeric, cummin, cayenne and chilli and fry for a further minute. Remove from the heat and add the yoghurt and season with salt, then chill. Stir in the fresh coriander just before serving.

To make the marinade, purée the chillies and garlic with the turmeric, salt and oil; this is the sort of operation for a mortar and pestle, because such small amounts of bulky material will not purée in a liquidizer or food blender. (I have a very small food processor made by Molyneux which is ideal for such jobs.)

Paint the pollack fillets with this marinade, using a pastry brush.

## TO MAKE THE KACHUMBER SALAD

Mix the vegetables in a small salad bowl with the salt, mint, and vinegar. Chill.

Make the batter 10 minutes before frying the fish.

Heat up a deep fryer to 360°F (180°C). Dip the fish first in the flour, then the batter, and fry till golden brown.

Serve with the raita and kachumber, and some plainly boiled rice and a sweet chutney together with some poppadoms.

# CHAR-GRILLED SHARK STEAKS WITH KEITH FLOYD'S SHARP SAUCE

Keith Floyd, who has now made three television series about food, is not only a very good cook but has, I think, succeeded in showing that cookery is fun and need not be impossibly difficult. He is not afraid to make mistakes on camera (or indulge in the odd glass or three while cooking). He decided to do two dishes at our restaurant, one for the series

*Floyd on Fish* and a second for *Floyd on Food*. This is one of those dishes; the other is the sea bass with a sorrel sauce on pp. 234–5.

Porbeagle is the best-flavoured of sharks. It looks and cooks like veal.

Four 10-oz. (300-g) steaks of porbeagle (you could also use tope; and monkfish is nice cooked this way)

---

### THE MARINADE

2 fl. oz. (60 ml) olive oil
2 bayleaves, cut into slices
1 spray of fennel (foliage and stem), chopped

A small sprig of thyme
Juice of a quarter lemon

---

### THE SHARP SAUCE

1 teaspoon (5 ml) peppercorns
5 fl. oz. (150 ml) red wine vinegar
2 fl. oz. (60 ml) sherry
1 oz. (30 g) brown sugar
4 oz. (120 g) onion, peeled and chopped
2 cloves of garlic, peeled and chopped
1 bayleaf

½ teaspoon (2.5 ml) salt
½ teaspoon (2.5 ml) Tabasco sauce
1 teaspoon (5 ml) Worcestershire sauce
4 oz. (120 g) tomato
1 tablespoon (15 ml) tomato purée
2 fl. oz. (60 ml) olive oil
5 fl. oz. (150 ml) water

Place the marinade ingredients in a shallow dish with the fish and marinate for at least an hour, turning occasionally.

Light your barbecue, or turn on your char grill or overhead grill (see the remarks on grilling on pp. 75–6).

Crush the peppercorns and put them in a shallow pan with the vinegar, sherry, brown sugar, onions and garlic. Place on a high heat and reduce rapidly till there is virtually no liquid left. Add all the other ingredients and most of the marinade (keeping a little back to baste the steaks as you cook them). Bring to the boil and simmer for 10 minutes. Strain the sauce through a conical strainer, using a ladle to push as much flavour through as possible. Grill the steaks for about 4 minutes on each side and serve with the sauce either hot or cold. A pleasant wine to go with this would be a chilled bottle of Rosé de Provence.

# ESCALOPES OF SHARK
# WITH NOISETTE BUTTER

Four 4-oz. (120-g) escalopes of
    porbeagle shark
4 slices fresh white bread
6 fillets of anchovy
1 tablespoon (15 ml) chopped parsley
1 oz. (30 g) flour
1 egg

1 tablespoon (15 ml) milk
1½ oz. (45 g) butter
1½ oz. (45 g) oil
4 oz. (120 g) salted butter
Juice of half a lemon
Lemon wedges

The escalopes should be thin slices cut from a large piece of shark. They
cannot be batted out like veal, since they break up, but it is fairly easy to
get some reasonable slices from the middle. Alternatively you could use
two thin slices per person from the tail, with the central cartilage
removed. In both cases the thick skin should be cut off.

Turn the bread into crumbs in a food processor or liquidizer, adding
the anchovy fillets and parsley at the same time. Put this in a shallow
dish. Lightly beat the egg with the milk. Pass the escalopes first through
the flour, then the egg mixture, and finally the breadcrumbs. Heat the
butter and oil in a large frying pan and fry the escalopes to a nice golden
brown. Do this in batches; don't overcrowd the pan. Pour out the butter
and oil. Heat the 4 oz. (120 g) of butter until it foams and smells nutty,
then add the lemon juice and pour over the escalopes. Serve with extra
wedges of lemon and some Parmentier potatoes (see p. 272). To go with
this, I would like a bottle of DOC Soave, ice-cold and with that slightly
bitter dryness some Italian wines have.

# A *FRICASSÉE* OF SKATE
# WITH MUSHROOMS

Skate is normally but not always sold skinned. Refer to p. 58 for details
on skinning, which unfortunately is not particularly easy – one for the
fishmonger if possible. For this recipe, you should buy good thick slabs of
skate wing from a big fish; the smaller wings would take up too much
room in the pan.

4 oz. (120 g) fresh white mushrooms
1 teaspoon (5 ml) freshly chopped
  parsley
2 oz. (60 g) butter

4 pieces of skinned skate each
  weighing about 8 oz. (240 g)
1 oz. (30 g) flour
1 pint (600 ml) fish stock (see p. 92)
1 egg yolk
2 fl. oz. (60 ml) double cream
Juice of a quarter lemon

Thinly slice the mushrooms. Chop the parsley. Heat the butter in a sauté pan big enough to take all four fillets in a single layer. Put them in the pan, season with salt, cover with a lid and cook gently for 2 minutes on each side.

Add the flour and mix it in around the fish. Cook it for 2 minutes, then gradually add the fish stock. Bring to the boil and simmer till the fish is cooked through (about 20 minutes).

Remove the fillets with a perforated spoon and keep them warm in a serving dish. Simmer the sauce for a further 10 minutes and add any juice that has drained out of the fish. Add the mushrooms to the sauce and cook for a further 2 minutes. Remove from the heat.

Whisk the egg and cream together in a small bowl (this is called a liaison), then pour in a little of the boiling sauce. Stir the mixture back into the sauce. Do not reboil after this. Add the lemon juice and parsley, test the seasoning and pour over the skate. Serve with a green salad and boiled potatoes.

## SKATE WITH BLACK BUTTER

The secret of many good fish recipes lies in contrasting the fish with a slightly sharp sauce. At its simplest this would be malt vinegar on fish and chips, more elaborately mackerel with gooseberry sauce or sea bass with *beurre blanc*. Skate with black butter, a personal favourite, is just such a fish dish where the nut-brown butter sauce is sharpened with wine vinegar and capers.

This dish can also be made with great success using nasturtium buds or seeds which are first salted and then pickled in white wine vinegar to which a handful of tarragon (including stalks) has been added.

2 lb. (900 g) skate wings
The *court bouillon* on p. 93
½ oz. (15 g) capers
6 oz. (180 g) salted butter

2 tablespoons (30 ml) wine vinegar (I use red for this recipe)
½ oz. (15 g) freshly chopped parsley

Cut the skate into four portions and place in a wide shallow pan. Pour the *court bouillon* over the fish, bring to the boil and simmer very gently for 15 to 20 minutes, depending on the thickness of the skate. Drain the fish and keep it warm on a serving dish; sprinkle them with capers.

Heat the butter in a frying pan until it foams, begins to go dark and smells nutty. Pour the vinegar into the pan, then the parsley, and immediately pour it all over the fish. Serve at once with plainly boiled potatoes and a nice bottle of dry white wine like a Sancerre.

# BOUILLABAISSE

This is my recipe for *bouillabaisse*, and is not intended to be the definitive account of the dish. It is not possible, in Britain, to obtain the correct small rock fish, including the essential rascasse, which go into the Mediterranean *bouillabaisse*. The dish should be made with a large variety of small fish which are all cooked unfilleted. Sometimes at the restaurant, if we are lucky enough to get an odd box of small gurnard, red mullet, weever, black bream or John Dory, we produce a *bouillabaisse* using whole fish, but normally we use fillets of larger fish, so that we can put five or six different varieties into the stew and still sell it for only one or two people.

This then is a *bouillabaisse* made as authentically as possible using what is best available around Padstow. If you take a severe view on my naming it thus, maybe you'd like to think of it as a 'Padstow Fish Stew'. It's *bouillabaisse* to me, though, and pretty evocative of that charmed part of France.

One change that I have made to the recipe is to prepare a fish stock out of the bones of the fish I am using. Then I boil the fillets in the stock, having added the olive oil, vegetables and herbs. This increases the strength of the finished soup.

4 lb. (2.4 kg) of any of the following fish: wrasse, dogfish, black bream, red bream, monkfish, cod, or hake, weever, trigger fish, gurnard, red mullet, bass, John Dory, bream, skate, conger eel, grey mullet – the more variety the better

The *rouille* recipe on p. 99

3 medium onions, peeled and roughly chopped

1 lb. (450 g) tomatoes, peeled and chopped, reserving the skins

3 pints (1.7 litres) water

3 fl. oz. (90 ml) olive oil

12 thin slices of French bread

The white of a large leek, washed and roughly chopped

2 sticks of celery, thinly sliced

1 large bulb of Florence fennel, thinly sliced

5 cloves of garlic, chopped

Freshly ground black pepper

A 2-inch (5-cm) piece of orange peel

1 level teaspoon saffron

1 sprig of thyme

2 bayleaves

1 lb. (450 g) mussels, washed and scraped clean of barnacles, with beards pulled out

½ lb. (225 g) shellfish: slices of lobster or crawfish, or langoustine or prawns in the shell

1 teaspoon (2.5 ml) of chopped fennel herb, with a few leaves of thyme, to sprinkle over the cooked fish

Salt

---

## ORDER OF WORK

1. Fillet the fish and prepare the vegetables.
2. Make the *rouille*.
3. Make the fish stock.
4. Fry the croutons.
5. Make the *bouillabaisse*.

Fillet all the fish except skate (if you are using it). Cut the fillets so that they are all about the same size.

Make a bowl of *rouille* using the recipe on p. 99.

Put one third of the onions in the bottom of a large pan with the tomato skins. Place all the fish trimmings on top and add the water. Bring to the boil and simmer gently for 20 minutes. Strain the stock.

Fry the French bread croutons in a little olive oil till a light gold colour. Rub with garlic and keep warm.

Heat the olive oil in a saucepan large enough to hold all the fish and stock. Soften the rest of the onions, the leek, celery, Florence fennel and garlic. Season with black pepper. Add the orange peel, tomatoes, saffron, thyme, bayleaves and the fish stock and bring to the boil, whisking as it comes to the boil to aid the emulsion of oil and stock. Now add the fish, putting the firmer-fleshed fish like conger eel, dogfish and skate in first. Add the softer fish and mussels a couple of minutes later. Boil only till the fish is just cooked (about 5 minutes).

Add the shellfish and boil for a further half minute. Strain the soup through a colander and place all the fish, mussels, shellfish and vegetables in a large warm dish. The mussels and shellfish should be left in the shell. Scatter with the chopped fennel and thyme and put the croutons on top.

Return the strained soup to the saucepan and test for seasoning. Boil the soup very vigorously for one more minute, whisking as you do to liaise oil and water. Now pour some of the soup over the fish and croutons.

Serve the rest of the soup in a warm tureen. I think the nicest way to eat the *bouillabaisse* is to spoon both fish and soup into a soup bowl and stir in a dollop of *rouille*; but you can if you like treat the fish and soup as two separate courses. Certainly the fish cooked this way, in stock rather than water, will not have lost all its flavour to the soup.

# RETSINA FISH STEW

There can be few tastes which better exemplify the phrase 'You either love it or you hate it' than retsina, the pine-resin-flavoured white wine of Greece. But it can be used to advantage in fish cookery when most of the insistent mouthwash flavour is driven off, leaving a subtle and aromatic suggestion of the original wine.

Retsina does not improve with age; it loses its freshness, so buy from a shop with a good turnover of stock. Some types are nicer than others (Kourtaki is good). In this fish stew, the retsina is added in quantity at the beginning, then a few drops more are splashed over it just at the end to give a flash of pine trees when the dish is taken to the table. The stew is finished by laying fried aubergines and rings of squid across the surface which contrast with the stewed fish and vegetables beneath. It is served with *skorthalia*, a garlic mayonnaise made with ground almonds which you stir in to thicken it (if you wish). I hope you like it.

The recipe is for six.

*Skorthalia* (recipe on p. 100)

5 lb. (2.3 kg) or a selection from the following; grey mullet, hake, conger eel, John Dory, red mullet, black bream, gurnard, sea bass, sea scorpion, garfish, red fish (Norway haddock), wrasse, red bream, small whiting, monkfish, wolf fish

1 squid, weighing about 8 oz. (240 g)

4 oz. (120 g) Florence fennel, washed and sliced

4 oz. (120 g) celery, washed and sliced

4 oz. (120 g) onion, peeled and chopped

1 oz. (30 g) garlic, peeled and chopped

5 fl. oz. (150 ml) good olive oil

5 fl. oz. (150 ml) retsina

6 oz. (180 g) tomato, peeled and sliced

6 oz. (180 g) potatoes, peeled and sliced

2 teaspoons (10 ml) tomato purée

¾ oz. (20 g) salt

1 tablespoon (15 ml) chopped fennel herb

1 aubergine, thinly sliced

A little olive oil

Milk and seasoned flour for coating the aubergine

---

## ORDER OF WORK

1. Make the *skorthalia*.
2. Fillet the fish.
3. Make fish stock.
4. Make the fish stew.
5. Cook squid and aubergine.

---

Prepare the *skorthalia*. You can cook the fish for this stew whole if you like, in which case just use 4 pints of water rather than fish stock. (We have to fillet the fish in stews at the restaurant because our customers don't like bones; so we make a fish stock from the heads and bones and use this with the filleted but not skinned fish in the stew.) Otherwise, fillet the fish and make a fish stock with the trimmings, using the same weight of vegetables as in the recipe on p. 92 but with 4 pints of water rather than 3.

Clean the squid (see pp. 62–3 for instructions); slice it into rounds and the tentacles and fins into strips.

In a large pan, cook the sliced fennel, celery, onion and garlic in the olive oil on a medium heat so that the flavour is drawn out of the vegetables but they are not burnt at all. Add all but about 3 tablespoons (45 ml) of the retsina, the tomato, potatoes and tomato purée, and cook for about 3 minutes. Add the fish stock and bring to the boil. Turn down the heat to a slow simmer, add the salt, half the chopped fennel herb and the fish fillets. The fillets can all go in at the same time if they are roughly the same thickness; but if some are much thicker, put them in a couple of minutes before the rest. If any of the fish is particularly soft, like hake or whiting, put it in a couple of minutes after the rest. Poach the fillets for 5 minutes (longer – up to 15 minutes – if you are using whole fish).

Carefully strain the fish and vegetables through a large colander over a large bowl and put them into a warmed dish suitable for serving the stew in, perhaps a Le Creuset casserole or a large soup tureen.

Return the soup to the original saucepan and boil it fiercely while you fry the squid and aubergine. The object of this boiling is to amalgamate the oil and fish stock and also to reduce the volume a little to concentrate the flavour.

Put a little olive oil in a frying pan, heat it up and quickly fry the squid. Take them out, pass the aubergine slices through the milk and then the seasoned flour, add more oil to the pan and quickly fry them. Keep them warm. Pour the boiling *bouillon* over the fish and vegetables and splash the last of the retsina over. Arrange the squid and aubergine on top. Finally sprinkle the remainder of the chopped fennel over and serve with the *skorthalia*.

# FISH STEW
# WITH SAFFRON AND CREAM

Any fish will do for this stew, except oily ones like mackerel or herring. If possible use firm fish like monk, conger, turbot or brill, and some soft fish such as cod, whiting or plaice.

2½ lb. (1.2 kg) white fish on the bone
2 leeks
3 sticks of celery
2 medium potatoes
2 medium onions
4 cloves of garlic
4 good-sized tomatoes
8 oz. (240 g) prawns in the shell
3 pints (1.7 litres) water

Salt and ground black pepper
20 to 30 mussels
3 oz. (90 g) butter
A 2-inch (5-cm) piece of orange peel
1 teaspoon (5 ml) saffron
Juice of half a lemon
A ¼-pint (142-ml) carton double cream
Freshly chopped parsley

## Order of work

1. Prepare the vegetables and prawns.
2. Open the mussels.
3. Make the fish stock.
4. Cook the vegetables and fish.
5. Reduce the cooking liquor.
6. Assemble the stew.

Skin and fillet the fish, keeping all the trimmings. Trim and wash the leeks and sticks of celery. Peel the potatoes and the onions. Skin and chop the garlic. Skin and roughly chop the tomatoes. Chop the green parts of the leeks, the tops of the celery and one onion and place in a large saucepan. Peel the prawns and reserve the flesh. Add the shells and heads to the pan and put the fish trimmings on top of them. Add the water, season and bring to the boil. Simmer for 20 minutes.

While the stock ingredients are coming to the boil, scrape the mussels clean and wash them well. Place them in a saucepan over a high heat with the lid on. Remove from the heat when the shells have opened, and strain them through a colander into a bowl. Add the cooking juice to the stock, keeping back the last spoonful or so which will probably have grit in it. When the mussels have cooled, remove the beards, but leave them in their shells.

Slice the remaining onion, celery and leeks with the potatoes. Melt the butter in a large pan which will look good enough to serve the stew in, and cook the vegetables until softened, about 5 minutes.

Add the garlic, tomato, orange peel and saffron and cook gently for 5 minutes. Strain the fish stock, pour it on to the softened vegetables and simmer for about 10 minutes. Add the fish, cut into 1-inch (2.5-cm) pieces, the hard fish first, followed 2 minutes later by the soft. When the fish is just cooked, add the prawns and mussels and warm them through. Strain the cooking liquor through a colander and keep the fish and vegetables warm.

Bring the liquor back to the boil and add the lemon juice and cream and reduce by rapid boiling for 10 minutes. Season to taste with the salt and pepper and add the fish and vegetables. Sprinkle with parsley and serve.

# Thirteen

# SPECIAL MAIN COURSE
# FISH DISHES

The recipes in this chapter are dishes we would put on our *à la carte* menu. None of them will be cheap, and few of them are easy to prepare; but for a dinner party or a special meal, this is the place to look.

## GRILLED SEA BASS
## WITH SAMPHIRE

See the notes about samphire on p. 85.

1½ lb. (750 g) samphire
2 bass, each weighing about 1½ lb. (750 g)
Salt and ground black pepper
5 fl. oz. (150 ml) fish stock (see p. 92)

1 tablespoon (15 ml) white wine vinegar
2 fl. oz. (60 ml) groundnut oil
1 oz. (30 ml) finely chopped onion
1 teaspoon (5 ml) chopped chives

Thoroughly wash the samphire, leaving the root on. Snip off the fins of the bass, taking care to avoid spiking yourself. Scale the fish and remove the guts; wash and slash the fish two or three times on either side. Turn on your grill.

Brush the bass with a little groundnut oil and season inside and out with salt and ground black pepper.

Bring a pan of unsalted water to the boil and cook the samphire for about 5 to 8 minutes. To test whether it is cooked, take a piece by the root and bite the green fleshy part away from the stalk centre. If it comes away easily it is cooked, but it still should be firm to the bite. At the restaurant we remove the stalks before serving the samphire; this is very labour-intensive and perhaps not necessary at home.

Grill the bass for about 8 minutes on either side.

Put the fish stock in a sauteuse and reduce the volume by rapid boiling down to a couple of tablespoons. Add the white wine vinegar, the groundnut oil, and the chopped onion to the reduced fish stock, season with salt and ground black pepper and warm through on a very low heat. Add the chopped chives just before you serve.

Serve the fish whole and fillet it at the table on to four warmed plates. Add samphire and spoon the sauce over the filleted fish and the samphire. Some new potatoes covered in freshly chopped parsley would make a pleasing accompaniment to this dish of clean and simple tastes.

# ROAST SEA BASS
# WITH A SORREL SAUCE

Bass is excellent simply roasted in the oven and the slight acidity of this sorrel sauce highlights the flavour of the fish. If you cannot get hold of sorrel, use watercress and add a little lemon juice. This gives a totally different flavour but is also very nice.

Incidentally, you might find the high oven temperature a bit odd for fish but there's nothing to toughen up in a fish by fast roasting. The idea here is to subject the bass to a fierce heat to get a nice crisp skin before the flesh cooks too much.

1 3½-lb. (1.6-kg) bass
3 oz. (90 g) unsalted butter
2 oz. (60 g) celery, washed and sliced
2 oz. (60 g) carrot, peeled, washed and sliced

2 oz. (60 g) leek, washed and sliced
1 fl. oz. (30 ml) dry white wine
Salt and freshly ground black pepper

———————————————— SAUCE ————————————————

2 egg yolks
2 oz. (60 g) onions, chopped
1 fl. oz. (30 ml) white wine vinegar
1 fl. oz. (30 ml) dry white wine
4 fl. oz. (120 ml) fish stock (see p. 92)
8 oz. (240 g) butter

2 oz. (60 g) sorrel
2 or 3 spinach leaves (to improve the colour of the sauce)
Salt
Sorrel leaves to garnish

Set the oven at 425°F (220°C; gas mark 7).

Gut, scale and remove the fins from the whole bass (see p. 52). Rinse and pat dry on a piece of kitchen paper.

Melt 2 oz. (60 g) of the butter in a small saucepan and gently cook the vegetables for about 4 minutes, adding the white wine halfway through. Season with the salt and pepper and leave to cool a little. Stuff the gut cavity of the fish with most of the vegetables, leaving some to rest the bass on when you roast it.

Butter the bass with 1 oz. (30 g) of the butter. Season well outside with salt and pepper. Place the whole fish in a roasting tin with some of the vegetables underneath and cook in the centre of the oven for about 30 minutes. Test whether the fish is cooked by cutting down on to the backbone at the thickest part and checking that the flesh has turned white right through.

You can make the sauce while the fish is roasting. Put the two egg yolks in the liquidizer. Place the chopped onions, vinegar, white wine and fish stock in a small pan, bring to the boil and continue to boil until all but a couple of spoonfuls of the liquid has evaporated. Add the butter, then the sorrel and spinach and soften these in the butter. Turn on the liquidizer and pour the contents of the pan through the small hole in the lid to make a quick hollandaise. Season. Pour the mixture through a sieve into a warm sauce boat.

When the bass is cooked, transfer to a serving dish, garnish with sorrel, and fillet it at the table, giving each person some of the roasted vegetables from under the fish as well as the vegetable stuffing. Serve with the sorrel sauce.

The wine to drink with this is undoubtedly a Puligny Montrachet, preferably a Premier Crû like Clavoillans from Leflaive in a good year.

# CASSOLETTE OF BRILL, SCALLOPS AND CRAB

Fish and shellfish cooked gently in a *cassolette* with the flavours of shellfish with tarragon and a little cream. A *cassolette* is a small round shallow copper pan. At the restaurant, this dish is cooked on top of the stove and served to the customer in the copper cooking pan. I have retained the name of the dish, because it sounds nice, but slightly changed the method to make it easier for you to cook at home.

| | |
|---|---|
| 10 oz. (360 g) skinned brill fillet | 1 teaspoon (5 ml) fresh lemon juice |
| 8 scallops | 3 tomatoes, skinned, deseeded and |
| ½ oz. (15 g) butter | chopped |
| 2 fl. oz. (60 ml) shellfish reduction | 1 teaspoon (5 ml) chopped tarragon |
| (see pp. 92–3) | Pinch cayenne pepper |
| 4 fl. oz. (120 ml) double cream | 8 oz. (240 g) white crab meat |

Slice the brill into ½-inch (1.25-cm) pieces. Cut the scallops into three.

Select either a clean large non-stick or a thick-bottomed enamel frying pan (all steel frying pans leave a metallic taste). Melt the butter in the pan; add the fish and a little later the scallops. Cook very gently in the butter.

As soon as the fish and scallops change from opaque to white, remove them to a warm plate with a fish slice. Add shellfish reduction and cream to the pan, turn up the heat and reduce the sauce until it is thick enough to coat the back of a spoon.

Add lemon juice, tomatoes, tarragon and cayenne. Return the fish and scallops to the pan and add the crab. Heat through, turning gently, and serve on four warm plates.

# FILLETS OF BRILL *DUGLÉRÉ*

Brill is similar in taste and texture to turbot, and this good dish of classical French cuisine is pleasantly simple; the brill is poached in Muscadet with tomatoes and butter and served with a sauce made from the reduced poaching liquor and *velouté*. If you don't want to go to the trouble of making *velouté* you can substitute the same quantity of double cream, but this is one of those dishes which show how nice a *velouté*-based sauce can be.

1 oz. (30 g) onion, finely chopped
3 good-sized tomatoes, skinned, deseeded and chopped
4 skinned fillets of brill, each weighing 6 oz. (180 g)
3 fl. oz. (90 ml) Muscadet

Salt and freshly ground white pepper
4 fl. oz. (120 ml) fish *velouté* (see p. 94)
2 oz. (60 g) unsalted butter
1 teaspoon (5 ml) chopped parsley
Lemon juice
2 fl. oz. (60 ml) double cream

Turn on your oven to 350°F (180°C; gas mark 4).

Butter a shallow oven dish and sprinkle with the onion and tomato. Lay the fish fillets on top, add the Muscadet, and season lightly with salt and freshly ground white pepper (black pepper is a bit harsh for this recipe). Cover with a butter paper and poach in the oven for about 7–10 minutes.

Pour off the cooking liquor into a small pan and reduce it by half by rapid boiling. Add the fish *velouté*, butter, parsley and a few drops of lemon juice. Whisk to a smooth consistency, add the double cream, pour over the fish, *et voilà*, it's done.

# CRAWFISH *EN CROÛTE*

You may feel that a crawfish should best be served plainly cooked with mayonnaise or a hot butter sauce, but I think you will agree that this dish has a certain style, with the firm slices of langouste surrounded by a delicate mousseline of crawfish, and the shellfish flavour further echoed by the sauce. When crawfish is served in this way, a relatively small one is enough for 8 people.

A 4-lb (2-kg) crawfish

## THE MOUSSELINE

| | |
|---|---|
| 4 fl. oz. (120 ml) shellfish reduction | 1 egg and 1 egg white |
| 1 lb. (500 g) skinned whiting fillet | 12 fl. oz. (360 ml) double cream |
| ½ oz. (15 g) onion | 2 oz. (60 g) butter |
| 1⅔ teaspoons (8 ml) salt | |

1 lb. (500 g) puff pastry (see pp. 107–9)
1 beaten egg (for egg wash)

## THE SAUCE

| | |
|---|---|
| The rest of the shellfish reduction | 3 oz. (90 g) butter |
| 1 teaspoon (5 ml) chopped tarragon | 3 oz. (90 g) tomato, peeled, deseeded |
| 8 fl. oz. (240 ml) double cream | and chopped |

## ORDER OF WORK

1. Cook the crawfish and remove the meat.
2. Make a shellfish reduction.
3. Make the mousseline.
4. Wrap mousseline and crawfish in puff pastry.
5. Bake.
6. Make the sauce.

Bring a large pan of well-salted water to the boil and cook the crawfish for 30 minutes. Leave to cool, then remove all the meat (see pp. 61–2 for advice on cooking shellfish and removing meat).

Make a shellfish reduction to the recipe on pp. 92–3. You can use some of the body section of the crawfish as well as prawns, but crawfish shell on its own doesn't have as good a flavour as prawns. Reduce the reduction by rapid boiling if it seems a little lacking in flavour; you will need 4 fl. oz. (120 ml) of it for the mousseline, which you should chill before adding. The rest of the reduction will be for the sauce.

If the crawfish has coral, keep this; put a quarter of it in with the mousseline, and the rest should be cut up with the crawfish meat.

Place the whiting fillet, onion, salt, eggs and butter in a food processor and purée them. Add the 4 fl. oz. (120 ml) of shellfish reduction, and then pour the cream in steadily over about 15 seconds. Turn off as soon as the cream is added and chill again.

Preheat your oven to 400°F (200°C; gas mark 6).

Roll out the pastry thinly and trim to approximately 20 by 12 inches (50 by 30 cm). Place half the mousseline down the centre of the pastry, leaving room at the ends to fold over. Lay all the crawfish along this, and put the rest of the mousseline on top. Fold in the ends, cutting part of the corner off so that the pastry is not too thick at the ends. Then fold one side over, brush with water, fold the other side over, and seal. Turn over on to a baking tray. Decorate if you like with leaves and vines. Brush with beaten egg and bake in the oven for about 25 to 30 minutes until golden brown.

While the crawfish is baking, finish the sauce. Put the rest of the shellfish reduction in a small saucepan with all the other sauce ingredients except the chopped tomato. Boil rapidly to reduce the sauce till it coats the back of a spoon. Take off the heat, add the tomato, and serve with the crawfish, which should be cut into thick slices.

# SLICED CRAWFISH SALAD WITH TOMATO, CHERVIL AND FISH *FUMET*

The crawfish is taken out of the shell and sliced and served with a garden salad dressed with walnut oil. The *fumet* is flavoured with tomato and chervil and a small amount of soya sauce, which, though not detectable, has the effect of lifting the flavour.

1 crawfish weighing 4–5 lb. (1.8–2.3 kg)

1 pint (600 ml) of good clear fish stock, made to the recipe on p. 92 and using only the bones of flat fish or the cod family

1 teaspoon (5 ml) soya sauce (Kikkoman Japanese soya is good)

Salad leaves for four, a mixture of bitter leaves like chicory and endive and lettuce like Salad Bowl and Lollo Red

2 fl. oz. (60 ml) walnut oil dressing (see p. 105)

2 oz. (60 g) tomato, peeled, deseeded and finely chopped

Small bunch of chervil, picked off the stalks

Cook the crawfish according to the instructions on p. 61. It will take 30 to 35 minutes.

While the crawfish is boiling, put the fish stock on to boil and reduce the volume by two-thirds by rapid boiling. Add the soya sauce.

While the crawfish is still warm, cut it in half lengthways (see the grilled lobster recipe (p. 251) for how to cut a lobster or crawfish in half). Remove the tail meat, slice and keep it warm while you work through the feelers, claws and legs, removing the meat. I shouldn't bother to remove the meat from all of these; there will be quite enough in the tail and a few of the legs. (You can save most of the legs and the meat in the body cavity for something the next day – perhaps a *feuilletée* of crawfish with hollandaise sauce made like the similar crab recipe on p. 181.)

Toss the salad in the dressing and put on four plates. Arrange the sliced crawfish on the plate next to it.

Just before serving, add the tomato to the hot *fumet* with the chervil, which you should quickly chop at the last minute to preserve its delicate flavour. Pour over the crawfish.

# GRILLED DOVER SOLE
# WITH OUR OWN PARSLEY BUTTER

It is possible to grill soles over a barbecue-type grill as long as they are well oiled first and the grill bars are extremely hot. In this way the bars will sear and carbonize the flesh of the sole and prevent it from sticking. If you haven't got a large and professional barbecue arrangement, I should stick to using your domestic grill. You can, if you like, heat a poker to red-hot in a gas flame or on an electric element and make grill bar marks on the fish, which looks very impressive.

Lemon sole, brill, small (chicken) turbot or plaice can be treated in exactly the same way.

A small bunch of parsley
5 anchovy fillets
4 oz. (120 g) unsalted butter
Juice of a quarter lemon

5 turns of your black peppermill
½ teaspoon (2.5 ml) salt
4 soles, each weighing about 12 oz. to
    1 lb. (360 to 450 g)

Chop the parsley and anchovy fillets together, mix with the slightly softened butter, lemon juice, black pepper and salt. Place in the middle of a sheet of clingfilm and roll into a sausage shape in the film. Chill and slice into thin rounds to lay on the top of the fish when you have grilled it.

Grill the soles for 4 minutes per side.

# BRAISED DUBLIN BAY PRAWNS WITH ASPARAGUS AND A SHELLFISH CREAM

Slightly cooked langoustine with a green vegetable stock sauce and a *savarin*-shaped cream flavoured with the crushed langoustine shells.

36 whole raw Dublin Bay prawns (or cooked ones if you can't get them raw)

## THE VEGETABLE STOCK

1 oz. (30 g) celery
1 oz. (30 g) leek
1 oz. (30 g) fennel
1 oz. (30 g) mushrooms

½ bayleaf
Sprig of chervil
6 white peppercorns (lightly crushed)
1 pint (600 ml) water

## THE CREAMS

2 fl. oz. (60 ml) shellfish reduction (see pp. 92–3)
10 fl. oz. (300 ml) double cream

3 eggs
¼ teaspoon (2 ml) salt

## THE VEGETABLES

8 asparagus spears, washed and peeled
8 oz. (240 g) spinach, well washed

## TO FINISH THE SAUCE

4 oz. (120 ml) double cream
1 oz. (30 g) butter

## ORDER OF WORK

1. Make a shellfish reduction.
2. Simmer the vegetable stock.
3. Cook the langoustine creams.
4. Blanch the vegetables.
5. Braise the langoustine.
6. Make the sauce.
7. Assemble the dish.

Set the oven to 350°F (180°C; gas mark 4).

Peel the langoustine and make a shellfish reduction with the shells and heads following the instructions on pp. 92–3.

Simmer all the vegetable stock ingredients for 30 minutes.

Mix the ingredients for the langoustine creams and place them in four buttered individual *savarin* moulds. Place these in a tray and add enough water to come halfway up the moulds. Bring to the boil on top of the stove, cover with a butter paper and bake in the oven for 20 minutes.

While the vegetable stock is simmering, poach the asparagus in it and cut the spears into three. Blanch the spinach for half a minute in boiling water. Pound a couple of the leaves in a mortar, or liquidize them, force them through a sieve with the back of a spoon, and reserve (to add to the sauce at the end with the cream to give a nice green colour). Strain the stock through a conical strainer, forcing as much liquid through as possible with the back of a ladle. Reduce by rapid boiling down to about 3 fl. oz. (90 ml).

Braise the langoustine in a little of the reduced vegetable stock in a shallow pan covered with a butter paper. They will cook very quickly; be careful not to overcook them. If you have to use cooked prawns, just warm them through in the stock. Return the cooking juice to the stock reduction and keep the langoustine warm. Add the cream to the vegetable stock and reduce a little more till the sauce coats the back of a spoon. Finally whisk in the butter.

Put a bed of spinach into the centres of four warmed plates and turn out a langoustine cream on top. Pour all the sauce around the outsides of the plates and arrange the Dublin Bay prawns and asparagus all the way round.

# A GRILLADE OF SEAFOOD

The *grillade* is extremely popular at the restaurant and is precisely the sort of food that I like the best. This and the *fruits de mer* (pp. 244–7) are perfect for eating outdoors – on a warm summer's day, in the case of the *fruits de mer*, or evening in the case of the *grillade*. I would suggest a wine of fairly robust character for the *grillade*, maybe a chilled bottle of retsina.

## FOR THE MARINADE

2 fl. oz. (60 ml) olive oil
1 teaspoon (5 ml) chopped fennel
3 bayleaves, sliced

Salt and freshly ground black pepper
Juice of a quarter lemon

2 lobsters, cooked, each weighing
   about 1 lb. (450 g)
24 Dublin Bay prawns (or 12
   Mediterranean prawns or 36 North
   Atlantic prawns)
Four 4 oz. (120 g) steaks of monkfish

Four 3-oz. (90-g) steaks of either grey
   mullet, conger eel, dogfish, tope,
   shark, whole small mackerel, red
   mullet, sardines, pilchards, black
   bream, small John Dory, gurnard or
   sea bass
Half a pint (300 ml) of *aïoli* (see
   pp. 98–9)
4 wedges of lemon

## FOR THE FENNEL DRESSING

Mix together:

5 fl. oz. (150 ml) olive oil
1 fl. oz. (30 ml) red wine vinegar
½ teaspoon (1.5 ml) of salt and some
   freshly ground black pepper

1 tablespoon (15 ml) chopped fennel
½ small onion finely chopped

At least one hour before cooking, put all the marinade ingredients in a shallow dish and add the fish; turn over in the marinade 2 or 3 times during the hour. Prepare and light your charcoal grill at least 40 minutes before cooking. Cut the lobsters in half lengthways and crack their claws.

Cook the steaks of fish for about 3 minutes on each side.

The lobsters and the prawns, being cooked already, don't need to go on the grill for very long; they can just be warmed through. This also slightly chars the shells, giving the *grillade* an aroma which is one of its great attractions. Brush the shells with some of the marinade you used for the fish and put the lobsters on the grill for about 2 minutes per side, prawns for about 1 minute.

Serve everything on one large serving dish. Add any of the marinade left to the dressing and pour the dressing over the plates. Serve with lemon and *aïoli* in a large bowl and plenty of French bread to mop up the dressing.

# MIXED DEEP-FRIED FISH AND SHELLFISH IN TEMPURA BATTER WITH AÏOLI

The choice of what to fry in this dish is yours; it should include both fish and shellfish. Here is a recipe for the sort of *mélange* we serve in the restaurant.

| | |
|---|---|
| 4 scallops | 4 Dublin Bay prawns |
| 1 small squid | The tempura batter on p. 107 |
| 2 small red mullet | The *aïoli* on pp. 98–9 |
| 4 oz. (120 g) monkfish fillet | Wedges of lemon |

Slice the scallops in half. Clean and skin the squid according to the instructions on pp. 62–3; slice the body into circles about ¼ inch (6 mm) wide and the tentacles and fins into strips. Fillet the two small red mullet. Cut the monkfish into 1-inch (2.5-cm) slices.

Set your deep fryer to 365°F (185°C).

Fry in small quantities, one portion at a time. Drain on kitchen paper. Tell the first person served not to wait.

# THE *FRUITS DE MER*

Seafood in a French style: lobsters, crabs and plenty of other shellfish, all left in the shell and presented on a base of crushed ice and seaweed with lemons, mayonnaise, and a particular kind of sharp sauce, shallot vinegar, made with red wine, red wine vinegar and chopped shallots.

A wonderful dish for a leisurely outdoor lunch by the sea on a hot summer's day, with plenty of chilled white wine and nothing else to do but sit and pick and chat.

You might feel that assembling the ingredients for a *fruits de mer* is beyond the scope of the average family on holiday, but this is not so. The dish is built up around crabs and lobsters, and once you have got hold of these, the other shellfish can quite easily be found in a day's gathering of the fruits of a rocky beach at low tide. Mussels, winkles, shore crabs are easy to find, as well as the seaweed essential to decorate the dish (bladderwrack is the best). Cockles too are not hard to come by; and where I live, soft-shelled clams, winkles, shrimps and sometimes prawns are quite common.

If, like me, you prefer your mussels, cockles, clams and carpet shells raw, take care to gather them from areas free from pollution. At the restaurant we find that most people prefer everything except oysters to be lightly cooked.

The suggested ingredients are for six people.

3 lobsters, each weighing about 1 lb. (450 g)

3 crabs, each weighing about 1½ lb. (775 g)

36 mussels

36 unshelled prawns (Dublin Bay prawns if you are lucky enough to get them)

1 lb. (450 g) shrimps

18 oysters

36 winkles

Plus any of the following: whelks, shore crabs, all types of clam, cockles, scallops, sea urchins

1 pint (600 ml) mustard mayonnaise (see p. 98)

¼ pint (150 ml) shallot vinegar (see p. 106)

Half a small bucket of seaweed, blanched in boiling water (unless from a clean beach), then rinsed in cold water and chilled

3 lemons

2 or 3 lobster picks

A claw cracker

## COOKING AND ASSEMBLING THE *FRUITS DE MER*

Lobsters and crabs: Cook the lobsters and crabs in plenty of boiling water salted at the rate of 5 oz. (150 g) to the gallon (5 litres). (This is the salinity of seawater.) The crabs should be pierced with a skewer once between the eyes and once under the tail flap up through the body to the eyes to kill them before boiling. Both crabs and lobsters should be dropped into boiling water, brought back to the boil and simmered for 20 minutes, then drained and left to go cold. They taste better if not refrigerated, so cook them on the day you intend to eat your *fruits de mer*.

Mussels: Clean the mussels (see p. 65), place them in a large saucepan, and add a splash of water. Place on a fierce heat with the lid on and let the mussels open in the steam produced by the water and the liquid which comes out of them. As soon as they open, remove from the heat and drain through a colander into a bowl. Keep the cooking liquor for another dish (perhaps a fish soup, which would be an ideal first course to be followed by the *fruits de mer*). Remove the beards from the mussels.

Prawns, shrimps, Dublin Bay prawns: You normally buy these cooked; if not, place them in a pan of boiling salted water, bring back to the boil and simmer for one minute for shrimps, two minutes for either type of prawn.

Oysters: Open by inserting the blade of an oyster knife in the hinge of the two shells. Protect the hand in which you are holding the oyster by wrapping it in a tea towel.

Winkles: Place in a pan of boiling salted water, bring back to the boil and drain.

Whelks: As for winkles, but simmer for 4 minutes.

Shore crabs: Place in a pan of boiling salted water, bring back to the boil and simmer for 5 minutes. Drain.

Clams and cockles: Cook in the same way as mussels.

Scallops: Clean the scallops as described in Chapter 3 (pp. 64–5) but leave them in the deep bottom shell; discard the top shell. Steam the scallops in a perforated tray over boiling water till they have turned from opaque to white.

Sea urchins: Cut in half, drain off the water.

## Making the mayonnaise

Use the recipe for mustard mayonnaise on p. 98. This is the sort of mayonnaise you would normally be given with a *fruits de mer* in Brittany. Mayonnaise is better hand-beaten than made in a processor.

## Shallot vinegar

Follow the recipe on p. 106.

To assemble the *fruits de mer*, take a large tray; a circular tin tea tray is ideal but a wooden tray would be fine too. Get the cubes out of about four ice trays, place in a polythene bag and crush with a rolling pin.

Place ice and chilled seaweed on the tray and assemble the shellfish and crustaceans in any form of still life you find exciting. The chefs at the restaurant seem to favour Dublin Bay prawns locked in mortal combat, with lobsters and crabs looking on. Decorate the tray with halves of lemon and carry it into the garden to tumultuous applause. Return with mayonnaise, shallot vinegar and bowls of water and napkins for washing and drying your hands – and naturally a number of bottles of ice-cold acidic wine like a Gros Plant or a Sauvignon de Touraine, or perhaps our house wine, Sauvignon de Haut Poitou.

# POACHED HALIBUT STEAKS WITH HOLLANDAISE SAUCE

I like to bake steaks of fish in foil with a little liquid; in this way, the fish is poached in its own juices and no flavour is lost.

| | |
|---|---|
| 4 halibut steaks, each weighing 7 oz (175 g) | Salt |
| 1 fl. oz. (30 ml) dry white wine | About 8 oz. (240 g) of the lightest hollandaise sauce (see p. 95) |

Set your oven to 375°F (190°C; gas mark 5).

Cut a piece of foil big enough to wrap up the halibut steaks easily, and butter one side of it. Season the steaks and place them side by side on the buttered foil. Splash with the white wine and wrap the steaks loosely, turning the two edges over a couple of times to make a good seal. Bake in the oven for 15 to 20 minutes. Open the parcel and place the steaks on a warm serving dish. Season them, pour the cooking juices over and serve with the hollandaise sauce.

# POACHED HALIBUT WITH DILL

In the south of England, halibut is very rare, and turbot would be a better buy; but in the north, what a wonderful fish! I have given this marvellous flat fish some of the flavours of northern Europe to complement it.

| | |
|---|---|
| 2 sticks of celery, finely sliced | 2 fl. oz. (60 ml) water |
| 1 carrot, peeled and sliced | 1 fl. oz. (30 ml) aquavit (optional) |
| Half a medium onion, chopped | Salt and freshly ground white pepper |
| 4 oz. (120 g) unsalted butter | 1 tablespoon (15 ml) chopped dill |
| 4 steaks of halibut, each weighing 10–12 oz. (300–360 g) | |

Preheat your oven at 425°F (220°C; gas mark 7).

Choose an oven dish large enough to take the steaks of halibut, and soften the vegetables in the butter over a gentle heat for 4 minutes. Place the halibut fillets on top, pour over the water and aquavit, season, sprinkle with some of the chopped dill, and cover with a buttered paper. Poach in the oven for about 12 minutes.

Remove from the oven, take the steaks out with a fish slice and put them on a warmed serving dish. Reduce the cooking liquor in the dish by half by rapid boiling, then whisk in the rest of the butter while still boiling.

Finally stir in the rest of the dill, pour over the halibut steaks and serve with some plainly boiled potatoes.

# GRILLED JOHN DORY
# WITH A CHIVE AND FENNEL DRESSING

If you are cooking fish under a domestic grill you might like to consider using a red-hot poker to make grill bar marks across it. This gives the fish a charred flavour which doesn't totally dominate the taste, and it looks tremendous.

Because of its enormous head, John Dory has considerably less edible fillet in relation to bone than most, so the large weight I suggest in this recipe will not be too much for four people as a main course.

| | |
|---|---|
| 4 John Dory, each weighing about 1½ lb. (750 g); or 6 lb. (2.75 kg) of larger fish | ¾ teaspoon (4 ml) salt |
| | Freshly ground black pepper |
| | 1 chopped shallot |
| 8 fl. oz. (240 g) olive oil | 1 tablespoon (15 ml) chopped chives |
| Juice of a lemon | 1 tablespoon (15 ml) chopped fennel |

Turn on the grill. Place a poker in an open gas flame or in contact with an electric element. Pass the fish through seasoned flour and pat them to remove any surplus. Brush lightly with oil and sear the sides with the hot poker marking diagonally across the fish and spacing the marks equally. You can mark the other way too to make a crisscross pattern, but I think just so much is enough.

Put the fish in a fish grilling wire and cook under the grill, with a tray underneath to catch the juices. When the fish is cooked, combine all the rest of the ingredients to make the dressing and pour it into the tray which was under the grilling fish. Put the fish on one large plate and pour the dressing right over them. Spoon the dressing over the fish as you serve them. A bottle of Bourgogne Aligoté and some Parmentier potatoes (see p. 272) would go well with this.

# STEAMED FILLETS OF JOHN DORY WITH A LIME AND GINGER HOLLANDAISE

At the restaurant, we have two steamers worth about £5,000 between them: rather a lot of money, I sometimes think, for generating a bit of steam. One of them, a pressure steamer, works just like a pressure cooker except that the steam is always on tap and is relatively dry. The other is slower but much more gentle, working without pressure, and this is the one we would use for this dish. To construct a steamer at home all you need is a large saucepan, some sort of trivet and a dinner plate (see p. 70).

In this recipe, I have incorporated the liquid from steaming the fish into the sauce. You don't need to do this, because you can make a perfectly nice hollandaise without, but it is the sort of touch that will make your hollandaise sauce somehow nicer. I have used the quick liquidizer method for hollandaise here, because if you're incorporating the cooking liquor, you need to make the sauce quickly so as not to keep the cooked fish waiting.

| | |
|---|---|
| 1 lime | 4 fillets of John Dory, each weighing |
| 2 egg yolks | 4 oz. (120 g) |
| Pinch of salt | ½ teaspoon (5 ml) of finely chopped |
| Pinch of cayenne pepper | fresh ginger |
| 1 pint (600 ml) of water | 6 oz. (180 g) unsalted butter |

Remove the zest from the lime using the fine side of a cheese grater. Squeeze the juice into the liquidizer and add the egg yolks, salt and cayenne.

Pour the pint of water into a large saucepan, put the fillets of John Dory on a dinner plate, skin side down, and place the plate on the trivet in the steamer. Sprinkle with the lime zest and the chopped ginger, lightly season with salt, bring to the boil, and steam until the fish is just cooked, i.e. when the flesh has turned from translucent to white; the flesh of John Dory is dense and takes longer to cook than most other fish. The only reliable way of telling whether it is done is simply to make a small cut into the centre and look.

While the Dory is cooking melt the butter in a small saucepan and keep it quite hot.

Take the fillets off the steamer plate and pour the cooking juices from the plate into the liquidizer. Blend for 10 seconds, then, with the liquidizer on maximum speed, pour the hot butter through the small hole in the top to make your quick hollandaise.

Decorate the serving dish with a twist of lime.

# GRILLED LOBSTERS
# WITH HOT HERB BUTTER

For this the lobsters are split in half while still alive and grilled. This is not as barbaric as you might think, because as long as you cleave the lobsters in two efficiently, they are quickly killed. If you don't like the idea, however, you can plunge them into boiling salted water and simmer them for ten minutes, then remove them, cut them in half and finish cooking them under the grill.

2 lobsters, each weighing about
   2½ lb. (1.2 kg)
Melted butter for basting the lobster
3 fl. oz. (90 ml) fish stock (see p. 92)
   or water

1 oz. (30 g) chopped fresh herbs
   (equal quantities of chervil, chives
   and basil)
Juice of a quarter lemon
4 oz. (120 g) unsalted butter, cut into
   pieces

Preheat your grill.

To cut the lobster in half, place it on a chopping board and drive a large knife through the middle of the carapace (the body section) and cut down towards and between the eyes. Then turn the knife around, place it in the original cut and bring the knife down right through the tail to split that in half. Pull off the claws, cut off the rubber bands that will be binding the claws, and crack open each of the three claw sections with a short, sharp chop from the thickest part of your knife blade.

Place the lobster, flesh side up, on a grilling tray and paint copiously with melted butter. Cook under the grill till the flesh has set, then turn over, brush with melted butter again and grill the shell side till it has turned from blue to red.

Bring the fish stock or water to the boil, then add the herbs and lemon juice. Remove from the heat and whisk in the butter, a piece at a time. Pour over the lobsters and serve.

# LOBSTER
# WITH A VANILLA SAUCE

There is really very little that needs to be done with a lobster except to boil it and serve it with some mayonnaise or melted butter, the flavour is so good. But just a small amount of a very intense sauce like this vanilla *sabayon* makes the dish utterly memorable. The use of a flavour more commonly associated with sweet dishes is not so unusual: saffron, nutmeg, ginger, even sugar and jam, prunes, apricots, plums, raspberries, strawberries, figs and plenty more are used in fish and meat dishes. You will find in this recipe that the vanilla and the slight sweetness of the Noilly Prat go remarkably well with moist collops of freshly cooked lobster.

I don't claim to have originated this dish; I first ate something very similar at a restaurant in Paris, L'Archestrate, run by a chef whose work I greatly admire, Alain Senderens. Monsieur Senderens has since gone on to open a larger and even more famous restaurant in Paris, Lucas Carton.

I have described in detail below how we present a lobster taken out of its shell. It requires a great deal of concentration to do this; if you get it right it looks stunning, but if you are doubtful about succeeding, it is better to serve the lobster still in the half shell. Random pieces of lobster on a plate compare most unfavourably with the splendour of the original. (See the recipe for grilled lobster on p. 251 for details on cutting a lobster in half.)

2 live lobsters, each weighing about
   1¾ lb. (840 g)
10 fl. oz. (300 ml) fish stock (see
   p. 92)
Half a vanilla pod
1 fl. oz. (30 ml) Noilly Prat

2 egg yolks
2 oz. (60 g) unsalted butter, cut into
   small pieces
Lemon juice to taste
Small pinch of cayenne pepper

## ORDER OF WORK

1. Cook the lobsters.
2. Reduce the fish stock and vanilla.
3. Remove the meat from the shells.
4. Make the sauce.

The lobsters must be freshly cooked and the meat removed from the shell while still warm. Bring a large pan of well-salted water to the boil and put the lobsters in (see the notes on killing shellfish on pp. 60–61). Put the lid on, bring back to the boil and simmer for 20 minutes. Remove from the water and leave to cool till you can handle the lobsters. While you are boiling them, put the fish stock, vanilla pod and Noilly Prat on the heat to reduce in volume by half by rapid boiling. Remove from the heat and leave to cool.

Remove the lobster meat carefully from the shells as follows. You will need a large heavy knife. Pull off the claws and crack them open with the blade of the knife, using the heaviest thickest part of the blade near the handle. Almost let the weight of the knife do the work, so that you crack the shell but don't cut the claw in half. It cracks most easily if you cut down on the edges of the claw.

First crack open the big claw joint. Before pulling the two pieces of broken shell apart, pull the movable pincer back as far as it will go to break the joint (this makes removal of the claw meat in one piece much easier). Now pull the shells apart and (hopefully) remove the claw meat intact.

Crack open the remaining two parts of the claws and remove the meat carefully with a lobster pick.

After dealing with the claws, the bodies are relatively easy. Pull the head sections (called the carapace) away from the tail sections. Take a pair of kitchen scissors and cut the tail shells from the joint with the head right through the middle of the back down to the tail itself. Pull the shells off to leave the whole tail meat without the shell. Place the tails on a chopping board and slice them across into neat rounds, keeping the shape of the tails intact as you do so.

Take a large warmed serving dish, and use a palette knife to lift each tail off the chopping board on to the dish. Arrange the claw pieces on either side in the same shape as the original claws.

Cut the carapace from one of the lobsters in half lengthways. Remove and discard the stomach sac just behind the eyes. Remove the body section from the carapace shell. You will not need the body section for this recipe (see the recipe for shellfish bisque, pp. 127–8). Take the two carapace shells and lay them on the serving plate at the top of each sliced tail section. Cut off four legs from each of the body sections and lay them on either side of the carapace to suggest the configuration of the original lobster. Finally put the tail end shell at the tail end of the meat. Unless you have worked very quickly, you will probably now find that you need to warm the lobster gently in the oven.

Keep the lobster warm while you finish the sauce. You will need a steel mixing bowl and a saucepan into which the mixing bowl will fit. Quarter-fill the saucepan with hot water, and bring it to the boil. Put the egg yolks and the vanilla reduction into the mixing bowl and whisk over the boiling water till the sauce begins to thicken and you can see the marks of the whisk in it.

Remove from the heat and whisk in the butter, a few pieces at a time. Add a little lemon juice and a tiny pinch of cayenne pepper. Serve the sauce poured around the lobster.

# WARM LOBSTER SALAD
# WITH TOMATO AND BASIL

The meat is removed from a lobster and sliced and served with a green salad and a sauce made with lobster coral, basil, tomato, fish stock and cream. The salad is dressed and served on the same plate and is slightly wilted by being put under the grill at the very last minute. Not one of the easier dishes in this book, but a real stunner.

2 lobsters, preferably hen lobsters, each weighing about 2 lb. (1 kg)
A good green salad with plenty of variety
A walnut oil dressing (see p. 105)
½ pint (300 ml) fish stock (see p. 92)

3 fl. oz. (90 ml) double cream
3 good-sized tomatoes, peeled, deseeded and chopped
10 basil leaves
Salt
A little lemon juice

The lobsters are cooked and prepared in exactly the same way as in the lobster with vanilla sauce recipe (p. 253), except that in this dish the coral and tomalley are used in the sauce. The coral is the dark green, slightly gelatinous part of the body cavity of the female lobster; the tomalley is the light greeny brown material. Both of these are protein, and, like egg yolk, they coagulate if they are heated too much but can be used to thicken a sauce if heated gently. They are added right at the end, and the coral gives the sauce a splendid red colour; but if you only have cock lobsters the tomalley will be enough to thicken the sauce satisfactorily.

Cook the lobsters, remove the meat and lay out as for lobster with vanilla. As long as the lobsters are not cooked too far in advance, it is best to let them cool down to make it easier to remove the meat. The lobster is served warm, not hot, and is in fact slightly rewarmed by being placed under your grill which you should now turn on.

Prepare your salad and dressing and have it ready.

Place the fish stock in a small pan, add the cream and reduce by half. Meanwhile place the chopped tomato on a board and chop the tomalley, coral and basil leaves into it.

Take the cream and fish stock reduction off the heat and whisk this mixture into it. Return the pan to the heat and stir constantly until the sauce thickens slightly and turns red. Remove from the heat at once and taste for seasoning; adjust with salt and add the lemon juice. Keep the sauce in a warm place while you warm the lobsters under the grill.

Just before serving add the salad and put the dishes back under the grill for no more than 20 seconds to wilt the leaves.

# MONKFISH COOKED LIKE
# A *GIGOT* OF LAMB WITH
# FENNEL AND GARLIC

Monkfish larded with slivers of garlic and pot-roasted in the oven with fennel, accompanied by a garlic sauce incorporating the roasting juice. This recipe describes the way we serve the fish in the restaurant, but you may find it more convenient to use one large monk tail, in which case buy one about 2½ lb. (1.2 kg) and cook for about 45 minutes. For a special occasion, though, a whole tail each is a pleasant surprise, and as a reward for the extra work involved, small monk tails are cheaper than large ones.

4 monk tails, each weighing
   10–12 oz. (300–360 g)
2 cloves of garlic
1 bulb of Florence fennel
3 oz. (90 g) butter

Salt and ground black pepper
½ pint (300 ml) fish stock (see p. 92)
2 oz. (60 g) *aïoli* (pp. 98–9), or 2
   crushed cloves of garlic with 2 oz.
   (60 g) mayonnaise

---
## ORDER OF WORK
---

1. Make the fish stock.
2. Make the *aïoli*.
3. Prepare the monkfish and fennel.
4. Roast the monkfish.
5. Make the sauce.

Preheat the oven to 350°F (180°C; gas mark 4).

Cut the fins off the tails and pull away the thick black skin. Cut away the thin membrane that runs along the bottom of the tails. This is quite difficult; if you cannot manage it, carefully sever the membrane in two or three places (if left intact it contracts in cooking and spoils the shape of the tail).

Cut about 1½ inches (4 cm) off the cartilage at the thick end of the tails back into the flesh (otherwise they stick out too much when the fish is cooked). Cut the garlic into thin slivers, make small incisions in the fish with the point of a knife and push the garlic into them.

Cut off the base of the fennel and pull off the outer leaves if stringy or discoloured. Cut the fennel into four quarters and slice these up. Chop up the fennel tops for sprinkling across the finished dish. Place the fennel with half the butter in the bottom of a casserole dish. Put the monkfish on top, season and dot with the rest of the butter. Bake with the lid on for 20 minutes. Baste the fish with the butter 3 times. Leave the lid off the casserole for the last 5 minutes to colour the fish.

Remove the fish and fennel with a perforated spoon and keep warm. Add the fish stock to the roasting juice and reduce by half by rapid boiling. Take off the heat, whisk a ladleful of the liquid into the *aïoli*, then pour this mixture back into the rest of the liquid. Reheat slightly but don't boil. Serve the monkfish down the centre of a large warmed oval dish. Arrange the fennel around the outside. Pour some of the sauce across the fish and sprinkle with chopped fennel. Serve the rest of the sauce separately.

# GRILLED RED MULLET
# WITH MEDITERRANEAN FLAVOURS

An elaborate dish designed to give a sense of occasion to this favourite fish of mine. The fillets of fish are cooked under the grill with a few leaves of celery. The livers of the mullet are mixed with garlic and shallots and spread on croutons. The fish is accompanied by celery, garlic, red peppers and leeks, all cooked in such a way as not to overpower the fish. The dish is served with a saffron *bouillon* reduced down to a light, concentrated sauce.

4 red mullet, each weighing about
8 oz. (240 g)

---

### THE *BOUCHÉES* AND FILLING

8 oz. (240 g) butter puff pastry (see pp. 107–9)
1 quarter of one large red pepper
2 oz. (60 g) of the white part of a leek
1 tablespoon (15 ml) white wine vinegar

2 fl. oz. (60 ml) dry white wine
2 fl. oz (60 ml) fish stock (see p. 92)
1 oz. (30 g) butter
Salt and black pepper

2 slices of white bread

---

### THE MULLET LIVER PÂTÉ

The livers from the mullet
½ oz. (15 g) butter
Half a clove of garlic, very finely chopped

½ oz. (15 g) very finely chopped shallot or onion
A few drops of cognac

---

### THE MILD GARLIC WITH CELERY

The heart of one head of celery, with inner leaves
8 cloves of garlic, split into two

5 fl. oz. (150 ml) milk
½ oz. (15 g) butter

## THE SAUCE

5 fl. oz. (150 ml) dry white wine
8 fl. oz. (240 ml) water
A 2-inch (5-cm) strip of orange peel,
  thinly peeled without pith
1 oz. (30 g) sliced onion
1 oz. (30 g) sliced celery

2 cloves of garlic
Pinch of curry powder
Pinch of saffron
Squeeze of lemon juice
1 oz. (30 g) butter

## ORDER OF WORK

1. Clean and fillet the fish.
2. Cook the *bouchées* and croutons.
3. Cook the *bouchée* filling.
4. Cook the pâté.
5. Cook the garlic and celery.
6. Make the sauce.
7. Cook the fish.
8. Assemble the dish.

I suggest that steps 1 to 5 are done some time before serving.

Clean and fillet the fish, making sure you keep back the livers.

Roll out the puff pastry to about ³⁄₁₆ inch (5 mm) thick. Cut out sixteen 1¼-inch (3-cm) disks. Cut ½-inch (1.25-cm) holes in eight of these. Brush the eight solid disks with a little water and place the eight circle disks on top. The ½-inch (1.25-cm) cut-outs will make lids. (Note: for good results, work with cold pastry.)

Preheat the oven to 450°F (230°C; gas mark 8).

Place the puff pastry *bouchées* on a baking tray and chill for half an hour. Bake for 10 minutes, but take the lids out after about 8 minutes.

Cut eight ¾-inch (20-mm) disks out of the white bread and fry gently in oil to a golden brown.

Turn on the grill. Brush the red pepper with oil and roast under the grill to blister the skin. Take out and remove the skin. Chop the red pepper in a fine dice and blanch for half a minute in boiling water. Drain. Finely chop the leek and place in a sauteuse with the vinegar, wine and fish stock. Simmer gently to cook the leek, then boil away all the liquid. Add the butter and the diced red pepper. Season.

Melt the butter for the pâté in a small pan and soften the garlic and shallots in it. Chop the liver very finely and stir through the garlic and shallot, season and add the cognac. Cook the liver only very lightly: it must remain slightly pink and soft.

Cut the celery into pieces about the same length and width as the split garlic cloves. Put the celery leaves to one side. Blanch the garlic in the milk for 3 minutes and drain. Heat the butter in a small pan till it smells nutty, remove from the heat immediately and put the garlic and celery in. Turn them over in the butter, then put the pan on a very low heat with a lid on for 20 minutes.

Put wine, water, orange peel, onion, celery, garlic, curry powder and saffron in a pan. Simmer for 10 minutes, then reduce by rapid boiling to about 4 fl. oz. (120 ml). Strain and add the lemon juice; whisk in the 1 oz. (30 g) of butter. Warm a very large serving dish.

Fill the *bouchées* with the leek and red pepper mixture; put the lids on them. Spread the croutons with the mullet liver pâté. Put the *bouchées*, croutons and garlic and celery in a low oven to warm through. Put the fish fillets on a grilling tray and brush with melted butter and season. Place a small sprig of celery leaf on each fillet and brush with butter. Place the fillets under the grill.

Pour some of the sauce over the bottom of the serving plate. Place the *bouchées* all around the outside interspersed with the croutons spread with the pâté. Put four little piles of garlic and celery on the plate. Finally lay the red mullet down the centre of the plate diagonally and slightly overlapping one another. Serve the rest of the sauce separately.

# ESCALOPES OF SALMON TROISGROS

From the Troisgros brothers, this is one of the most well-known of *nouvelle cuisine* recipes, and one of the best. The thin escalopes of salmon are cooked so quickly that they are almost raw inside, which seems to me the best way to eat salmon, or salmon trout (which you can equally well use in this recipe). I find both fish disappointing when cooked right through, because they become dry. This recipe, though based on the original Troisgros version, has slightly changed, as always happens in the trade, through constant use by another chef.

1½ lb. (775 g) salmon fillet from a good-sized salmon
Groundnut oil
Salt
1 pint (300 ml) fish stock (see p. 92)
1 fl. oz. (30 ml) dry white wine

1 fl. oz. (30 ml) Noilly Prat
2 oz. (60 g) sorrel leaves
3 fl. oz. (90 ml) double cream
3 oz. (90 g) butter
Juice of a quarter lemon

Remove any bones in the fillet of salmon with tweezers, long-nosed pliers or by trapping them between the point of a small office knife and your thumb. With a sharp filleting knife or carving knife cut the salmon into 12 diagonal slices about ¼ inch (6 mm) thick, rather as if you were cutting thick slices of smoked salmon, i.e. cutting on the slant down to the skin. Brush a grilling tray with oil and place the 12 escalopes of salmon on it. Brush them lightly with oil and season lightly with salt.

Turn on your grill and put four large plates in the oven to warm. Place the fish stock, wine and vermouth in a small pan and reduce by three-quarters by rapid boiling. While this is reducing, wash and pick the stalks from the sorrel and slice the leaves into a thin *chiffonade*. When the fish stock has reduced, add the cream, reduce still further, then whisk in the butter. Add the lemon juice and stir in the sorrel. Take off the heat.

Put the fillets under the grill. You don't need to turn them; they are done when the flesh changes colour from dark pink to light pink (about 30 seconds). Pour the sauce over the warm plates. Carefully lift the escalopes off the grilling tray with a palette knife and lay them on the plates slightly overlapping. Sprinkle a little chopped sorrel over them.

# POACHED SALMON
# WITH *SAUCE VERTE*

I prefer to poach salmon in salted water rather than in a *court bouillon*, because I don't think that fish as fine-flavoured as salmon needs anything added to it.

If you would prefer a *sauce verte* with a little more spice, use some coriander leaves as well as the ingredients below.

| | |
|---|---|
| A piece of salmon weighing about 2½–3 lb. (1.2–1.4 kg) | 1 oz. (30 g) parsley, chervil, tarragon and chives (in roughly equal quantities) |
| 1 oz. (30 g) spinach leaves | |
| 1 oz. (30 g) watercress | ½ pint (300 ml) olive oil mayonnaise (see pp. 97–8) |

Place the salmon in a fish kettle and pour on enough cold water to cover it. Add salt at the rate of 5 oz. (150 g) to each gallon (5 litres). Bring the kettle to the boil, but then allow it to boil for only about 5 seconds.

Remove it at once from the heat and let the salmon go quite cold in the water. This will produce a cooked salmon which is underdone and moist next to the bone.

Blanch all the green leaves in boiling water for one minute. Refresh in ice-cold water. Strain the herbs through a sieve, then squeeze them dry and liquidize them with a little of the mayonnaise. Mix in the rest of the mayonnaise and serve with the salmon.

# SALMON IN PUFF PASTRY WITH A CHAMPAGNE SAUCE

A fillet of salmon stuffed with tarragon butter and wrapped in puff pastry served with a champagne sauce with fresh *fines herbes*. This is one of the most successful dishes we ever dreamt up and though rather time-consuming it is not difficult to make, and, I think, is successful because quite simply flavoured. Note that champagne is not essential; you can substitute Muscadet, Vouvray or a Sauvignon, but *not*, in this case, any cheap dry white wine – it is too special a dish.

You will find it quite tricky to wrap the fillet with pastry this thin. A cold work surface, a cool room and speed are important. You could just make up one big fillet and portion it out when cooked, but I find that individual portions give a perfect balance between fish and pastry and also allow for very precise cooking, which is most important with a fish that can be so dry if overcooked.

> 1 lb. (450 g) butter puff pastry (see
> pp. 107–9) or frozen puff pastry

---
## THE TARRAGON BUTTER
---

6 oz. (180 g) unsalted butter
1 tablespoon (15 ml) fresh tarragon
½ teaspoon (15 g) salt
Juice of a quarter lemon

4 turns of the black peppermill
1¼ lb. (600 g) salmon fillet, skinned
1 beaten egg (for egg wash)

—————————— THE CHAMPAGNE SAUCE ——————————

½ pint (300 ml) fish stock (see p. 92)   6 fl. oz. (180 ml) double cream
4 fl. oz. (120 ml) champagne   1 tablespoon (15 ml) chopped *fines*
½ oz. (15 g) mushrooms   *herbes* (parsley, tarragon, chives
½ oz. (15 g) chopped onion   and chervil)

—————————— ORDER OF WORK ——————————

1. Make the pastry.                 5. Make the sauce.
2. Make the tarragon butter.        6. Cook the salmon.
3. Skin the salmon.                 7. Finish the sauce.
4. Wrap the salmon.

Prepare the pastry. Make the tarragon butter by softening the butter slightly and mixing in the tarragon, salt, pepper and lemon juice. Remove the skin from the salmon (see p. 56 for the technique). Unless the fillet is a tail piece, you will find a row of small bones down the centre of the fillet. These should be removed either with a pair of tweezers or by gripping the bone between your thumb and the point of a small knife and pulling them out.

Cut the fillet into four equal portions, then cut a pocket in the side of each, trying to make this as deep as possible without cutting through to the other side of the fillet. Divide the tarragon butter into four and put a piece in each of the pockets.

Roll out the puff pastry extremely thinly, no more than ⅛ inch (4 mm) thick. Cut a piece of pastry about 6 inches (15 cm) square depending on the size of the fillet. Lightly brush the surface with water, place the fillet along one edge of the pastry ensuring that there is spare pastry on either side. Roll the fillet right over, lifting the pastry up and over too until the near edge touches the pastry on the other side. Press down a little to seal and cut away any surplus. Tamp down the ends to seal them and cut away any surplus. Brush the fillets with egg wash and chill for at least half an hour.

Turn your oven full on.

To make the sauce, put the fish stock, champagne, mushrooms and onion in a small saucepan and reduce by half. Add 4 fl. oz. (120 ml) of the cream and reduce until it coats the back of a spoon. Pass through a sieve, then keep warm. While you are reducing the sauce, whisk the remaining double cream in a bowl until it is beginning to thicken.

Bake the salmon for 12 minutes. Slice each portion into 4 or 5 pieces slightly diagonally, so that when you place them on four warm plates each slice lies against the next. Move the slices apart a little so that you can see the salmon inside the pastry; it should be moist and slightly pink.

Finish off the champagne sauce by adding the chopped herbs and whisking the whipped cream into the sauce just before serving.

# A RAGOÛT OF TURBOT
# AND SCALLOPS WITH CREAM
# AND BASIL

The turbot and scallops are braised on top of some sliced vegetables with Vouvray and a splash of fish stock. The dish is finished off with cream and some freshly chopped basil. Not a cheap dish, but always extremely popular at the restaurant.

2 lb. (900 g) turbot
8 large or 12 small scallops
1 pint (600 ml) fish stock made from the turbot bones (see p. 92)
2 oz. (60 g) carrot, peeled
2 oz. (60 g) celeriac, peeled
2 oz. (60 g) white of leek
2 oz. (60 g) fresh white button mushrooms

3 oz. (90 g) butter
2 fl. oz. (60 ml) Vouvray (or other dry white wine)
5 fl. oz. (150 ml) double cream
10 fresh basil leaves
Salt and ground white pepper
Lemon juice

Fillet and skin the turbot (see pp. 54–6) or ask your fishmonger to do it, but you must have the trimmings for making the stock. Make a fish stock with the turbot bones and concentrate the strength of this by reducing the volume by rapid boiling down to about 5 fl. oz. (150 ml).

Slice the turbot into ¾-inch (20 -mm) slices across the fillet. Cut the scallops into two rounds (or three if they are large ones).

Prepare the rest of the ingredients while the fish stock is simmering. Slice the carrots, celeriac and leek into strips 1 by ⅛ inch (3 cm by 3 mm). Thinly slice the mushrooms. Place the butter and half the Vouvray in a wide and shallow pan, preferably with a thick bottom, and gently cook the carrots, celeriac and leek in it with the lid on for about 5 minutes until *al dente*, then add the sliced mushrooms. Season lightly.

Place the slices of turbot on top of the vegetables, moisten with the rest of the Vouvray and the fish stock. Lightly season. Cook the turbot very gently on top of the vegetables with the lid on for 3 minutes. Now add the scallops and continue to cook gently till turbot and scallops are just, but only just, cooked, that is when they have turned a marble white colour. The entire operation of cooking the fish should take no more than 5 minutes.

Now remove the lid and take out the fish and scallops. Add the cream and the basil, which you should chop only at this stage, so as to preserve its delicate perfume. Boil vigorously to thicken the sauce and emulsify cream and cooking juices. Finally, season the sauce and add some lemon juice to sharpen it up a little if you think it needs it (such considerations are a matter of personal taste). Now return the fish to the pan.

This *ragoût* looks much better turned out on to four warmed plates than served in one dish. Use the biggest plates you've got, and group the fish, scallops and vegetables in a pleasing arrangement of colour and shape. I always try to arrange food to look as if no thought has gone into its position on the plate though in fact a lot has.

# FILLETS OF TURBOT
# WITH LOVAGE, A CHARDONNAY SAUCE
# AND A GREEN TERRINE

There is a lot of work involved in this dish, so I have written it for a large dinner party of 8 to 10 people. The terrine will be enough for 10, as will the sauce.

It is not necessary to stick rigidly to the green ingredients that we use in the terrine, but if you are omitting sorrel, add a teaspoon (5 ml) of lemon juice. A more elaborate terrine can be made by lining the mould with spinach leaves, so that the slices have a dark green surround. To simplify the production of this dish, you can make the terrine a day before and refrigerate it, then slice it and warm it through in the oven.

Fishmongers seem reluctant to sell turbot in filleted form; you will have to insist. Brill is a perfectly acceptable substitute.

## THE TERRINE

1 oz. (30 g) spinach
1 oz. (30 g) watercress
1 oz. (30 g) rocket
½ oz. (15 g) parsley
12 oz. (360 g) lemon sole fillet,
    skinned and free from bone

1 teaspoon (5 ml) salt
1 egg and half an egg white
1 oz. (30 g) sorrel
¼ oz. (7.5 g) fresh basil
12.5 fl. oz. (375 ml) double cream

5 oz. (150 g) unsalted butter
5 oz. (150 g) onion, finely chopped
3 oz. (150 g) white button
    mushrooms, thinly sliced
Up to 10 fillets of turbot, each
    weighing about 6 oz. (180 g)
3 fl. oz. (90 ml) Chardonnay or other
    full-bodied dry white wine
10 fl. oz. (300 ml) water

10 leaves of lovage, blanched in
    boiling water for 2 minutes, then
    refreshed in ice-cold water (use
    celery leaves if you can't get the
    lovage; these need not be
    blanched)
Salt and white pepper
10 fl. oz. (300 ml) double cream
Lemon juice

## ORDER OF WORK

1. Make the terrine and cook an hour before serving.
2. Poach the fillets of fish.
3. Make the sauce.
4. Assemble the dish.

## THE TERRINE

You will need some sort of mould for the terrine; I use a small bread tin holding 1½ pints (850 ml). Blanch the spinach, watercress, rocket and parsley in boiling water for 30 seconds. Refresh in cold water, drain in a colander, and pat dry with a teatowel.

Put the fish fillet, salt and eggs in a food processor and blend till smooth. Add the blanched leaves, the sorrel and the basil, and blend till these are smooth. Chill the mixture, still in the processor bowl; the cream should be well chilled too. Return the bowl to the motor and blend in the cream over a period of about 15 seconds. Blend only till the mixture thickens enough to hold its shape, then turn out into a well-buttered terrine.

Set your oven to 350°F (180°C; gas mark 4).

Place some buttered foil on top of the mould and put in a metal tray. Pour into the tray enough hot water to come halfway up the side of the mould and bring to the boil on the top of the cooker. Place the tray in the oven and cook for about 45 minutes.

Keep the terrine in the mould in a warm place while you cook the fish and make the sauce.

## COOKING THE FILLETS OF FISH

Take a large, solid roasting tray or similar shallow dish, big enough to take the ten fillets of turbot side by side. Melt half the butter in it and add the onions and mushrooms. Soften them in the oven without colouring. Remove from the oven and lay the fillets of fish on top. Pour the wine and water over. Lay a leaf of lovage on top of each fillet, and season with salt and freshly ground white pepper. Bring to a simmer on top of the cooker, then bake in the oven for 5 to 10 minutes, depending on the thickness of the fillets.

Take out of the oven and keep warm while you quickly make the sauce. Pour the contents of the tray through a sieve into a shallow saucepan and bring to the boil. Add the cream and lemon juice to the boiling sauce and reduce a little. Remove the pan from the heat and whisk in the rest of the butter.

Warm two large serving dishes.

Remove the terrine from its mould by laying a tray over the top and inverting both, causing the terrine to slip out on to the tray. Slice the terrine carefully with a serrated knife. Place five portions around the outside of one serving dish and five around the outside of the other.

Place five fillets of turbot slightly overlapping down the centre of each serving dish and spoon a little sauce over the turbot. Serve the rest of the sauce separately.

# Fourteen

# VEGETABLE RECIPES

'I must say that cabbage with grilled lobster was a bit of a surprise,' a customer said after his meal the other night, 'but cooked the way it was, I'm a convert!' We tend to regard fish as something to be served as a separate course, and it is hard to imagine what vegetables will combine well with it. But I see no reason why any vegetable which isn't too strongly flavoured shouldn't be served with fish: why not cabbage with lobster if it's the undercooked cabbage with a butter and chive sauce below, or perhaps Florence fennel with parsley and mild garlic?

At the Seafood Restaurant, we always serve our vegetables on a separate plate, as Chinese and Indian restaurants do, so that a combination of flavours can be enjoyed at the same time without swamping one another. I would even prefer to treat vegetables as another course, served after the main dish; in this way the meal can be prolonged, digestion aided and life sweetened.

## FRENCH BEANS
## WITH LEMON BUTTER

Top and tail 1 lb. (450 g) beans and drop them into boiling salted water. Cook till *al dente*, then drain, keeping some of the water. Boil about 3 fl. oz. (90 ml) of the water, and put in 3 oz. (90 g) butter. Boil rapidly to liaise the two and add the juice of half a lemon and a teaspoon or so of freshly chopped parsley. Pour over the beans.

## CABBAGE
## WITH BUTTER AND CHIVES

| | |
|---|---|
| 1 small cabbage | Salt and freshly ground pepper |
| 3 oz. (90 g) butter | 1 tablespoon (15 ml) chopped chives |
| 1 teaspoon (5 ml) lemon juice | or chopped spring onions |

Put 5 pints (3 litres) of salted water on to boil. Take off the outer leaves of the cabbage, cut it in quarters and then remove the thickest part of the stalk. Cut into ½-inch (15-mm) slices and put in the water when it is rapidly boiling. Bring back to the boil and cook for 5 minutes. Drain immediately in a colander.

Melt the butter in a large frying pan and add the lemon juice. Put in the well-drained cabbage and warm through, turning it over a few times. (All you are doing here is drying the cabbage out and replacing moisture with butter, so do not overheat.) Finally season with salt and pepper from the peppermill and add the chives or spring onions.

## FLORENCE FENNEL
## WITH PARSLEY AND MILD GARLIC

| | |
|---|---|
| 1 lb. (500 g) Florence fennel | Salt and freshly ground black pepper |
| 8 cloves garlic | 1 tablespoon (15 ml) freshly chopped |
| 3 oz. (90 g) butter | parsley |

Pull off and discard the outer leaves of the fennel bulb. Cut off the bottom and any damaged tops, then cut it into quarters. Slice into ¼-inch (6-mm) slices. Peel the garlic cloves and cut them into quarters. Cook the fennel and garlic in boiling salted water for 4 minutes. Drain. Melt the butter in a large frying pan, add the drained fennel and garlic and cook gently, turning a few times, till dried out and buttery. Don't let it catch. Season and add the chopped parsley.

Cooking the garlic in this way removes its harshness.

## MANGE-TOUT PEAS
## À LA FRANÇAISE

| | |
|---|---|
| 12 oz. (360 g) mange-tout peas | 2 oz. (60 g) unsalted butter |
| 6 spring onions | A good pinch of sugar |
| 3 oz. (90 g) lettuce | A good pinch of salt |

Top and tail the mange-tout peas. Peel the spring onions and chop into ½-inch (1.25-cm) lengths. Slice the lettuce thinly. Melt the butter in a pan and add the spring onions and mange-tout peas and a couple of tablespoons (30 ml) of water. Add sugar and salt, then sweat for 5 minutes with a lid on the pan. Finally add the lettuce. Leave the pan on the heat only while you turn the lettuce over with the peas and spring onions, then serve.

## BOILED NEW POTATOES
## WITH PARSLEY AND MINT

Boil your potatoes with salt and a sprig of mint. Serve them tossed in butter and half chopped mint and half chopped parsley. Spearmint is the best type for cooking with potatoes.

## COQ D'OR POTATOES

This recipe comes from the old Coq d'Or restaurant in Stratton Street, London, now Langan's Brasserie. Most potato dishes, I think, are too overpowering for fish, but this one, a single layer of thinly sliced potatoes baked in a *gratin* dish till quite crisp is just right.

A tiny piece of garlic
1 lb. (450 g) potatoes
½ pint (300 ml) chicken stock

2 oz. (60 g) unsalted butter
Salt and pepper

Set your oven to 400°F (200°C; gas mark 6).

You can use chicken stock or duck stock for this dish (or indeed fish stock); it should be a clear clean white stock rather than one made from the roast carcases.

Butter a shallow *gratin* dish and rub it with a peeled clove of garlic. Peel the potatoes. Trim a thin slice off one side to steady the potato, then slice it thinly, keeping the slices in place in the shape of the potato as you work; make sure that your knife cuts right through as you cut each slice. Now push down on the slices with the flat of your hand, forcing them into a natural fan shape. Lift the whole lot up with a palette knife and place them carefully in the *gratin* dish. Repeat with the other potatoes, laying them side by side. Pour the stock over the potatoes, dot with the butter and season with salt and ground black pepper. Bake in the oven until all the stock has cooked away and the crust of the potatoes is golden brown and crisp.

# PARMENTIER POTATOES

Diced potatoes fried in butter and served with freshly chopped chives.

1½ lb. (700 g) medium or large
    potatoes
Clarified butter

Salt and freshly ground black pepper
1 teaspoon (5 ml) chopped chives

Peel the potatoes. Trim two sides so that the potato will stay firmly on the chopping board when you slice it. Cut the potato into ½-inch (1.2-cm) slices. Cut these into ½-inch (1.2-cm) strips, then into ½-inch (1.2-cm) dice.

Wash these dice, drain, and dry them in a cloth. Fry them in a frying pan in the clarified butter till golden brown. Season with salt and pepper. Serve with the chopped chives.

# POTATO *DAUBE*

This recipe comes from Richard Olney's *Simple French Food*, which as well as being full of good recipes is rare among cookery books in that it is a pleasure to read. We often use this dish.

5 cloves of garlic, crushed and peeled
¾ pint (1 litre) salted water
4–5 tablespoons (60–75 ml) olive oil

2 lb. (1 kg) firm, yellow-fleshed
    potatoes, sliced thinly and wiped
    dry
3 or 4 bayleaves

Set your oven at 400°F (200°C; gas mark 6).

Cook the garlic cloves in the salted water, at a simmer, covered, for about 15 minutes, then purée the garlic through a sieve back into its cooking water. Rub an oven casserole with olive oil. Pack in half the potatoes, distribute the bayleaves, salt lightly (or not at all, depending on the saltiness of the garlic water) and add the remaining potatoes. Pour over the garlic purée and water: the potatoes should be well covered with liquid, but not drowned. Dribble olive oil over the surface and cook in the oven for 45 to 60 minutes.

# POTATO PANCAKES
# WITH SOURED CREAM AND JUNIPER

| | |
|---|---|
| 2 oz. (60 g) flour | ½ teaspoon (15 ml) salt |
| 1 egg | 5 turns of the peppermill |
| A 5-fl.-oz. (150-ml) carton of soured cream | 5 crushed juniper berries |
| | 1½ lb. (700 g) potatoes |

Mix all the ingredients except the potatoes together to make the batter.

Peel the potatoes and grate them into thin strips using the grating plate on your food processor, or the coarse plate of a cheese grater. Keep the grated potato in a bowl of water till you want it, then drain and dry out in batches in a tea towel.

To make an individual pancake, mix about 2 oz. (60 g) of potato with enough batter just to bind the potato together. Heat up some clarified butter in a small frying pan and flatten the mixture out in the bottom with the back of a wooden spoon. Cook on a medium heat for about 4 minutes, then turn the pancake over and cook on the other side.

# SAMPHIRE

Instructions for cleaning and cooking samphire are on p. 85 and in the recipe for bass with samphire (p. 233).

# SPINACH

Probably the most successful vegetable for serving with fish and a useful salad leaf as well. I used to like spinach cooked by blanching and then stewing for some time in plenty of good unsalted butter, but now I favour just blanching it or, even better, steaming it till it has little more than wilted, then tossing it in melted butter.

# ACKNOWLEDGEMENTS

I would like to thank the following:

My wife, Jill, for so much sensible criticism of the many dishes I cooked for her.

The staff at the Seafood Restaurant who sat in on the 'cookery book lunches', Marie, Chris, Roger, Di, Sue, Linda and Wendy, whose great enjoyment of those meals spurred me on.

Christine France and the cookery staff at *Woman's Realm* magazine for helping me so much in the early days of recipe writing.

Lastly I'd like to thank Paul Sellars, our *sous chef*, who spent a winter cooking recipes with me and whose skill and imaginative ideas have been an invaluable help to me.

# INDEX